Social Theory
and the
Crisis of Marxism

V

Social Theory
and the
Crisis of Marxism

JOSEPH McCARNEY

VERSO

London · New York

First published by Verso 1990
© Joseph McCarney 1990
All rights reserved

Verso
UK: 6 Meard Street, London W1V 3HR
USA: 29 West 35th Street, New York, NY 10001-2291

Verso is the imprint of New Left Books

British Library Cataloguing in Publication Data
McCarney, Joseph *1941-*
    Social theory and the crisis of Marxism.
    1. Marxism
    I. Title
    335.4

    ISBN 0-86091-231-0
    ISBN 0-86091-948-X pbk

US Library of Congress Cataloging-in-Publication Data
McCarney, Joe.
        Social theory and the crisis of Marxism / Joseph McCarney.
            p.   cm.
        Includes bibliographical references.
        ISBN 0-86091-231-0. — ISBN 0-86091-948-X (pbk.)
        1. Marxian school of sociology.   I. Title.
        HM24.M354   1990
        301—dc20

Printed in Great Britain by Bookcraft (Bath) Ltd
Typeset in Times by Leaper & Gard Ltd

Contents

Preface

It is frequently asserted, and still more frequently assumed, that Marxism as an intellectual tradition is currently in a state of crisis. These assertions are sometimes made in tones of triumph or gloating by declared opponents of everything the tradition is taken to represent. Sometimes, however, they come regretfully or despairingly from its friends; indeed from those who locate themselves within the tradition, or would do so, were it not for what they regard as its present pathological condition. It seems to be of the nature of a tradition of thought that if substantial groups of such people believe it to be in crisis, this is itself grounds for accepting that it is. Hence, the diagnosis has to be taken seriously. It is given added weight by the ease with which an impressive set of historical determinants may be invoked as background. The list is a familiar one, and will in any case have to be reviewed in the later course of this discussion. Here one may simply mention the many defeats and disappointments suffered by the socialist and working-class movements in the West, more immediately in the past two decades. There is also the profound absence of working models of a fully achieved socialist society. Those who seek such a model are confronted instead by 'actually existing socialism' with its moribund official doctrines and apparent shift towards market solutions to its economic problems. The effects of these determinants are felt in chronic low morale among Marxist intellectuals, a dearth of rich or compelling new lines of inquiry, the development of various kinds of 'post-Marxist' thought, and the surrender of the ideological initiative to the motley forces of the radical right. It is of course worth bearing in mind, as Louis Althusser reminded us near the start of the latest episode of 'crisis talk', that 'the crisis of Marxism is not a recent phenomenon' and that 'Marxism has in its history passed through a long series of crises and transformations'.[1] Such reminders are of value in helping to place current developments in perspective. Yet in themselves they take away nothing of the gravity and ominous implications of such developments. In particular, they can offer no reassurance that what we are witnessing is not indeed the final phase of an epoch in intellectual history. The possibility that the present 'crisis of Marxism' may be terminal has still to be considered in the light of whatever powers of judgement we can bring to bear. Any temptation to treat references to it as cries of 'Wolf!' has to be restrained by remembering also that in the story the cry proved in the end all too justified, a cry from the heart.

There seems little room for doubt as to what is the chief question of a philosophical kind to arise at this point. It is the mundane and obstinate one of what precisely may be supposed to be in crisis; of how the identity of the tradition alleged to be at risk is to be specified. In asking this, one need not be assuming that 'Marxism' denotes some fixed object with an essence to be captured if one has the necessary metaphysical skills. The question may be understood in historical terms, and posed in the interests of disclosing whatever distinctions are needed to make sense of the history. It will be focused initially on a determinate body of work: the achievement of Marx and, more broadly, of 'classical Marxism'. It becomes the question of whether a set of theses can be identified to which this body of work may be said to be inescapably committed, and which demands some similar commitment from all who claim a substantial allegiance to it. In asking it one may draw comfort from the fact that Marx, although not given to essentialism, had an acute sense of these matters, as shown most pungently in the notorious denial that he was a 'Marxist'. Our problem, it may be said, is that of reconstructing the criteria which serve to make such a judgement intelligible. The rewards of doing so are not the polemical ones of being able to separate sheep from goats, whichever way round the evaluative force of the classification is supposed to work. The discussion of who is and who is not a 'Marxist' is by now almost entirely pointless, and perhaps never had much point for anyone other than Marx himself. There remains a need to become clear about the underlying conceptual realities, however one then chooses to situate oneself in relation to them, and with whatever nuances and qualifications. It should be added that, of course, there already exists a superabundance of answers to our question. The present attempt presupposes that there is still something new to be said or, more accurately, that there are some old and neglected truths which need urgently to be restated. The responsibility for vindicating this will rest on the discussion that follows.

Even in a prefatory sketch it should be possible to state the main task more precisely. For one may hope to discern the core of the difficulties to be tackled, the crux from whose resolution a means of dealing with the others may be derived. This key issue may be approached by asking how Marx conceived, in the most general terms, the nature of his intellectual life-work; that is, of the logical status of his science of society. Put in these terms the problem may be said, without much risk of being contentious or question-begging, to turn on a quite specific range of considerations. Marx, it may be suggested, thought of himself – and his view has been generally endorsed, at least by Marxists – as, above all else, a revolutionary thinker and theorist of revolution. He insists on the revolutionary character of his work in terms that suggest that its whole significance derives from being in some way or other at the service of revolutionary social change. It would not be too much to say that the work demands to be conceived as being, just in virtue of its own nature, a force for such change or an element of it. To put it more soberly, the point is that his science asks to be considered as having not merely the usual descriptive and explanatory relationship to its object, but a practical significance or bearing for it also. The question is: how did Marx conceive of this integral dimension of the practical? What is the precise relationship of his revolutionary theory to revolutionary practice by virtue of which the theory is constituted as revolutionary? It will be demonstrated in what follows that, when the key question is formulated in this way, a certain kind of answer forces itself on one's attention with overwhelming textual authority and unrivalled hermeneutic power for making sense of the Marxist project. It is this answer that is presently ignored or overlaid with accretions, and that needs urgently to be reconstructed and placed at the forefront of debate.

If one seeks to explain our contemporary cloud of unknowing it is plainly to history that one must turn; to the changing fortunes of Marx's intellectual legacy. It will be necessary to take account of the barriers imposed in the Second International period against the transmission of some crucial features of that legacy. More significant in the present context, and much more difficult to deal with, is the smoke-screen laid down by the historical tendency known as 'Western Marxism'. The price for removing these obstacles to understanding is that any idea of a unified Marxist tradition, rich in continuous achievement, has to be abandoned. The tradition emerges as irremediably twisted and riven, indeed as broken-backed. For the main forms of Marxism in the West will be seen to have failed to carry forward anything of substance from the classical programme for social theory. From this perspective, claims of a crisis must appear to have deeper foundations than is usually suspected even by those who press them most vociferously. On the other hand, it may be suggested that our situation is such that only the most radical ground-clearing can now offer prospects of an adequate space on which to build. Moreover, the resource represented by the original legacy is not thereby destroyed or made inaccessible. It may still be possible to establish organic links with it. These in turn may encourage the kinds of creative development needed to make Marxism once again a living force in the intellectual world. Those whose approach to the issues is shaped in any measure by Hegelian dialectic will be accustomed to the idea that a crisis may be 'a time of birth and transition to a new period'.[2] But such thoughts are more generally available. Thus Althusser, perhaps the most determined contemporary opponent of the Hegel connection, insists that the phrase 'the crisis of Marxism' must be given 'a completely different sense from collapse and death'. Then we can say: 'At last the crisis of Marxism has exploded! At last it is in full view! At last something vital and alive can be liberated by this crisis and in this crisis.'[3]

These are stirring words. The aim of the present work is to discover what, if any, rational grounds there are for such optimism.

* * *

I wish to acknowledge my indebtedness, extending over a number of years, for conversations on the topics of this book, and for criticisms of earlier versions of parts of it, to Chris Arthur, István Mészáros, Peter Osborne, Sean Sayers, Tony Smith and, most of all, to Roy Edgley. They will understand when I say that I am almost equally struck by the amount we found to agree on in these exchanges and by the way they bore out the dialectical truth that 'Opposition is true Friendship'.

I am indebted to Robin Blackburn for helpful suggestions concerning Herbert Marcuse, and for his interest in, and encouragement of, the project as a whole.

Finally, I would like to express my thanks to Aine Murtagh and Carin Dean for the exemplary skill and patience with which they typed the manuscript.

1

The Nature of the Problem

This book is a study of a central aspect of the Marxist intellectual tradition. It is addressed to concepts of social theory within that tradition, and, more especially, to concepts of the nature and status of Marxist social theory itself. Thus its topic comprises forms of self-understanding that are at the same time views on the proper or optimal ways of doing certain kinds of theoretical work. It seeks both to explicate these ideas and to assess them critically. If its primary objectives are achieved, some further questions should come into view. Provided, at any rate, that some measure of viability is accorded the Marxist project, one may ask how far it has actually been carried through and what are its future prospects. These further questions will not be treated systematically here. Nevertheless, the main discussion should yield a necessary condition of saying something useful about them, as well as a strong temptation to try to do so.

To sketch even our primary tasks is to delineate a field of study too vast to be treated satisfactorily within the compass of the present work. It may be well to make clear that there will be no attempt to deal equally here with all of its regions. To do so should also serve to indicate the historical range of the discussion. The main limitation may be described as follows. There is a large body of work conventionally located within the confines of Marxism which views Marxist social theory as essentially a descriptive and explanatory theory of unique authority and scope. Its major achievement is asserted, or assumed, to be the discovery of scientific laws of history and, specifically, of the mechanism that ensures the downfall of capitalism and its replacement by socialism. Using a familiar shorthand, this may be labelled the Marxism of the Second International. There are a number of reasons for not treating it here in its own right. The first is that there seems to be no substantial set of philosophical issues peculiar to the 'Marxist' version of such a science of

1

historical laws. If there are any, they could in any case be reached only through an analysis of the coherence and feasibility of the general programme, a task that lies well beyond our scope. A second, and related, point is that the 'Marxist' version cannot, as will become clear, be said to draw its inspiration from what is most distinctive and persistent in Marx's own meta-theoretical reflections. Finally, one should note that it does not figure at all prominently in current debates in the West, and indeed, could scarcely be said to represent a live option in them. That there are good reasons for this state of affairs is itself implied by the thesis of the present work. It would be perverse to seek to revive the Second International doctrine merely to knock it on the head again. To do so would be to introduce a pointless loop into the argument. Setting the doctrine aside, one can, using some more conventional shorthand, identify our chief areas of concern as 'classical' and 'Western' Marxism.

The linking of these areas may be given a positive justification. It consists in a thematic affinity between them. The nature of the affinity will be indicated roughly at first and then more precisely as the discussion proceeds. It concerns the relationship of theory to practice and, more specifically, the assumption of the peculiarly intimate character of this relationship. Some well-known formulations can serve to give an immediate purchase on the theme. Classical Marxism may be represented by Engels's designation 'scientific socialism'. This has usually been taken, as was plainly intended, as postulating a socialism informed through and through by the insights and authority of science. Engels's use of the term seems also to carry the suggestion of a science that has somehow, in virtue of its own constitution, a socialist character. Thus, he provides the gloss that scientific socialism is 'the theoretical expression of the proletarian movement'.[1] This in turn has a certain canonical status as an echo of various programmatic statements by Marx.[2] The relationship 'being the expression of' seems to promise as immediate and transparent a connection between theory and practice as may be conceived.

If one seeks a Western Marxist illustration of the theme, there is a vast field from which to choose. It may suffice to cite a similarly notorious instance: Gramsci's adoption of Labriola's phrase 'the philosophy of practice' as his name for Marxism. Clearly, this gives practice an integral, indeed definitional, role in conceptualizing theory. In Gramsci's discussion a central place is taken by 'the concept of the unity of theory and practice'. The identification of theory and practice is, he declares, 'a critical act, through which practice is demonstrated rational and necessary, and theory realistic and rational'.[3] These are striking claims: the reciprocally constituting and life-giving roles of theory and practice could scarcely be more dramatically affirmed. It should also be said that, in mediating these roles through the category of rationality, Gramsci is signalling a central concern of the present discussion, a concern that will recur many times in it. Here one may simply note that, taken together, our illustrations establish at least a *prima facie* case for the tightness of the theory–practice bond as a thematic affinity between classical and Western Marxism.

The theme seems bound to exclude Second International Marxism. An active intervention in events is scarcely called for if their course may safely be left to the workings of impersonal laws. Hence, where historical inevitability is emphasized the problem of how to conceptualize the theory–practice nexus does not acquire any urgency. Even apart from this substantive emphasis, the characteristic Second International stance on the formal question of science's relation to its object has little to offer the present inquiry. A science is assumed to be the systematic pursuit of knowledge of whatever causal relationships fall within its field of reference. Such an assumption does not in itself exclude the effectivity of human agency. Indeed, a systematic grasp of causal connections must prove useful to individual agents by informing their adaptation of means to ends. This, however, assures for science only a technical or instrumental role which cannot capture all that is involved in our thematic illustrations. It promises neither a scientific socialism nor a socialist science, but, at most, the conjunction of science and socialism. This would achieve not the unity of theory and practice but the external linking of theory to a practice towards which it is in itself indifferent. Any organized body of empirical knowledge may be said to have a practical significance in this sense. It applies as well to metallurgy as to historical materialism. Moreover, it readily accommodates orthodox, 'bourgeois' conceptions of the relation of social science to society. These conceptions have typically allowed that the science may be the basis for social engineering once it is harnessed to a specification of goals. The formulation of the goals is, however, taken to be a matter of normative commitment arrived at independently of the cognitive work of science. This engineering model must disappoint anyone who expects Marxism to embody a relationship with practice that is a radical alternative to that postulated in bourgeois thought.

Some light may be shed on the nature of that expectation if one considers a line of argument that seems conceptually well designed to satisfy it. In general terms, what is required, one may suppose, is that Marxist social theory be shown to have a practical dimension that does not arise from external linkages but is, in some sense, intrinsic to it. This supposition may be sharpened by using a terminology which is in current fashion and also has impeccable credentials from classical Marxism. What is required, it may be said, is that the theory be exhibited as a vehicle of, or a form of the movement towards, 'human emancipation'. Two problems arise at once. The first is that of saying what an emancipated human existence would be like, and the second is that of showing how social theory may be conceived as operating, by virtue of its own nature, on behalf of such existence. It is tempting to suppose that the two may be solved together. For an account of the goal should also yield a set of standards by which existing reality may be judged. Herein, it may be suggested, lies the practical significance of social theory: it is emancipatory through being evaluative, negatively evaluative, of non-emancipated society in the light of standards derived from the goal of emancipation. In being negatively evaluative it provides, one may add, reasons for acting so as to change what is being evaluated. Such reasons, however, are surely practical if anything is: with them the search for practicality reaches rock-bottom. Thus, the practical dimension of social theory comes to consist in its role as a systematically grounded and elaborated negative evaluation, a 'critique' of society. Moreover, this role may reasonably be regarded as intrinsic to it. The explanatory and critical aspects may be thought to be individually necessary to, and jointly constitutive of, its identity. By this route one arrives at a view which has been widely held in Western Marxism and may be accounted among its characteristic features. Its distinctive conception of the status of Marxist social theory is that it is in essence a critique of capitalist society. Here, as elsewhere, Western Marxism may be seen as reacting against the positivism of the Second International. The reaction is wholly justified, at least in the sense that it seeks to recover an authentic element in their supposed common ancestor, the Marxism of the classical period. It is a central contention of this book, however, that while the instinct of recovery is sound, the form of its expression has been profoundly misconceived and, indeed, has been a source of major dislocation within the Marxist tradition as a whole.

I

It is natural to wish to ground the process of justifying this contention in the relevant portions of the original Marxist legacy. An obvious starting-point is provided by the meta-theoretical reflections which were referred to earlier. The crux of them is Marx's insistence that his science employs a 'dialectical' method. The writers we have to consider have generally taken this insistence as a basic premise and guiding light. It has been seen as the key to reconstituting Marx's conception of his own work and, specifically, of its relation to practice. The appeal of such an approach is not hard to discern. The concept of dialectic is both protean and contested. An aspect that is not usually contested, however, is the sense of some essential connection with whatever is dynamic and in process of development. In the context of human society this must imply a connection with social change and, thereby, one might suppose, with organized attempts to achieve such change; that is, with radical practice. It is significant that in one of Marx's best-known expositions he explicitly links the dialectical character of his science to its 'revolutionary' status as 'a scandal and an abomination to the bourgeoisie'. In the same breath he insists no less strongly that it is 'in its very essence' a 'critical' method.[4] The present discussion assumes that a satisfactory elaboration of these remarks would reveal the core of classical Marxism's self-conception as social theory. The assumption itself is quite in keeping with Western Marxist tradition. The tradition has generally had little difficulty in focusing on the centrality for these matters of the dialectic. What has to be criticized are the ways in which it has typically sought to pose and resolve that central question.

At this point our concerns should begin to take more concrete forms. The chief task is one of reconstructing the practical dimension of Marxist social theory. It is uncontentious, and has massive textual support, to suppose that this practicality, however it is exercised, is exercised on the side of what Engels calls, in the statement cited above, the 'proletarian movement'. Within Marxism it is that movement which provides the agency through which the emancipated society is to be achieved. The question is how the theory's mode of operation as a constituent of the proletarian movement is to be understood. How, one may ask, is social theory to be conceived within a Marxist perspective as serving the interests of the working class, which are also the interests of human emancipation? There is a conceptual resource which has some advantages at this point as serving to pose the issues more sharply and, potentially at least, to systematize the treatment of a large area of classical Marxism. It will not in its fully explicit form be acceptable to everyone. It should, however, be possible to concede, if need be, the element most likely to upset settled convictions without losing what are, for present purposes, the chief benefits of the analysis. This is in effect to suggest that the recalcitrant element may be regarded, so far as those purposes are concerned, as being of largely terminological significance.

The basic idea may be put in its starkest form straight away. It is that to ask how social theory serves the interests of the working class is, within the framework of classical Marxism, to ask how it functions as working-class ideology. This idea could be fully vindicated only by providing a detailed account of the classical Marxist conception of ideology, a task which lies outside the scope of the present inquiry.[5] Here one should simply note that the heart of such an account would consist in a proposed definition of ideology as thought which serves class interests. It is the theoretical, rather than textual, difficulties to which this proposal gives rise that concern us now. They are chiefly ones of spelling out precisely how it is that the ideology of a class is to be conceived of as serving its interests. It is not difficult to see that it must be a matter of some kind of intelligible inner connection. The service is internal or conceptual, performed by virtue of the nature of the ideas themselves, not, for instance, through the causal consequences of their dissemination. There are two basic models in terms of which such a process may be understood. In the 'semantic' version, ideological forms serve class interests by being evaluative of the social practices and arrangements which constitute them. It is this model which is most prominent in Marx's own exercises in ideological analysis, as in the case of the ideologies of the Young Hegelians and of the political economists. In the second, 'syntactic', version the ideological effect is achieved through postulating, or assuming, formal analogies between the social arrangements constitutive of the class interests and the universe at large. The arrangements are legitimated by being, as it were, inscribed in reality itself, so that wherever people look the forms of their society are enacted over and over again. Studies of traditional societies offer the most striking illustrations of this mechanism, but it also sheds light on Weber's Protestant capitalists and on Goldmann's tragic visionaries of the *noblesse de robe*. The clearest expression in Marx's work is to be found in the treatment of religion and, in particular, of Christianity as the form of religion 'most fitting' for capitalism.[6]

It may readily be shown that the syntactic model cannot provide a basis for understanding Marxist social theory as ideology. Most obviously, and decisively, this is so because it presupposes a cosmological dimension which the theory does not possess. It may also be noted that the natural affinities of the model are with conservative thought. Its primary function is to shed light on the process of conceptually underpinning existing arrangements, and the examples that occur most readily to mind have that character. The basic message is: 'This is how things are, and must be.' It is also possible to envisage a reactionary use of the same conceptual resources. In it the existing arrangements would be viewed as being out of tune with the cosmos and as requiring accordingly to be changed. This is most easily taken as a proposal to return to some prelapsarian state of harmony. Such a restoration of the homology of society and extra-social reality is an unlikely programme for a theory professing to be socialist and dialectical, and is certainly not that of Marxism. The semantic model is, on the other hand, a serious candidate for the role we have in mind. For if it is accepted, Marxist social theory will again emerge as systematic negative evaluation: it is proletarian ideology by virtue of being a critique of capitalism. Thus, the path we have been exploring leads once more to the conception of social theory as social criticism. This is, it appears, the form in which the solution to our problem must be cast.

It should be emphasized that a reading of the situation in terms of 'ideology' is not obligatory, provided that the underlying conceptual realities are clear. The discussion has sought to draw attention to the complexity of the relationship of theory and social reality, and, specifically, of the case where the theory is presumed to bear practically on the reality. Whatever light it has shed may be maintained, whether this is agreed to be the ideological case or not. To reject the ideological reading is, it may be suggested, to forego an opportunity of achieving a synoptic view of the classical Marxist treatment of forms of social consciousness. That achievement requires above all a satisfactory placing of the categories 'science' and 'ideology'. It has been systematically obstructed by the tendency in Western Marxism to assume a dichotomy here or, at any rate, to regard ideology as a category for collecting forms of consciousness that are in one way or another cognitively defective. The interpretation outlined above breaks decisively with that tendency. Its advantages seem sufficiently marked to be worth adverting to from time to time. No attempt will be made, however, to secure them definitively, and the discussion will not presuppose the correctness of the interpretation. Its purpose is to explicate conceptions of social theory within the Marxist tradition. The delineation of a more comprehensive picture, taking in other areas of the tradition, would, however desirable in itself, be a bonus. We shall have to be content with glimpses of that larger picture.[7]

It is possible to trace yet another path over the terrain of the preceding argument. The starting-point is the view that social theory may be practical just in virtue of being dialectical. To formulate it is, one should note, to pose a problem, not to announce a solution. There is, it must be admitted, something in the charge that the friends of dialectic have tended to use it as a magic formula whose invocation can settle outstanding questions by itself. Yet a focus on the dialectical character of Marx's procedure offers no guarantee of exegetical success. Even commentators who offer detailed accounts going well beyond slogans do not always generate more than superficial insights here. These remarks may be filled out by considering a recent ambitious and sophisticated treatment of the matter. It is, moreover, a peculiarly useful source of warnings and guidelines for further inquiry. It yields, to anticipate the discussion, one particularly significant and melancholy moral. In this region at any rate what is more recent is not necessarily richer or more penetrating. Even work at the forefront of contemporary debates may turn out to involve a regression from achievements of the past. That this should be so accords well with the suggestion, which will recur in the present study, that Western Marxism as a whole traces a more or less consistent path of intellectual decline from its origins. The process is best encapsulated in the progressive slackening of its grip on the essentials of the tradition in which it locates itself. There is, of course, a sense in which a materialist explanation of this phenomenon is readily available. The fortunes of ideas are bound to the movement of material reality. If circumstances have been systematically unfavourable to socialist practice in the West, one can hardly expect the theory to thrive. From another perspective, however, the situation poses a peculiar difficulty for a theory professing to be dialectical. Other kinds of theory may suffer neglect or misunderstanding or dwindle to be the possession of a few without being damaged in their own being. For theories of the kind proposed by Hegel and Marx, which claim to be in touch with the emergent rationality of human society, matters are, it may be thought, more serious. The decay of the tradition seems of itself to constitute a criticism of the founding theses. The loss of insight into what those theses originally affirmed suggests that we are far from having to deal with a series of *Aufhebungen* through which all that is valuable in what has gone before has been preserved and raised to higher levels. Here, as elsewhere, a dialectical perspective forces attention on the true gravity of the contemporary crisis of Marxism, a crisis which may be masked by other approaches. This, too, is a theme which will recur in our discussion.

II

The source of guidelines referred to above is the 'vindication of dialectics' proposed by Jon Elster and developed in a series of writings. It is, as he puts it, an attempt 'to make explicit the logical structure (which one could call dialectical) of the non-methodological writings of Hegel and Marx'.[8] Elster's vindication has for its declared focus 'the idea of a contradiction'.[9] A fundamental thesis is that: 'There are situations in reality that can only be described by means of the concept of a logical contradiction'.[10] The interest of such situations lies in their centrality for the study of social change. Thus, among many similar formulations, one is told that 'the notion of a real contradiction can and should be the core of a theory of social change' and that 'the notion of a social contradiction has the theoretical function of identifying causes of instability and change'.[11] This project is, for Elster, attended with the largest consequences in view of his 'basic postulate' that '*the goal of the social sciences is the liberation of man*'.[12] It is plain that here is a rich mix of ingredients and one of great interest for our inquiry. In particular, it seems to promise just the kind of theoretical specification of the practical dimension of dialectical thought that we require. The outcome is, however, strangely disappointing, and also instructive in a high degree.

For Marx's theory of social contradictions, and, hence, his dialectical method, to be viable, it is essential, Elster believes, that the contradictions be construed as 'real contradictions' which are 'firmly tied to the logical concept'. This is achieved once they are seen as obtaining 'when several individuals simultaneously entertain beliefs about each other which are such that, although any one of them may well be true, it is logically impossible that they all be.' The social scientific interest of these situations lies in the fact that: 'If the individuals having these mutually invalidating beliefs about each other all act as if they were true, their actions will come to grief through the mechanism of unintended consequences.' This result is what Elster, borrowing from Sartre, calls 'counterfinality'.[13] The stock example is also due to Sartre: 'Each individual Chinese peasant ... seeks to obtain more land by cutting down trees, but a general deforestation induces erosion with *less* land available to each peasant than at the outset.'[14] The understanding of such situations represents, in Elster's opinion, 'Marx's central contribution to the methodology of social science'.[15]

It should be noted that Elster recognizes a second variety of social contradictions which he terms 'suboptimality'. It is formally defined as 'the deliberate realization of a non-cooperative solution that is Pareto-inferior to some other pay-off set obtainable by individual choices of strategy'. This is explained as the situation that arises 'when all the players adopt the solution strategies, fully aware that the others will do so as well and that they could all have obtained at least as much, and one of them more, than in the solution if some or all of them had diverged from the solution strategies'.[16]

The most striking difference between suboptimality and counterfinality is that the former involves intended and the latter unintended consequences. This, however, just reflects that fact that suboptimality, unlike counterfinality, is a game-theoretic notion. As such it presupposes 'strategic' rationality on the part of the players, in contrast to the merely 'parametric' rationality of counterfinality. 'The purposive-parametric actor assumes that he is free to adjust optimally in a constant or parametric situation. This assumption is in itself quite consistent . . . but if entertained simultaneously by all actors it generates counterfinality.' The 'purposive strategic man' on the other hand, is 'the actor of game theory who knows that his environment is composed of other strategic actors and that he is part of their environment'. It follows that he will be able 'to realize his goals without any danger of counterfinality'.[17] Thus, strategic behaviour is distinguished by the fact that it depends on choices 'that take account of the conjectured or anticipated choices of other agents'.[18] The 'paradigm case' of suboptimality, as thus conceived, is the Prisoner's Dilemma, a structure of which the social sciences provide, Elster believes, 'innumerable examples'.[19]

The prospect of the notion of a social contradiction being the core of a theory of social change seems both clear and inviting. When one looks more closely at Elster's argument however, this prospect begins to dissolve. It emerges that what the notion can and should be the core of is, more precisely stated, 'a dual theory of social change'. This is a theory not of the two aspects or varieties of change but of change on the one hand and of its absence on the other. The 'main thesis' Elster wishes to defend is that 'given certain structural conditions ... contradictions tend to generate collective action for the purpose of overcoming the con-tradictions'.[20] It is a dual theory in the sense that: 'Depending upon the kind of contradiction involved, the structural conditions for political organization may function both as obstacles to change and as agents of change.'[21] Thus, in some cases the contradiction is itself a 'form' of change, and then the action to which it leads 'may have the effect of reversing or halting the process of change'. These cases may, in Elster's view, safely be identified with counterfinality, which is itself *an economic variety of change'* engendering political action 'to restore the *status quo'*. Given a suboptimality, on the other hand, a collective action 'will represent the *political variety of change,* a departure from the *status quo'*.[22] In the working out of these ideas the dualism is firmly main-tained: counterfinality is itself change and generates action to counteract change, while suboptimality leads to a political process which achieves change if it is successful.

There are strong elements of paradox in this position. What Elster is offering is, one might suggest, the core of a theory of the genesis of collective political action. In this context the specific function of the variety of social contradiction he calls 'counterfinality' is to theorize the roots of conservative and reactionary politics. The oddity of identifying Marx's methodological achievement with this theme hardly needs labouring. Moreover, it should be borne in mind that counterfinality is the primary case of social contradiction and that suboptimalities only qualify in so far as they manage to be indistinguishable from it. Hence, Elster's thesis would be more accurately expressed by saying that, while social contradictions may themselves be forms of economic change, the causes which they have the theoretical function of identifying are causes of social stability and stasis. It is surely surprising to find such a view associated with traditional dialectics, still more to have it regarded as part of its vindication.

This point deserves to be taken a little further. What the dual theory proposes are parallel links between contradictions on the one hand and change or stability on the other. This seems not at all in keeping with the spirit in which these elements are treated in the classic texts. It is surely difficult to reconcile with the constant Hegelian refrain that contradiction is 'the root of all movement and vitality', 'the very moving principle of the world'.[23] The term used for such declarations is, in the original, *Widerspruch*, and Elster has usefully drawn attention to the carelessness of Marx's translators 'whereby not only "Widerspruch" but also "Gegensatz" are rendered into English (and French) by "contradiction"'.[24] Viewing Marx's usage in the light of this warning, it is evident that, where he differentiates the two terms, it is precisely the restless, crisis-signifying element that marks the moment of *Widerspruch*. An instance is provided in a passage cited by Elster from the *Economic and Philosophic Manuscripts*: 'The antithesis (*Gegensatz*) between *lack of property* and *property*, so long as it is not comprehended as the antithesis of *labour* and *capital*, still remains an indifferent antithesis, not grasped in its *active connection*, in its *integral relation*, not yet grasped as a *contradiction* (*Widerspruch*).'[25] The point emerges still more clearly in the continuation which is not used by Elster: 'labour . . . and capital . . . constitute *private property* as its developed state of contradiction (*Widerspruch*) – hence a dynamic relationship driving towards resolution.'[26] This dynamism is the constant hallmark of the relation of contradiction in Hegel and Marx. It pervades not merely their methodological pronouncements but also the details of their practice. Nowhere does it seem to occur to them to view the relation as a potential mode or instrument of immobility. It is exhibited rather in processes in which the successive stages, while retaining something of their origins, are perpetually driven beyond to realize also what is discrepant and unprecedented. A social science which even-handedly links contradictions with 'conditions for stability' and with 'conditions for change' can scarcely claim a significant part of this intellectual legacy.[27]

To do Elster justice as an interpreter of Hegel and Marx, it is necessary to move at this point to a more concrete level of analysis. In particular, one should focus on the cases where he specifically connects the perception of what he regards as social contradictions with change; that is, on the suboptimalities. The question to be asked is what is the precise nature of the connection in these cases. It will be useful here to consider what Elster regards as a 'transparently simple example' illustrating his ideas about social contradictions. The situation is one foreshadowed by Marx and identified in Keynesian economics as an 'essential paradox of capitalism': 'each capitalist wants low wages for his own workers (this makes for high profits) and high wages for the workers of all other capitalists (this makes for high demand)'. The capitalists are, however, capable of learning, and may end up by understanding the paradox, and understanding that they all understand it, in which case, as Elster remarks, 'the situation is transformed into a game'. Clearly, this development is one from counterfinality to suboptimality, mediated by the actors coming to perceive the contradiction in the original situation. When the transition is accomplished:

> The suboptimality of the situation makes for paradox and tension; it is hard to accept misery when everyone could better their lot if everyone behaved differently. The outcome, given certain structural conditions, is a pressure towards organization, collective action, or government intervention: a case of *contradictions inducing change.*[28]

A key role in this account is played by the assumption of the difficulty of accepting misery when it is seen to be avoidable. Thus, it is played by what may be regarded as a simplistic, but presumably uncontentious, psychological generalization. Elster is conscious of the sketchiness of his suggestions in this area, and wishes to defend it before 'the empirically oriented reader', for whom he is 'primarily writing'. His hope is that social scientists will be 'tempted into filling in some of the holes' in his outline sketches, so as to specify 'the precise mechanism for change'.[29] Clearly, what is envisaged is a causal mechanism working through individual psychology. Given the purely contingent nature of the relationships this would involve, on Elster's conception of causality, it is not surprising that he should be just as willing to link contradictions with stability as with change. Invoking again the contrast with Hegel and Marx, however, it has to be said that for them the link with change is internal to, and indeed partly constitutive of, the relation of contradiction. It is by its nature the vehicle of the new: 'to think the contradiction' is, we are given to understand, to think 'pure change'.[30] The point may be put by noting that something vital in the classical doctrine has fallen between the gaps of Elster's reconstruction. He recognizes the primitive variety of social contradiction, the unperceived counterfinality, as itself a form of change. Furthermore, he asserts that the second variety, the perceived suboptimality, may activate a mechanism making for change. What is missing is the traditional notion that the perception of contradictions is, in and of itself, a creative, transforming force in human life. Without this element it is difficult to grasp what, historically, the fuss over the dialectic has been about, or what there is in it that stands in any significant need of vindication. Thus, Elster's mission succeeds only at the cost of trivializing whatever it manages to rescue.

A convenient way to develop the point is provided by his discussion of the *Phenomenology of Spirit.* It is for him 'without comparison

Hegel's greatest work', and Marx's theory of social contradictions is said to be 'derived largely' from it.[31] Elster displays, however, a somewhat coarse-grained understanding of how the dialectical transitions in the work are accomplished. He notes that its 'moving force' is 'the emergence and then the overcoming' of certain kinds of contradictions of beliefs and desires: 'the subject itself discovers the inconsistency of its current "form" (*Gestalt*) when comparing its own mental structure with its own criteria of adequacy'. This is so far an unexceptionable, indeed enlightening, account. In pointing the moral, Elster's touch is, however, less sure: 'The "surfacing" of the contradiction to an explicit object of consciousness induces a change in the form of the consciousness, but the new form always turns out to harbour a contradiction of its own, and so on until the level of absolute knowledge has been reached.'[32] The language of causal mechanism which serves him everywhere else to link contradictions with change seems conspicuously out of place here. The lesson of Hegel's text is not that the discovery of self-contradictions 'induces' a change in the form of consciousness: it is in a literal sense already itself such a change. The mental structure which carried the contradiction does not survive its 'surfacing' pending the working out of a causal process, but is immediately overturned by it. This issue is of great importance for our argument. It may, however, be best to postpone its detailed consideration to a later stage. For the present we should be grateful to Elster for focusing on the *Phenomenology* in connection with the roots of Marx's theory of social contradictions. It is a hint that will in due course be developed. We should be grateful for even more basic insights; in particular, the identification of contradiction as the key category of dialectical science and the insistence that to achieve significant results it must retain its 'logical' character. It remains to be seen what conception of the scope of logic is needed to accommodate this, but it represents what is surely a salutary emphasis.

It is still the case, however, that the exemplary value of Elster's discussion is largely negative. At the core of it there is, we have seen, an empirical thesis concerning the efficacy of a social-psychological mechanism. According to it, the perception of contradictions of a certain kind sets up pressures to overcome the contradictions, where such overcoming involves social change. Even if this thesis were firmly established it could scarcely make a significant contribution to, still less constitute a vindication of, the dialectics of Hegel and Marx. As the discussion has shown, these dialectics presuppose some stronger, more intimate connection between thought and change than may be accounted for along such lines. It is surely obvious that the basic relationship postulated in the thesis would need drastic modal strengthening for it to have any serious chance of success. At this point it seems natural to turn once again to the idea of critique. For it offers a prospect of conceiving of the key items as internally related to each other. In criticizing what is unsatisfactory, theory, it may be suggested, yields the practical conclusion that it should be changed and, thereby, licenses action to change it. To act on the basis of such theory is not a matter of bowing to psychological pressure, but of being convinced by a process of argument. Hence, the possibility arises that a vindication of dialectics may have at its core not an empirical regularity but a movement of reason, a movement that will be causally efficacious in so far as the audience for critique is itself rational.

The discussion has led by a variety of routes to the conclusion that any further progress must lie through the doctrine of critique. The first section of the book will be an examination of that doctrine. It is natural to start by considering it in its seminal formulation for Western Marxism, the critical theory of society of the so-called 'Frankfurt School'. This is the subject of Chapters 2 and 3. The discussion turns in Chapters 4 and 5 to consider some versions of the doctrine which have been proposed by recent writers with intellectual roots in the analytical tradition in philosophy. They will, for convenience, be grouped under the heading 'scientific critique'. These two main forms of the critique approach are united in their stress on the requirement to be dialectical; what they offer is in its self-conception a critical and dialectical theory. Yet, as one might expect, they also differ significantly in their preconceptions, style of argument and substantive conclusions. Each is, in its own way, exemplary for our purposes, and, taken together, they provide a reasonably complete view of the strengths and weaknesses of the approach as a whole. It is important in the light of what follows to stress that the strengths are considerable, and must be preserved in any solution that is eventually proposed. What is proposed here will, it is hoped, be itself dialectical in that sense as well as in others. Such a proposal will be elaborated in the final section of this study.

PART I

The Critique of Society

2

The Frankfurt School: Adorno

This chapter is concerned with the doctrine of social critique in its most influential form, the critical theory of society of the Frankfurt School. It will be assumed for the present that to be critical is to be practical in a sense that fulfils all that may legitimately be demanded of social theory. The first question to be considered is how the critical character of Frankfurt School theory is to be understood. What constitutes it as critical and not simply explanatory theory? It is a question which gets little systematic attention from the critical theorists themselves, nor, surprisingly, has it occasioned much reflection by commentators. The tendency of the literature is for the critical claim to be made and accepted, while the problem of how it should be conceptualized is ignored, or negotiated with vague generalities. Yet it is perhaps the chief question of philosophical interest that arises in this area. The answers shed much light on the kind of structure a critique of society needs to possess. They also exhibit a pattern with a still more direct relevance to the present discussion. They show that in all major versions of Frankfurt School theory what constitutes it as critical is at odds with its explanatory aspect. The aspiration to be critical cannot, it appears, be reconciled with the theorists' deepest sense of what is actually going on in society and of the logic of that process. The conflict arises, it should be stressed, precisely because the aspiration is cast in a self-consciously 'dialectical' mould. It is the critical theorists' insight into, and wish to satisfy, the requirements for theory to be dialectical that is the source of the dilemma in which they found themselves. This dilemma ensures their exemplary status for our inquiry. A grasp of it reveals, as perhaps nothing else could, the deep problems faced by the project of dialectical social critique and, more generally, by any theory that in contemporary conditions aims to be dialectical and emancipatory.

A text often given canonical status, both inside and outside the

17

Frankfurt School, so far as the statement of a programme is concerned, is Horkheimer's 1937 essay 'Traditional and Critical Theory'.[1] It is, in spite of this status, or in partial explanation of it, remarkably elusive even on quite basic points. Nevertheless, the historical loyalties of the method it advocates are clearly, if half-heartedly, declared. The term 'critical', we are told in a footnote, 'is used here less in the sense it has in the idealist critique of pure reason than in the sense it has in the dialectical critique of political economy'.[2] It will be convenient to borrow for these contrasting elements in the idea of critique the labels 'reconstruction' on the one hand and 'criticism' on the other.[3] The idealist programme of reconstructive critique is one of specifying the conditions of the possibility of the exercise of reason, either in general or in some specific practice. The critique of political economy has, however, to be understood as criticism; that is, as systematic negative evaluation. It seems from Horkheimer's declaration that it is with this second version of critique that we have essentially to deal.

The question posed at the start of the chapter may now be re-formulated. What has to be conceptualized is a system of negative evaluation. Such a system, it may be assumed, will necessarily involve some standards of evaluation. There must be criteria of judgement mediating the transition from the starting-points of the enterprise to its practical conclusions. The question is what is the nature of the standards in the case of the critical theory of society of the Frankfurt School.

It may be well to start by noting the most general ways in which the critical theorists themselves characterize their practice. The most general epithet of all has already been encountered in the quotation from Horkheimer and is invoked on innumerable occasions elsewhere: their critique is, first and foremost, 'dialectical'. Thus, the critical theorists seize on Marx's master clue to methodology as resolutely as one could wish. For them dialectical social theory is necessarily critique, a critique that works in the mode of 'immanence'. Adorno speaks for all when he insists: 'Dialectic's very procedure is immanent critique.'[4] He is fully representative also when he goes on to claim the authority of Hegel for this view. The reference cited is from a section of the *Science of Logic* which offers one of Hegel's most explicit presentations of dialectic as immanent criticism. Its immediate concern is the question of the correct approach to philosophical systems:

the refutation must not come from outside, that is, it must not proceed from assumptions lying outside the system in question and inconsistent with it. The system need only refuse to recognize those assumptions; the *defect* is a defect only for him who starts from the requirements and demands based on those assumptions.[5]

Hegel goes on to make the comment quoted by Adorno: 'Genuine refutation must penetrate the power of the opponent and meet him on the ground of his strength; the case is not won by attacking him somewhere else and defeating him where he is not.'[6]

The standards of dialectical criticism must not, it appears, be externally imposed on the object, but must in some sense arise within it. This is still not a perspicuous requirement, and perhaps the best way to bring it into a sharper focus is to see how it is interpreted in practice. What is needed are some models of immanent method at work. No attempt can be made here to follow up all the many and varied hints dropped by the critical theorists as to how social criticism might proceed. The discussion will have to be confined to conceptions which have some substantial presence in their writings. It should also be said that although there is an element of chronological order in what follows, it is not a historical study and the basic divisions of the subject matter are framed on conceptual grounds alone.

I

The obvious place to start is with a procedure that seems to apply the lessons of the *Science of Logic* as directly as possible. It is advocated in Horkheimer's 'Notes on Institute Activities' of 1941, his most self-conscious attempt as Director to 'summarize the research project' of the Institute of Social Research. The question of standards is dealt with in the following way:

> The critical nature of societal concepts may best be elucidated through the problem of value judgments that animates current discussion among social scientists.... Social theory may be able to circumvent a sceptical spurning of value judgments without succumbing to normative dogmatism. This may be accomplished by relating social institutions and activities to the values they themselves set forth as their standards and ideals.... If subjected to such an analysis, the social agencies most representative of the present pattern of society will disclose a pervasive discrepancy between what they actually are and the values they accept.... The ambivalent relation between prevailing values and the social context forces the categories of social theory to become critical and thus to reflect the actual rift between the social reality and the values it posits.[7]

On this model, immanent criticism lives off the gap between what society professes and what it performs. Much of its appeal, as Horkheimer's account suggests, derives from the way it appears to resolve the problem of standards without the need for elaborate and difficult theorizing. They are constituted by values posited by the social reality itself. Thus they are, as it were, taken ready-formed from the object of criticism: it is made to condemn itself out of its own mouth.

There is a strong case for holding that such a conception was indeed central to the Institute's work at this period. It is often explicitly invoked by the leading theorists, and many of their illustrations of critical method are intelligible only in terms of it. Characteristically, it is what Adorno was later to call 'liberal society's pretensions to freedom and equality' that are the chief target.[8] The model is somewhat less prominent in Marcuse's writings, but he too declares:

> The critical rationality derives from the principles of autonomy which individualistic society itself had declared to be its self-evident truths. Measuring these principles against the form in which individualistic society has actualized them, critical rationality accuses social injustice in the name of individualistic society's own ideology.[9]

A version of the same idea supplies, on the author's own account, the methodology of *Soviet Marxism*.[10]

The practice of criticism conceived along these lines has figured large in commentaries on the Frankfurt School. In these works it is frequently subsumed under, and provides the chief substance of, the category 'critique of ideology' (*Ideologiekritik*). It will help in exploring the subject to reflect on the misleading nature of this heading. As Marcuse's statement suggests, what we have here is not, in its standard employment by the critical theorists, a conception in which ideology forms the object of criticism. Instead, ideology, in the shape of the values of society, is held constant as the yardstick against which social reality is measured. It is, in Horkheimer's words, a method for criticizing 'social institutions and activities in the light of the values they themselves set forth'. Adorno is just as explicit: the 'spokesmen' of dialectical materialism 'questioned not the ideas of humanity, freedom and justice but rather the claim of bourgeois society to have realized those ideas'.[11] Thus, the project is not one of a critique of ideology but of what might be called an ideological critique of society.

This issue opens the way to something more fundamental. It brings home the need to make explicit a condition which must obtain if one is to speak of critique here at all. On the face of things, it may be said, all that the procedure achieves is, in Horkheimer's terminology, to 'disclose a discrepancy' or 'reflect a rift' between ideology and reality. Such a gap is in itself, however, no more a deficiency for a liberal society than it would be for any other. It would be odd to assume that one must be criticizing a community that claims to follow the precept 'thou shalt not suffer a witch to live' if one shows that it does not in fact manage to kill all the individuals meeting its requirements for being witches. The difficulty here was anticipated by Hegel: it concerns the ease with which the force of the criticism may be evaded by stepping outside the assumptions that define the field of immanence. The method has critical significance only in so far as one accepts, however provisionally, the ideology used as a yardstick. It will have greatest impact on those who subscribe to it with fewest reservations, and are most likely to be outraged by seeing it flouted. Hence, the method, as standardly employed by the Frankfurt School, is in its deepest meaning a method of bourgeois self-criticism.

These points emerge clearly enough in Adorno's discussion of the method in connection with 'radical bourgeois thought' of the nineteenth century. At that time: 'Critics confronted bourgeois society not only economically but morally with its own norms.'[12] The representative figure is the Ibsen of *Hedda Gabler*. Adorno's discussion shows from another aspect the basic limitation of the ideological method, its inability to enforce conclusions hostile to the existing state of things. At best, its disclosure of the contradiction of ideology and reality may be said to confront its audience with a need to choose. In the case in question, some of them at least were inclined to jump in the opposite direction to the critics. Thus, the criticism 'left the ruling stratum ... with no other defence than to reject the very principle by which society was judged, its own morality'.[13] Later in the same work Adorno sheds fresh light on the bourgeois character of the model by developing a refinement of it in terms of the notion of 'irony'. The mode of irony is not content with flatly confronting social reality with its own ideology, but, more subtly, 'convicts its object by presenting it as what it purports to be'. It is a quintessentially insider style of criticism whose 'formal *a priori*' is agreement on 'binding norms'.[14] Here the representative example is the work of Karl Kraus.

Adorno is plainly sensitive to the suspicion that the procedure achieves its immanence, its insider status, only at the expense of its radicalism, only by accepting the confines of the bourgeois horizon. Thus, he insists that 'the motives of intransigent bourgeois self-criticism coincide in fact with those of materialism, through which the former attain self-awareness'.[15] This claim seems in a general way unconvincing. The motives of materialism include the abolishing of bourgeois society, and bourgeois self-criticism, however intransigent, could hardly stretch so far without losing its bourgeois identity: its self-awareness at that point would be suicidal. In relation to our overall concerns, however, the issue may best be pursued by direct reference to the work of Marx. No extensive citation is needed to show that he did not take bourgeois ideology as a guiding light, but instead subjected it throughout his career to radical criticism. There is, for example, the treatment of the doctrine of the 'rights of man' in the early essay 'On the Jewish Question'. The objection is not that these rights fail to be realized in bourgeois society: it is directed against the entire tradition of thought in itself.[16] On this issue at least there is no failure of continuity between the young and the mature Marx. This is sufficiently shown by the mockery directed in the first volume of *Capital* at the sphere of commodity exchange as 'a very Eden of the innate rights of man ... the exclusive realm of Freedom, Equality, Property and Bentham'.[17] No doubt the significance of Marx's career is open to many interpretations. But any tendency to assimilate him to the role of bourgeois ironist must surely be misconceived.

It may not be necessary to labour the difficulties faced by ideological critique. For the model did not remain for long at the centre of the Frankfurt School's conception of its project. It began to founder for reasons that are eloquently depicted in Adorno's account of the fate of bourgeois irony:

> Irony's medium, the difference between ideology and reality, has disappeared. The former resigns itself to confirmation of reality by its mere duplication. Irony used to say: such it claims to be, but such it is; today, however, the world, even in its most radical lie, falls back on the argument that things are like this, a simple finding which coincides, for it, with the good. There is not a crevice in the cliff of the established order into which the ironist might hook a fingernail.[18]

With variations of idiom, this diagnosis is repeated by all our subjects. In the era of liberal capitalism it was possible, the argument runs, to confront reality with its own aspirations. But in the total, one-dimensional world of administered capitalism no such possibility appears. Ideological critique presupposes a gap between what thought projects and what is actually performed. But thought has now become a reflex of the established order and projects nothing beyond it: ideology in the original sense has evaporated. Thus, the programme of ideological critique could not be carried through because it proved incompatible with the School's central vision of the nature of contemporary society. It had to be given up and replaced by something else. Resources for this were, of course, available. The failure of ideological critique is, nevertheless, ominous in its signalling of the problem of reconciling the explanatory thrust of the School's social theory with the ambition to be critical.

II

It was noted above that critique as criticism requires an element that sets standards of judgement. This cannot now be constituted by ideals avowed by the object itself. It seems natural, however, to suppose that whatever fills the role will have to have a similar conceptual shape. This suggests that it should consist in a set of values which, as before, function as principles of social organization and, taken together, specify a state of human existence held to be superior to that obtaining in the present. It is not even necessary in virtue of the collapse of ideological critique to renounce the particular values by which it had operated, though it will, of course, be necessary to conceptualize their claim to be immanent in a different way. It remains to be seen whether this can be achieved. The first step towards an alternative model is, at any rate, easy enough to take. For the vision of a preferred state of society, of 'the good life' for human beings, is a pervasive presence in the writings of the critical theorists. It will accord with a familiar usage, and is encouraged by that of our subjects themselves, if what is warranted by this vision is identified as a specifically 'moral' version of critique.[19]

The main questions that arise at this point may be distinguished as follows. The first is simply that of specifying the Frankfurt School's ideal of human existence as precisely as the evidence allows. The second concerns its foundational aspect, the justification of the values it embodies. The third, closely related to the other two, is the question of how criticism in terms of such values can be immanent so far as existing society is concerned. What hangs on this is, as we have seen, the claim of criticism to be part of, or organically linked to, the tradition of dialectical thought. It is in the end the crucial issue for the present inquiry, but something must be said on the others in order to clear the ground for dealing with it.

The search for answers to the first question quickly runs up against the notorious reluctance of the members of the School to spell out in any detail the features of the future society. This reluctance reflects a tendency in Marxist thought stemming from Marx himself, though with Adorno in particular it takes a peculiarly emphatic form, amounting almost to a taboo. Nevertheless, the literature of critical theory contains enough in the way of characterization for our immediate purposes. The society towards which the theory is orientated, the first 'truly human' society, will be structured in accordance with principles of freedom and justice. Beyond that, at the individual existential level, Marcuse supplies a reasonably rich specification in terms of the achievement of happiness. For Horkheimer too, at least in some phases of his thought, critical theory has 'the happiness of all individuals as its goal'.[20] Adorno's characteristic stance is perhaps best shown in his reaction to the fact that 'He who asks what is the goal of an emancipated society is given answers such as the fulfilment of human possibilities or the richness of life'.[21] What this elicits is an immediate condemnation both of the 'illegitimate' character of the question and the 'repellent assurance' of the answer. Yet even in this very section of text Adorno is willing to provide some content for conceptions of everyday life in the emancipated society. Admittedly, the note that is struck is one not often heard in the precincts of Marxism:

> *Rien faire comme une bête*, lying on water and looking peacefully at the sky, 'being, nothing else, without any further definition and fulfilment', might take the place of process, act, satisfaction and so truly keep the promise of dialectical logic that it would culminate in its origin. None of the abstract concepts come closer to fulfilled utopia than that of eternal peace.[22]

There is also a contrast to be drawn between Adorno on the one hand and Horkheimer and Marcuse on the other as regards the question of foundations. The section of *Minima Moralia* which has just been cited offers a starting-point for considering Adorno's distinctive views in this area. Having rejected both question and answer concerning the goal of an emancipated society, he adds at once: 'There is tenderness only in the coarsest demand: that no one shall go hungry any more.' This 'coarseness' is, it may be said, the hallmark of Adorno's version of moral critique. In *Negative Dialectics* he envisages a society 'so organized as the productive forces would directly permit it here and now, and as the conditions of production on either side relentlessly prevent it', and comments: 'The *telos* of such an organization of society would be to negate the physical suffering of even the least of its members and to negate the internal reflexive forms of that suffering.'[23] Elsewhere in the work the drive towards the great moral simplicities takes even starker form: 'It is not in their nauseating parody, sexual repression, that moral questions are succinctly posed; it is in lines such as: No man should be tortured; there should be no concentration camps....' What is striking here from a foundational viewpoint is the unwillingness to allow these 'lines' to be a subject for theorizing: 'The lines are true as an impulse, as a reaction to the news that torture is going on somewhere. They must not be rationalized.'[24] Later on, the stakes are raised yet higher, and theory seems still more out of place:

> A new categorical imperative has been imposed by Hitler upon unfree mankind: to arrange their thoughts and actions so that Auschwitz will not repeat itself, so that nothing similar will happen. When we want to find

reasons for it, this imperative is as refractory as the given one of Kant was once upon a time. Dealing discursively with it would be an outrage, for the new imperative gives us a bodily sensation of the moral addendum – bodily, because it is now the practical abhorrence of the unbearable physical agony to which individuals are exposed even with individuality about to vanish as a form of mental reflection.[25]

This refusal to be discursive is the most remarkable feature of Adorno's position. His wish is, it appears, to assimilate the relationship with the moral fundamentals to a purely natural, somatic reaction, an 'impulse', a 'bodily sensation'. Many philosophers have, of course, granted the primitive status of suffering and have placed it at the centre of their moral universe. But they have generally been willing to represent this view as, in some measure, the product of, and a fit subject for, ratiocination, if only in order to register it as an ultimate commitment or basic postulate. Such a recognition seems to involve a degree of theoretical placing, of conceptual mediation, that would be unacceptable to Adorno. His stance appears by contrast as frankly irrationalist. Having regard to the factors that shaped it, the stance is in human terms deserving only of deep respect. If, however, it is considered as an element in a foundational exercise, it can hardly be accepted as satisfactory. The difficulty is that, as with other forms of irrationalism, it is open to an immediate counter-thrust that has as much or as little authority as it does itself. Unfortunately, we know enough of human psychopathology, and Adorno has contributed to these insights, to realize that sympathy and indignation cannot be counted on as automatic responses to agony. The supply of torturers would not be what it is if there were not also at work spontaneous stirrings of a different kind. To acknowledge this, is not, of course, to suggest that Adorno's humane and generous anger belongs on one footing with the evil cravings of the sadist. But the differences do not emerge if they are considered merely in their character as natural impulses: to bring them out the willingness to find reasons, to deal discursively, is indispensable.

This willingness is much more marked in the writings of Horkheimer and Marcuse. Indeed, the position that emerges from them has a decidedly rationalist character, for in it 'reason' itself turns out to be the key foundational category. The basic claim is simply that the organization of society which realized justice, freedom and happiness would also be its rational organization. Beyond that, the tendency is to assume, in keeping with the philosophical tradition, that nothing need, or can, be said in its favour. For Horkeimer's views it may be most rewarding to turn to the earlier period before the development of the philosophy 'shared' with Adorno.[26] In 'Traditional and Critical Theory' the critical project is consistently placed under the authority of reason. Critical theory of society is described as 'a theory dominated at every turn by a concern for reasonable conditions of life'. The goal at which critical thought aims is 'the rational state of society'. More specifically, 'the critical theory in its concept formation and in all phases of its development very consciously makes its own that concern for the rational organization of human activity which it is its task to illumine and legitimate'. At the same time, the project is also tied to various substantive social considerations and primarily to ones of justice: 'the critical theory has no specific influence on its side, except concern for the abolition of social injustice'. Horkheimer taps in the final nail in the argument by adding: 'This negative formulation ... is the materialist content of the idealist concept of reason.'[27]

In a companion piece to Horkheimer's essay, Marcuse lays stress on the connection between reason and freedom: 'the concept of reason contains the concept of freedom as well.... Hegel was only drawing a conclusion from the entire philosophical tradition when he identified reason and freedom.' Elsewhere in the essay the goal of the 'rational organization of society' is explicitly linked with 'concern for human happiness', and 'man' is understood as 'a rational being' that 'requires freedom' and has happiness as 'his highest good'.[28] Another essay of the period strongly emphasizes the 'inner connection' of happiness and freedom: 'Happiness, as the fulfilment of all potentialities of the individual, presupposes freedom: at root, it is freedom. Conceptual analysis reveals them to be ultimately identical.'[29]

In plotting the internal ties that bind the concepts of reason, freedom and justice, Horkheimer and Marcuse were, as they well knew, drawing on powerful themes in the Western philosophical tradition. Freedom and justice have standardly been regarded there as the primary mediations through which reason makes its presence felt in the world: freedom is the indispensable medium of all attempts to implement its demands, and justice is the guarantee that their implementation bears no trace of arbitrariness; that is, of the irrational. The connections are less transparent in the case of happiness and Marcuse has to engage in more elaborate discussion to establish them. Nevertheless, the overall strategy is clear. What is offered is, in the end, a foundational theory in which the social ideal is specified in terms of principles that are themselves to be seen as articulations of reason. This is an entrenched and, within its limits, persuasive pattern of argument, and it will not be challenged here. Having fixed it as background, attention may now be shifted to an issue which is raised in an acute form by Horkheimer's and Adorno's rationalism. Their foundational strategy had relied on abstract, conceptual considerations not especially linked to any particular set of historical circumstances. The difficulty is to see how criticism in the light of standards established in that way can possibly qualify as immanent. But this issue is bound to become more pressing in the course of the move from ideological to any form of moral critique.

III

A response may be formulated in terms of a category which has a central place in dialectical tradition and recurs constantly throughout the writings of the critical theorists. It offers the most suitable heading under which to draw together the diversity of their views. The key category is potentiality. Criticism may intelligibly be said to be immanent provided that its object is, as it were, pregnant with its goal. But potentiality is notoriously a slippery notion, and the risks were obvious to our subjects. Thus, it is an organizing principle of Marcuse's essay on 'Philosophy and Critical Theory', and yet he is careful to warn: 'in phantasy one can imagine anything. But critical theory does not envision an endless horizon of possibilities.'[30]

In an essay written slightly later, Adorno, having insisted that dialectics 'would renounce itself in renouncing the idea of potentiality', goes on to ask: 'But how is potentiality to be conceived if it is not to be abstract and arbitrary, like the utopias dialectical philosophers proscribed?'[31] The danger in the idea is that it may give way under pressure and fail to place any significant controls on one's imaginings. It is then easy to drift into the possible worlds of the logicians, the accommodating domain of the not logically impossible. The potentialities that ground the immanence of dialectical critique, however, must be in some stronger sense real, objective possibilities of the material. The task for theory is to discipline the idea so as to achieve this. There are, it may be suggested, three main guidelines or forms of constraint at work in the writings of the Frankfurt School.

The first is a direct legacy of historical materialism. Genuine possibilities are warranted by the level of development of the productive forces. Significantly, this is the immediate recourse of both Marcuse and Adorno in the essays that have been cited. The second constraint derives from philosophical ontology. The limits of what is truly possible are set by the nature of whatever it is whose development is in question. In critical theory, the typical focus of such concern is, variously, the individual human subject, society or humanity as a whole. The third requirement may be seen as a distillation of the first two, their political expression, so to speak. It holds that there must be actual forces or tendencies at work in existing society which may be taken as the bearers of the possibility of its transformation. These guidelines are, of course, not mutually incompatible, but are readily found in association with one another. There are, however, significant variations of emphasis in the way they are treated in the different reaches of critical theory.

The variations emerge primarily in the treatment of the ontological guidelines. The historical materialist requirement tends to be assumed by all the critical theorists, but not in a way that differentiates them substantially. In relation to the modern period, it is usually taken as carrying the promise of the conquest of scarcity, which is itself the precondition of all the other achievements of the emancipated society. Accepting this requirement can, however, only be the starting-point for an understanding of potentiality. Theorists who claim any kinship with Marx will, after all, be unlikely to see much point in speculating about social possibilities which lack any roots in human productive powers. To delimit them significantly one has to consider the nature of the subjects of historical change.

Adorno's work in this area involves a theme that seems to offer a powerful response to the crisis of ideological critique. At least, it promises the smallest break with the origins of dialectical method. The attempt to base critique on values professed by the object itself turned out to be a failure. But it was, in any case, a procedure of limited scope which captured only a part of the Hegelian enterprise. To capture it fully one has to do justice to the diversity of working models of dialectic it contains. In particular, one has to move beyond the limitations of the model which was the basis for ideological critique, that of the immanent approach to philosophical systems. It is by no means the case that Hegel's dialectic is tied to objects with a level of consciousness capable of yielding standards for criticism ready formed. The means through which its range is extended beyond such instances are mainly ontological. Thus, the historical dialectic has as its 'presupposition' the idea that 'reason governs the world, and that world history is therefore a rational process'. As such, it is 'the rational and necessary evolution of the world spirit'.[32] The significance of this ontological commitment for immanent method is that it introduces a fresh element to serve as a pole of the oppositions on which the method depends. This element is the rational which stands opposed to the real and which yet, since the two are articulated together through the life of spirit, is inherent within it as potentiality. Method is not now limited to finding a gap between the object's self-image and its present existence. It may focus instead on that between one or both of those moments and the object as it is in its concept and in truth; that is, in the fulfilment of its role in the development of rational spirit. The difficulties in this conception have sponsored a vast literature, but they need not concern us in detail here.[33] What has to be noted is the new world it promises to open up for criticism. This is no longer confined to objects that may be said to possess their own ideology. Even what is most inarticulately locked 'in itself' may be posited in opposition to the rational form of its own existence. Thus, one arrives at the conception of a method of complete generality, a generality echoed in many of Adorno's formulations of his immanent dialectic; the 'confrontation of concept and reality', the 'cogitative confrontation of concept and thing'.[34]

It is scarcely surprising that Adorno feels able to retain such formulations, for he is far from any outright rejection of Hegelian ontology and, in particular, its problematic of the subject. An indication of how he wishes to rework that problematic is given in his contribution to the *Positivismusstreit*. The hallmark of positivist sociology is taken to be its treatment of 'the subject of all knowledge – society, the bearer of logical generality' as if it were simply an object: 'Here lies the innermost difference between a critical theory of society and what is commonly known as sociology ... critical theory is orientated towards the idea of society as subject, whilst sociology accepts reification.'[35] The most explicit development of this idea is to be found in *Negative Dialectics*. What is proposed there is a materialist unmasking of Hegelian *Geist*, an unmasking from which it emerges as identical with society.

> Alfred Sohn-Rethel was the first to point out that hidden in ... the general and necessary activity of the mind (*der allgemeinen und notwendigen Tätigkeit des Geistes*) lies work of an inalienably social nature. ... Beyond the philosophy of identity's magic circle the transcendental subject can be deciphered as society, unconscious of its own self (*als die ihrer selbst unbewusste Gesellschaft*).[36]

The theme recurs later in the work: 'In the name "world spirit" the spirit is affirmed and hypostatized only as that which it always was in itself ... what society worships in the world spirit is itself, the omnipotence of its own coercion.'[37]

This ontological thesis has, as might be expected, its implications for method. It is in the light of it that one should read the statement that negative dialectics 'assumes, *tel quel*, the abrupt immediacy, the formations which society and its evolution present to our thought; and it does this so that analysis may bare its mediations, according to the standard (*nach dem Mass*) of the immanent difference between phenomena and that which they claim to be in themselves (*was sie von sich aus zu sein beanspruchen*)'.[38]

Here, as in Hegel, the evolution of the subject is made to yield the standard for universal critique. It gives a purchase to the crucial idea of the tension between what things immediately are and what they implicitly (*von sich aus*) claim to be. In Adorno's version, however, difficulties begin to thicken when one considers how the process of history, through which alone such claims may be realized, is conceived.

The issue may be introduced by returning to the historical materialist constraint on potentiality. For Adorno, as for the other critical theorists, the key factor in the productive forces is technology. The development of this factor is subject to a historical dialectic, the 'dialectic of enlightenment': technology is the 'essence' of the knowledge that constitutes enlightenment.[39] The programme of enlightenment is 'the disenchantment of the world' through the exercise of reason.[40] What is involved is, however, a limited, 'formalized' conception of reason whose most significant feature for present purpose is its instrumentality.[41] It would be difficult to exaggerate the scope of the claims Adorno makes for the movement of disenchantment: 'As far back as we can trace it, the history of thought has been a dialectic of enlightenment.'[42] Given that enlightenment is, in essence, technical knowledge, history now appears as a unitary process, the 'history of the progressing mastery of nature'.[43] Seen in this way, it invites a complex response:

> Universal history must be construed and denied. After the catastrophes that have happened, and in view of the catastrophes to come, it would be cynical to say that a plan for a better world is manifested in history and unites it. Not to be denied for that reason, however, is the unity that cements the discontinuous, chaotically splintered moments and phases of history – the unity of the control of nature, progressing to rule over men, and finally to that over men's inner nature. No universal history leads from savagery to humanitarianism, but there is one leading from the slingshot to the megaton bomb.[44]

Thus, the progressing mastery of nature brings in its wake domination over human beings and over nature in human beings. Adorno goes on to display the reflection of this view of history back on the ontology that underlies it.

> History is the unity of continuity and discontinuity. Society stays alive, not despite its antagonism, but by means of it.... What historically made this possibility may as well destroy it. The world spirit, a worthy object of definition, would have to be defined as permanent catastrophe.[45]

If one now permits this image of the historical subject to be reflected back still further, on to the project of critique, the entire structure of thought is revealed to be fundamentally unstable.

This is so because its elements will not fit coherently together. The crux of the matter is that, assuming the ontology and the philosophy of history, critique may be either immanent or emancipatory, but not both.

Yet both are necessary if it is to keep within the orbit of dialectical social thought. It seems a minimal requirement of coherence to retain the bond between the ontological and the historical visions. This is to allow that what the phenomena claim to be has some efficacy in the world and that history is in some measure the record of its progressive satisfaction. But then, given the character of that record as depicted by Adorno, what the phenomena claim must merit condemnation as a harbinger of tyranny, not freedom. Critique focused on the gap between aspiration and achievement would be anticritique, which might well function immanently but only in the service of immanent catastrophe. If, however, one insists on the emancipatory role, critique will have to give up its immanence. Cut off from the malignant purposes of things and the course of events which embodies them, it must confront those realities as the most abstract *Sollen*, not simply as extrinsic, but as wholly antithetical. A critique that sets itself in that way in opposition to the movement of spirit is dialectically an absurdity. Within the framework of dialectical thought, the critical project cannot, it seems, be reconciled with the vision of history as universal domination. The dialectic of enlightenment annuls dialectical critique. Thus, it must be concluded that Adorno's version of moral critique comes to grief in much the same way as did ideological critique: it proves to be incompatible with the critic's understanding of what is actually going on in society. Once again, the critical and the explanatory dimensions of critical theory fall apart. This time, however, the obstacle to immanent criticism is not the character of a particular period, of administered as opposed to liberal capitalism. It is rather the logic of human enlightenment itself, a logic of domination that has been operative since the dawn of history. Immanent moral critique turns out in the end to be a delusion for the reason declared in *Dialectic of Enlightenment*: 'The conclusion that terror and civilization are inseparable ... is well-founded. ... It is impossible to abolish the terror and retain civilization.'[46] From one standpoint, Marcuse's intellectual career appears as a sustained resistance to this conclusion, a systematic attempt to reclaim civilization for 'pacified existence'.

Before considering this attempt, reference should be made to Adorno's treatment of the third constraint on potentiality, the need for its political expression. The position already outlined may be said to involve a response to this need. It is one that envisages the embodiment of the possibility of change as nothing other than the historical subject, society itself. Admittedly, it could be conceived of as a response only of a rather abstract and schematic kind. Instead of addressing the suggestion at length in its own terms, however, it may be more useful, in the light of our overall concerns, to refer it directly to the views of Marx. What is encountered there is a consistent and forceful rejection of the 'society as subject' idea. In *The German Ideology* it is condemned as a 'speculative-idealistic, i.e. fantastic, conception', and Max Stirner's partiality to it forms an important part of the case against him.[47] The *Grundrisse* warns: 'To regard society as one single subject is ... to look at it, wrongly; speculatively.'[48] The specific terms and context of this rejection give an extra resonance to Adorno's admission that in the critical theory of society 'one is forced back almost inevitably to the standpoint of Left Hegelianism, so scornfully criticized by Marx and Engels'.[49] It is reasonable to suppose that an aspect of what is, for Marx, unacceptably Left Hegelian about the society-subject idea is its tendency to undermine any prospect of organically linking theory with radical practice. To be told that society as a whole is the subject of change is little help to groups that have to struggle within society as it is: theory confronts practice here with a blank wall. Adorno was, of course, notoriously indifferent to the question of the objectification of his ideas in action. Hence, it might be claimed that the problem being discussed is at least not the source of serious internal tension in his work. In this respect, too, Marcuse presents a significant contrast.

3

The Frankfurt School: Marcuse

It has been shown that Adorno's ontology will not ground a form of potentiality suited to the needs of emancipatory critique. What is grounded there is rather a potentiality for domination and disaster. With Marcuse matters proceed more straightforwardly in this respect. The main features of his position are sufficiently familiar from his own accounts and the many excellent commentaries that a brief recapitulation should suffice. The prime object of his ontological concern is, as he usually puts it, 'man': he is from first to last an unrepentant philosophical anthropologist. An enduring emphasis is captured early on, in a review of the *Economic and Philosophical Manuscripts*, when 'the definition of man' is said to be 'the basis of the critique of political economy'.[1] From the *Manuscripts* Marcuse retained the themes of freedom as man's essential nature, and of labour as the process through which freedom is realized. To this anthropology he was later to add elements drawn from Freud's theory of instincts. The strategic purpose of the additions was to show that 'Freud's own theory provides reasons for rejecting his identification of civilization with repression'.[2] This may be taken, for present purposes, as a rejection of the same identification in Horkheimer and Adorno. Hence, one should not expect to find that their transhistorical pessimism is shared by Marcuse. He is not concerned to show that the logic of repression is inseparable from civilization as such and must disfigure the civilization of the future. It may be anticipated that the difficulties confronting dialectical critique in his system will not stem primarily from its basic philosophical disposition, its ontology and theory of history. As a first approximation, it may be said that they cluster instead around the political component of potentiality, the need for it to be demonstrable in real forces and tendencies.

There seems no room for doubt as to the seriousness with which

Marcuse views this requirement, a seriousness that sets him apart within critical theory. A central claim of the essay on 'Philosophy and Critical Theory' is that unlike philosophy, 'critical theory always derives its goals from only present tendencies of the social process'.[3] Many years later, this characteristic was to be spelled out still more forcibly in terms of the 'governing principle of dialectical thought' that negation should be determinate:

> The negation is determinate if it refers the established state of affairs to the basic factors and forces which make for its destructiveness, as well as for the possible alternatives beyond the status quo. In the human reality, they are *historical* factors and forces, and the determinate negation is ultimately a *political* negation.[4]

Thus, it appears that the dialectical approach to the established state of affairs is posited on the political negation of that state of affairs. Later still, however, the programme implicit in this view was to come under severe strain, as Marcuse developed a more systematic understanding of the society established around him.

The issue may be introduced by noting a persistent ambivalence, indeed equivocation, which characterizes the writings from *One-Dimensional Man* onwards. It has two aspects. The first is whether contemporary society actually contains elements that carry the possibility of its transformation. The second concerns the implications for the status of theory if the first question is answered in the negative. Equivocation on these matters runs so deep that the body of work as a whole displays signs of structural tension, even of an intellectual equivalent of trauma.

The key text here is *One-Dimensional Man* itself. Its exemplary value derives in part from the fact that both forms of equivocation are acknowledged in it. The first is depicted bluntly: '*One-Dimensional Man* will vacillate throughout between two contradictory hypotheses: (1) that advanced industrial society is capable of containing qualitative change for the foreseeable future; (2) that forces and tendencies exist which may break this containment and explode the society.'[5] The second gets a more muted recognition, though one that links it explicitly to the first. Marcuse writes of an 'ambiguous situation' in connection with an 'attempt to recapture the critical intent' of social categories. It 'appears from the outset to be regression from a theory joined with historical practice to abstract, speculative thought'. Yet, at the same time: 'the position of theory cannot be one of mere speculation. It must be a historical position in the sense that it must be grounded on the capabilities of the given society.'[6]

The ambiguity, as the discussion tacitly admits, is nowhere resolved in the text. Since the questions it raises are our chief concern at present, it may be well to look more closely at the background to Marcuse's statement of it.

At the start of *One-Dimensional Man* critical theory is presented in terms, characteristic of its moral employment, of potentiality for a better human existence. It is 'a theory which analyses society in the light of its used and unused or abused capabilities for improving the human condition'.[7] The notion of capabilities is then given the 'political' gloss familiar from early Marcuse:

> The 'possibilities' must be within the reach of the respective society; they must be definable goals of practice. By the same token, the abstraction from the established institutions must be expressive of an actual tendency – that is, their transformation must be the real need of the underlying population. Social theory is concerned with the historical alternatives which haunt the established society as subversive tendencies and forces.[8]

This specification at once encounters, however, the fundamental truth of established society as it is experienced in *One-Dimensional Man*:

> But here, advanced industrial society confronts the critique with a situation which seems to deprive it of its very basis. Technical progress, extended to a whole system of domination and coordination, creates forms of life (and of power) which appear to reconcile the forces opposing the system and to defeat or refute all protest in the name of the historical prospects of freedom from toil and domination.... This containment of social change is perhaps the most singular achievement of advanced industrial society.[9]

This may well strike one as a sufficiently clear stand on the first set of issues that were said above to be subject to equivocation. It also hints at implications for the second set which are then drawn out with what seems equal plainness: 'Confronted with the total character of the achievement of advanced industrial society, critical theory is left without the rationale for transcending this society. The vacuum empties the theoretical structure itself.'[10] It might now appear that the critical project is left wholly pointless or refuted. But this is a conclusion on which Marcuse is never willing finally to settle.

The 'Introduction' to *One-Dimensional Man* offers another, less drastic, way of reading the lessons of the integrated society. It is admitted that: 'In the absence of demonstrable agents and agencies of social change, the critique is ... thrown back to a high level of abstraction.' Nevertheless, 'this absence', it is implied, does not suffice to 'refute' the theory.[11] In the 'Conclusion' of the work, Marcuse returns to the topic, and comes down more firmly in favour of optimism. 'Dialectical theory', he asserts, 'is not refuted, but it cannot offer the remedy.'[12] He refers again to the contrast between the present situation of the theory and that which confronted its founders, when there were 'real forces (objective and subjective) *in* the established society which moved (or could be guided to move) towards more rational and freer institutions':

> Without the demonstration of such forces, the critique of society would still be valid and rational, but it would be incapable of translating its rationality into terms of historical practice. The conclusion? 'Liberation of inherent possibilities' no longer adequately expresses the historical alternative.[13]

It is difficult not to feel that Marcuse is here shrinking from the logic of his own analysis, from a conclusion whose grounds he had himself decisively established. If a theory professing a dialectical character is thrown back to a high level of abstraction, cannot be translated into historical practice and ceases to be focused on inherent possibilities, it is surely not just suffering from a regrettable weakness but is damaged in the very core of its being. It is a theory whose claim to be dialectical is bogus. Such a verdict is supported by Marcuse's reading of dialectical tradition.

Reference has already been made to his account of the 'governing principle' of determinate negation as requiring political negation through destructive factors and forces in established society. It is difficult to see how a theory that refuses to base itself on what is inherently possible could claim descent from such origins. It is equally difficult to see how an admission of untranslatability into practice could be accommodated to them. In Marcuse's understanding of Marx, practice is standardly taken to have a vital, indeed constitutive, significance for theory, to be a condition of its very possibility. Thus, Marx's bringing together of the master–servant dialectic and critique of political economy 'proves itself to be a *practical theory*, a theory whose immanent meaning ... is particular praxis'.[14] A theory cut off from praxis and thrown back to abstractions could hardly claim affinity with this model. It may be, however, that the most effective way to crystallize doubts about Marcuse's fidelity to his own dialectical insights is in terms of the treatment of the subject in his exegetical work. The theme is given strong, perhaps excessive, emphasis in his interpretation of Hegel.[15] Moreover, none of Marx's commentators have more firmly insisted that his revolutionary theory presupposes a revolutionary subject, the class that is the 'absolute negation', the 'living contradiction' of capitalist society.[16] The continuing validity of this line of thought seems to be affirmed in *One-Dimensional Man*: 'society would be rational and free to the extent to which it is organized, sustained and reproduced by an essentially new historical Subject'. Significantly, however, the theme has here moved into the subjunctive and is, in any case, immediately over-taken by the usual gloomy acknowledgement of reality. The existing system 'denies this exigency', and its dominant characteristics 'militate against the emergence of a new Subject'.[17] Marcuse's grasp of dialectical tradition should, strictly speaking, have ruled out the optimism over the viability of dialectical theory that he permits himself in this situation. It is, after all, one in which a basic assumption of the tradition, that theory moves in harmony with the movement of reality, is no longer tenable.

This discussion needs to be related to developments after *One-Dimensional Man*. The question of society's revolutionary potential as it figures in the later writings may be considered first. Marcuse's ambival-ence in this area is not of great interest in itself, but only as background to his thinking about the role of theory. To avoid the danger that one is simply charting legitimate shifts of opinion over a period, it may be well to conduct the discussion within the framework of individual texts. The case of *Counterrevolution and Revolt* is particularly interesting. It is marked by a dualism in which optimistic and pessimistic formulations are laid down close together in an inert opposition without either mutual reflection or movement of synthesis. Thus, capitalism is said to create transcending needs which it cannot meet, yet existing needs are, it seems, transformed only in the socialist revolution. Freedom is rooted in the human sensibility, so that the senses are the basis for the trans-formation of reality. Yet existing society is reproduced not only in the mind, the consciousness, of men but also in their senses. On the one hand, the fetishism of the commodity world is wearing thin, as people see behind it; Communist parties and unions are mass organizations with a potentially revolutionary force; the existential protest threatens the coherence of the social system. On the other hand, socialist Marxist theory and practice have no soil, no 'sufficient reason', among the large majority of the working population; the cultural revolution appears as the àbstract negation rather than the historical heir of bourgeois culture; in any case, the potential mass basis for social change may become a mass basis for Fascism.[18]

What is evident here is not so much readiness to embrace full-blown contradictions as a diversity of interpretation that suggests simply an inability to make up one's mind. So powerful an impression as the text conveys of facing in different directions at once could scarcely have been lost on Marcuse himself. Indeed, the nature of the issues is such as might be thought to bring them within the scope of the confession of vacillation in *One-Dimensional Man*. Some admirers have wished to interpret the tendency as a testimony to the dialectical character of his thought.[19] But he makes no attempt himself to represent it in such a light. In terms of his wholly orthodox understanding of dialectic as a dynamic process of resolving contradictions, it would be hard to imagine anything less dialectical than continuous vacillation between their opposing poles, the intellectual equivalent of running on the spot. Elsewhere in Marcuse's writings the unhappy, self-critical tone with which this area of tension is explored is strongly marked. In *An Essay on Liberation*, he refers to the 'vicious circle' consisting in the fact that 'the rupture with the self-propelling conservative continuum of needs must *precede* the revolution which is to usher in a free society, but such rupture itself can be envisaged only in a revolution'.[20] Similarly, he speaks in *Five Lectures* of 'what is unfortunately the greatest difficulty' in theorizing social transformation: 'for new, revolutionary needs to develop, the mechanisms that reproduce the old needs must be abolished. In order for the mechanisms to be abolished there must first be a need to abolish them.' He concludes sadly: 'That is the circle in which we are placed, and I do not know how to get out of it.'[21]

The circle may be said to have a vicious aspect in the everyday as well as the technical sense. There can be no doubt of Marcuse's life-long hostility to capitalism and of his commitment to its transformation into socialism. Moreover, he constantly sought to locate and identify with whatever elements of opposition offered prospects of advancing that end. In this way he remained always a political being to an extent unparalleled among the critical theorists. Thus, in human terms, his inability to see a way out of the circle may be thought to have a cruel, even tragic, significance. Such a judgement is acceptable up to a point, but it cannot, without sentimentality, be allowed to stand as a final verdict. The need for qualification arises when one begins to consider the consequences of the situation for the status of theory: that is, when one turns from questions concerning the assessment of revolutionary potential to questions concerning the viability of critique. It has then to be admitted that the tragic tension had been well dissipated by the time the vicious circle was acknowledged. The tension is partially maintained in *One-Dimensional Man* owing to the continued reliance on formu-lations that reflect the earlier conception of potentiality as determinate; that is, political, negation. But already these formulations cannot be said to represent the dominant strain. That is represented by the tendency to combine optimistic conclusions about the possibility of theory with pessimistic ones about the possibility of practice. Such a tendency itself presupposes a conception of theory and of its relation to practice which is not that of classical dialectics. Thus, the slackening of tension occurs because the traditional requirements for dialectical theory become eroded. This development gathers pace in Marcuse's later period.

Its most striking expression is the advice that critical theory should not, in contemporary circumstances, be afraid to be 'utopian', in deliberate contrast to its own past and to traditional Marxism. In a 'Foreword', written shortly after *One-Dimensional Man*, to a collection of Marcuse's essays from the 1930s, he compared the earlier situation with that obtaining at the time of writing. 'Today critical theory is essentially more abstract than it was at that time.... In view of the capacity and productivity of organized capitalism, should not the "first phase" of socialism be more and qualitatively other than it was projected to be in Marxian theory?'[22] The lesson to be drawn is: 'thought in contradiction must become more negative and more utopian in opposition to the status quo. This seems to me to be the imperative of the current situation in relation to my theoretical essays of the thirties.'[23]

The meaning of this proposal may be made more precise with the help of our preceding discussion. What it amounts to is the dropping of political conditions for potentiality in favour of relying on the contribution of the productive forces. The background of Freudian–Marxist anthropology continues to be assumed, but its effective significance is the negative one of serving to guarantee that domination is not destiny and that a non-repressive civilization is theoretically conceivable. The character of the position that results is revealed in the opening passage of *An Essay on Liberation*:

> Up to now, it has been one of the principal tenets of the critical theory of society (and particularly Marxian theory) to refrain from what might be reasonably called utopian speculation.... I believe that this restrictive conception must be revised, and that the revision is suggested, and even necessitated, by the actual evolution of contemporary societies. The dynamic of their productivity deprives 'utopia' of its traditional unreal content: what is denounced as 'utopian' is no longer that which has 'no place', . . . but rather that which is blocked from coming about by the power of the established societies. Utopian possibilities are inherent in the technical and technological forces of advanced capitalism and socialism.[24]

Once adopted, the utopian strain was to haunt Marcuse's thought to the end.[25] In one of his last pieces of writing, an essay on Rudolf Bahro, he insists that 'socialism shows itself to be a real possibility, and the basis of utopia is revealed in what already exists, only when the most extreme, integral "utopian" conception of socialism informs the analysis'.[26]

The utopian turn has important implications for the nature of critical theory. Even when the claim to be dealing in inherent possibilities is retained, what they turn out to be inherent in is simply the 'technical and technological forces', regardless of how they are blocked by the realities of power. Potentiality has itself become almost entirely technical here, and not to any significant degree political. What results is a species of moral critique without political mediations. In it judgement is formed in the light of a state of society representing the fulfilment of human nature whose material requirements can in principle be met with existing technology. As Marcuse is at least sometimes willing to admit, this conception involves a definite break with Marxist theory. The conclusion seems inescapable that it is precisely what the presentation suggests, a version of the utopian socialism that was so roundly condemned by Marx and Engels. Indeed, it involves a break with any form of dialectic that can claim descent from Hegel. Its merely utopian possibilities will not meet the required conditions of immanence. They must confront the present as an ideal and a rebuke, not as the revelation of its natural bent and the conclusion of its inner logic.

Some additional light may be shed by considering how the theme of the subject develops in Marcuse's later work. At the level of official doctrine, as it were, attachment to it never wavers. Its meaning within the overall structure of thought was, however, to shift considerably. There is continuing qualitative change, along the lines foreshadowed in *One-Dimensional Man*, in the significance of the theme for theory. In the original conception of Hegel and Marx, as Marcuse had shown, the consciousness and agency of the subject had been the indispensable medium of existence of dialectic. They have nothing resembling that status in the position Marcuse was to evolve under the pressure of the total society. Thus, *An Essay on Liberation* continues to use the language of the subject to posit the problem of social transformation, but, it is now, it appears, impossible to specify who the agents of such transformation might be, and futile to try.[27] Inability to identify the subject has become a difficulty, even 'the greatest difficulty', for theory, but still by no means what the naive student of dialectical tradition might expect, its death sentence. Clearly, the tradition has become seriously diluted at this point.

Another form of dilution appears in the way the concept of the subject begins to lose its original boundaries of reference. The result is that the concept becomes increasingly insubstantial and indeterminate. Already in *An Essay on Liberation*, there is a crucial shift of emphasis from the subject, in the old sense, to subjectivity.[28] Thus, the 'emergence of the new subject' is spoken of as if it were simply identical with 'radical change in consciousness'.[29] Moreover, the main event celebrated in the work is that the 'new sensibility has become a political factor', demanding to be taken account of by critical theory.[30] This new sensibility, even if it cannot be located in any specific agents of change, is itself *praxis*.[31]

Against this background, it is not surprising that Marcuse should have seized so enthusiastically on Bahro's notion of 'surplus consciousness'. This is 'that free human (*psychische*) capacity which is no longer absorbed by the struggle for existence'.[32] It is not 'the consciousness of a particular class', but 'the consciousness of individuals from all strata' comprising a 'diffuse, almost organizationless opposition' with 'no mass base'. Marcuse presents this thesis in the familiar idiom: the individuals from all strata are 'the potential subject of an oppositional *praxis*'.[33] But the concept of the subject has surely here reached its limiting case. For what we are dealing with is so amorphous as to be scarcely intelligible as an individual centre, even a 'potential' centre, of thought and action.

Some help with the problem is provided elsewhere in the Bahro essay. Marcuse cites, and accepts, the claim by Bahro that surplus consciousness as 'transforming power' is 'embodied' in the 'intellectualized layers of the collective worker', and only beyond this does it exist 'in all strata of the dependent population, in an obstructed and inactive form'.[34] He goes on to spell out and defend the thesis of the 'leading role' of the intelligentsia, even in the provocative form of socialism's alleged need for an 'elite of intelligence'.[35] These references to the intelligentsia are the nearest he comes to the identification of a determinate group sustaining the new consciousness. Belief in the leading role of intellectuals as a group in promoting social change has had considerable appeal for intellectuals in modern times. In spite of its durability it is a belief which has difficulty mustering significant theoretical, not to speak of empirical, support. Marxism seems almost the last source where such support might be expected. Indeed, when Marcuse achieves his belief in a new consciousness embodied in the intelligentsia it is hard to avoid the sense of a great circle closing in the history of ideas. The echoes of the revolution of consciousness which was proclaimed by the Left Hegelians, with themselves as its representatives, and was excoriated by Marx and Engels, seem unmistakable. To note this is to invoke another image of a pattern of thought closing in on itself, this time within critical theory. Given Adorno's identification with Left Hegelianism noted earlier, the development we have been tracing in Marcuse's work seems a reflection of the ultimate coming together of the views of the two most prominent critical theorists. In this respect as in others what results is a moment not of true *Aufhebung* but of almost complete assimilation and loss of identity on Marcuse's part.[36]

The difficulties encountered by Marcuse's version of moral critique have a familiar ring. Critical immanence has once more proved unable to find a fingerhold in reality. As in the case of ideological critique, the impregnable reality is that of contemporary, administered society. Just as it destroys ideology in the sense required to yield standards of criticism, so it eliminates the possibility of its own political negation. In these circumstances, critique is indeed thrown back to abstractions, to an appeal to the needs of human nature and the technical feasibility of their fulfilment. This in turn leads to changes in meta-theory, to Marcuse's abandonment of the criteria of immanence he knew to be crucial for classical dialectics, and to his attempt to equip critique for survival as a utopian enterprise. His concern with oppositional elements remains, but only as a biographical particularity, a survival of political instincts, no longer as the expression of a theory necessarily linked to practice. Here the entire project of renewing the Hegelian Marxist tradition by means of a critical theory of society may be seen as running honourably into the sand.

The conclusion of this discussion is that the Frankfurt School's programme of critique cannot be carried through in any of its main variants whether 'ideological' or 'moral'. In all of them the immanent, emancipatory evaluation of reality proves to be incompatible with, and is systematically subverted by, its understanding. To complete the picture one may note the final stances taken by our subjects in this situation, as its grip tightened fully. The evidence of Horkheimer's last years suggests that his response was in effect to abandon altogether the aim of constituting social theory in opposition to the established order. Instead he was to develop other intellectual interests, religious and metaphysical, and make his peace with the actually existing capitalism of the Federal Republic. Adorno's case is significantly different. He appears to have held to the end to his peculiar form of negativity, continuing to represent the spirit that always denies. Thus, he may be said to have kept alive the possibility of critique, though as a utopian enterprise convinced of its own impotence in the world. It is a critique embodied only in kindred, yet isolated, individuals, ironic points of light amid the darkness of the time. Marcuse, as we have seen, put up the most determined resistance to the logic of their common predicament. It is true that in the end his position comes very close to that of Adorno, most obviously in its utopianism and residual faith in intellectuals. Yet one may still detect a gap between the two, Marcuse's intellectuals are never merely 'beautiful souls', testifying to the conceivability of an alter-native order whose achievement they do not aspire to influence. They retain some potential, in however vague and attenuated a sense, to be active elements in a historical process directed towards that alternative. Nevertheless, in his case too one has to register the failure of the original programme. The central claim of dialectical thought to uncover and speak for a rationality emergent in ordinary existence has again proved impossible to sustain. In this failure lies the most distinctive contribution of the Frankfurt School to the theme of defeat that is often, and with justice, taken to be the hallmark of Western Marxism as a whole.

Against this background it appears natural that someone who retained critical ambitions for social theory should seek to realize them under different theoretical auspices, to move the methodology out of the shadow of Hegel. This may, at any rate, serve as a rough characterization of Habermas's work in critical theory. The divergence from the first generation Frankfurt School is expressed primarily in his foundational strategy. It is one in which critique as reconstruction is, so to speak, revived in order to bear the weight of critique as criticism. The standards of criticism are reconstructed by means of a transcendental argument as presuppositions of discourse.[37] Clearly, the intellectual ancestor of this strategy is Kant, rather than Hegel. Hence, one may speak of a shift in basic orientation whose consequences extend to all the concerns of this discussion. It is, of course, only superficially a paradox to suggest that transcendental arguments may yield immanent conclusions. For they establish what is required in virtue of the nature of the object if it is to be intelligible. Thus, the standards transcendentally established for critical theory may be said to be always immanent to the object of criticism. But this result, as so often with Kantian method, must appear from a Hegelian standpoint as too easily won, by a process that omits the painful, detailed labour of the negative. What the standards are held to be intrinsic to is the nature of language, and hence of social action, as such. They are not intrinsic to any one society or period in a way that distinguishes the relationship conceptually from that obtaining for any other. All human practices operate, as it were, at the same logical distance from the standards, even if, as a matter of fact, they differ in the extent to which they manage to realize them in practice. Immanence in Hegel and Marx is more determinate than this, shaped to the specificity of the object and not simply attributable to it in common with everything else. Their theory is a thoroughgoing historicism in which standards of reason have life and meaning only in the movement of societies, and are not independently accessible to timeless, transcendental reflection. It seems a pity if a body of thought with such a distinguished past were now to be given up without a struggle. Hence, it is tempting to explore the possibility of taking the opposite path to that of Habermas. If Hegelian Marxism proves unsuitable as a framework for critical theory of society, one might propose to retain the framework while dropping the assumption that within it social theory must be conceived as criticism.

This is, however, a proposal that can emerge in sharp focus only at a later stage of the discussion. It must await in particular the completion of our survey of the main forms of the social critique thesis. The other form to be considered is the achievement of some contemporary writers whose intellectual formation owes most to analytical philosophy. In it the standards for critique are supplied by values whose importance for Marx and for dialectical thought in general seems undeniable. They are the purely 'rational' or 'cognitive' values that are constitutive of all inquiry in science and logic. The possibility to be considered is that of exhibiting Marxist theory as a social critique which need appeal to no other criteria of judgement. This is a bold and appealing prospect which deserves close scrutiny.

Scientific Critique: Truth and Contradiction

The preceding chapters were concerned with the most sustained attempts by members of the Frankfurt School to develop versions of social critique. It was suggested that these by no means exhaust the possibilities envisaged at various points in their writings. There is another of them which merits particular attention, on account both of its intrinsic interest and of its elaboration by later writers. This elaboration seems to owe little to the direct influence of the Frankfurt theorists. That it may, nevertheless, be seen as a natural extension of views they held is in a sense all the more significant. It testifies to the richness of their thinking in this area, the extent to which they realize or anticipate a comprehensive set of alternatives and so deserve a central place in the study of the social critique thesis in relation to the Marxist tradition. Moreover, it suggests that the conception in question has an enduring and, as it were, spontaneous, appeal, at least in a certain historical situation. It is a conception that, if it works, seems to promise for critique the most secure and economical basis of all. The key idea is that the critique of society may be grounded in purely logical and cognitive values, the values constitutive of scientific inquiry itself. For convenience we may speak of this as a project of 'scientific critique'. The values in question are assumed to be constitutive in that they are conditions of rationality in relation to the inquiry: they specify the forms it must take to qualify as rational. Thus, the ultimate foundational category turns out, once again, to be nothing other than reason itself. This seems to secure the affinity with Frankfurt School theory at the deepest level. It is, of course, not surprising that such an affinity should exist between intellectual tendencies which profess to operate within the tradition of dialectics. For reason is the central category of that tradition, the source from which all others lead and to which they return. It must remain to be seen, however, what substance the suggestion of affinity has in the present case.

I

Within the Frankfurt School the prime source is the work of Adorno, the most inventive, or inconstant, of these thinkers where varieties of critique are concerned. A crucial element is supplied by the claim made in *Aesthetic Theory* that 'understanding is the same as criticism, a faculty that can distinguish true and false'.[1] Elsewhere, this element is more emphatically voiced: 'There is no knowledge which is not, at the same time, critical by virtue of its inherent distinction between true and false.'[2] The idea is that the basic cognitive categories of truth and falsity have themselves an evaluative role throughout the domain of their use. Hence, science as the systematic pursuit of knowledge is inescapably a critical activity. It is not surprising that Adorno's most extended treatment of the theme should occur in the contribution to the *Positivismusstreit*, a dispute in which he was obliged to appear at his most methodologically self-conscious, and specifically in relation to the issues being canvassed here. His chief opponent was Karl Popper, a thinker whose attachment to the idea of criticism is no less explicit and fervent than Adorno's own. The similarities between Adorno's critical theory and Popper's 'critical rationalism' go deeper than nomenclature. They extend to the recognition that science involves what Popper calls 'purely scientific values' and his belief that 'truth is our regulative principle, our decisive scientific value'.[3] This apparent congruence of view was obvious to commentators on the debate and was by no means lost on Adorno himself.[4]

His response takes the general form of contending that Popperian criticism, in contrast to critical theory, suffers from an arbitrary restriction of scope. Popper's 'purely cognitive or, possibly, "subjective" concept of criticism' is supposed to apply 'only to the unanimity of knowledge and not to the legitimation of the reality recognized', but 'thought cannot leave it at that'.[5] We are compelled 'to extend the concept of criticism beyond its limitations in Popper's work'.[6] Recognition of this is held by Adorno to be implicit in Popper's own formulations:

> if one takes the dependency of the method upon reality (*Sache*) as seriously as is inherent in some of Popper's definitions ... then the critical work of sociology could not be restricted to self-criticism – to reflection upon its statements, theorems, conceptual apparatus and methods. It is, at the same time, a critique of the object.

The moral is driven home with an explicit reference to the roots of the Frankfurt School tradition: 'The critical path is not merely formal but also material. If its concepts are to be true, critical sociology is, according to its own idea, necessarily also a critique of society, as Horkheimer developed it in his work on traditional and critical theory.'[7]

Adorno's thesis is that critical rationalism is, in virtue of its own constitution, compelled to pass from criticism of scientific theories to scientific criticism of society. A bridging role is played by the notion of truth: 'The idea of scientific truth cannot be split off from that of a true society.'[8] More fully specified, this form of mediation works as follows:

> The separation between the structures of science and reality is not absolute. Nor may the concept of truth be attributed solely to the structures of science. It is no less meaningful to speak of the truth of a societal institution than of the truth of theorems concerned with it. Legitimately, criticism does not normally imply merely self-criticism – which is what it actually amounts to for Popper – but also criticism of reality.

It may be no less meaningful to speak of the truth of a societal institution than of the truth of theorems about it, but it has presumably to be understood along different lines. Here, as generally in Adorno, the former truth is a matter of conformity to the 'concept' as the illustration he proceeds to give makes clear: 'The concept of society, which is specifically bourgeois and anti-feudal, implies the notion of an association of free and independent human subjects for the sake of the possibility of a better life and, consequently, the critique of natural societal relations.'[9] If criticism is to be grounded in the discrepancy between the object and its concept, a question that arises urgently is precisely how the concept is to be specified. The answers available in Adorno's work take one back along some familiar paths between which, it may be said, the illustration above is ambiguous. The first is that of ideological critique where the concept is understood as the avowed self-concept. The second is that of its ontological specification in terms of the nature of the transcendent subject in its materialist decipherment as society. The difficulties involved in both of these were discussed in previous chapters, and need not be rehearsed here. It may be enough for present purposes to note that a fresh impulse propelling critique along these paths has now been identified. It derives from reflection on what one is committed to by the practice of science in virtue of its 'regulative principle' and 'decisive value' of truth.

There is a second strand in Adorno's discussion which at least on the face of it offers a different kind of mediation, one that appeals more directly to a classic dialectical theme. Popper had maintained that 'the main instrument of logical criticism' is 'the logical contradiction'.[10] This is seized on by Adorno in his campaign to press on Popper the logic of his own position:

If Popper seeks the essence of criticism in the fact that progressive knowledge abolishes its own logical contradictions, then his own ideal becomes criticism of the object if the contradiction has its own recognizable location in it, and not merely in the knowledge of it. Consciousness which does not blind itself to the antagonistic nature of society, nor to society's immanent contradiction of rationality and irrationality, must proceed to the critique of society without *metabasis eis allo genos*, without means other than rational ones.[11]

The idea is that criticism of theorems implies criticism of society, for the category that grounds the one is instantiated no less truly and completely in the other. Thus, the bridge Adorno provides for Popper may be said to have two main planks, a distinctly 'epistemological' one, consisting in the notion of truth, and a more narrowly 'logical' one, consisting in the notion of contradiction. It will do no injustice to Adorno's thought to suppose that both may be regarded as elements of a social critique that proceeds 'without means other than rational ones'; that is, of what has been called here 'scientific critique'. If one seeks an account of either, or of their interrelations, there is, however, little further help to be gained from Adorno. What he has to say on the matter remains at the level of striking but undeveloped suggestions. To see how these may be theoretically articulated it is best to turn to the work of some contemporary writers whose roots lie in analytical philosophy.

II

There is, to start with, a recent discussion which shows particularly clearly some of the attractions and difficulties of scientific critique. It is close enough in spirit to Adorno's anticipations to be viewed as a form of their fulfilment. Yet it has the advantage of seeking to present the basic insights in a rigorous way. This starting-point is Roy Bhaskar's attempt to demonstrate that the human sciences may be, or provide, an 'explanatory critique' of their object, and that the possibility of such a critique constitutes 'the kernel of the emancipatory potential' of these sciences.[12] The core argument is, Bhaskar asserts, 'very simple'. It turns on the condition 'that the subject matter of the human sciences includes both social objects (including beliefs) and beliefs about those objects'. Fully laid out, it runs as follows:

if we possess (i) adequate grounds for supposing that a belief P (about some object O) is *false* and (ii) adequate grounds for supposing that S (co-) *explains* P, then we may, and must, pass immediately to (iii) a negative evaluation of S

(CP) and (iv) a positive evaluation of action rationally directed at the removal of S (CP). To elaborate; in as much as we can explain, that is to show the (perhaps contingent) necessity for some determinate false consciousness, or perhaps just some determinate consciousness under the determinable 'false', then the inferences to a negative evaluation of its source(s) and a positive evaluation of action orientated towards their dissolution are *ceteris paribus* mandatory.

Thus, science in exposing the falsity of beliefs and uncovering their social origins yields a criticism of those origins and approval of action to remove them. For Bhaskar, it is 'the causal relation of generation' that 'grounds the epistemological programme of critique'.[13]

Some features of this argument deserve a close look. Bhaskar views it as one in which 'we pass securely from statements of facts to value', thereby showing how the alleged gulf between the two may be bridged.[14] Thus, he takes the initial premises, statements of the form 'P is false', as 'value-neutral', not 'value-impregnated'. Hence, science's exposure of falsity is not itself an evaluative activity, though it entails evaluations. This position differs from that of Adorno, Popper and others who grant that truth and falsity themselves function as evaluative concepts in their scientific use. It is not easy to agree that it represents an improvement on such views. Bhaskar holds that what is not itself defective may be caused by what is and that it is the causal bond that provides the warrant for the attribution of defect. But if there is nothing wrong with the effects as such, it is hard to see how the negative evaluation, and prescription for removal, of the causes can arise in tracing the generative relation. Bhaskar's claim that it does lacks either intuitive obviousness or a proper discursive backing in his work. The issues involved need to be teased out a little, as they are crucial to the project of scientific critique.

A suggestion that might be made is that Bhaskar's argument runs counter to the familiar idea that 'effects resemble their causes'. In itself this idea is far too vague to be decisive here. In particular, without criteria specifying what kinds of differences are ruled out by it, one cannot be sure that being 'value-neutral' as opposed to 'value-impregnated' is among them. Nevertheless, whatever influence the idea has must work against the plausibility of Bhaskar's case. The point is perhaps best put the other way around, as it were. The trouble with the procedure Bhaskar adopts is, it may be said, that it deprives him of the support of an intuition that is genuinely operative in this area: namely, that finding a defect in something entitles one to infer a negative judgement on its cause. Some such assumption seems to underlie most attempts to tie genetic and evaluative reasoning together.[15] Stated in general terms the assumption is scarcely compelling. Thus, for instance, where objects embodying human values are attacked by natural forces, it seems a primitive kind of thinking to insist on reading the evaluative element involved in characterizing the effect back into the cause. If the cathedral is 'damaged' by lightning, it does not betoken anything 'wrong' with the lightning. At the very least the assumption in question would need careful explication to be acceptable. Nevertheless, it does have the merit of suggesting how, at least in principle, the programme of critique might draw support from the causal inquiry. Bhaskar's argument, by contrast, in seeking to make the gap between fact and value coincide with that between effect and cause, seems left with a double burden of transition which it is, as it stands, ill equipped to bear.

All this is said by way not of refutation but rather of exposing some difficulties in Bhaskar's version of scientific critique. It is in any case not easy to judge how serious such a line of thought is as an objection. For it is not altogether clear how substantial is his commitment to the value-neutrality of statements of the form 'P is false'. In response to the denial that such statements are value-neutral, his strategy seems to be to maintain that the basic thesis will survive even if the denial is accepted. This seems to suggest that what is at stake is of merely linguistic importance. The acceptance of different ways of characterizing the evaluative status of falsity-attributions will not then affect the critical significance of scientific explanation. It serves only to shift the point at which the crucial transition from fact to value takes place. Thus, according to Bhaskar, if 'P is false' is not value-neutral:

> then the value-judgement 'P is false' can be derived from premises concerning the lack of correspondence, or mismatch, of objects and beliefs (in the object domain) ... we do have here a transition that goes against the grain of Hume's Law, however precisely that is supposed to be here interpreted or applied.

This passage suggests that Bhaskar can accept, as an alternative to his original view, the somewhat more plausible claim that it is the activity, itself critical and evaluative, of exposing false beliefs that validates criticism of their sources. Yet he immediately adds, as if in renewed support of the original idea: 'On the other hand, if "P is false" is value-neutral then the inferences to "P ought not to be believed (CP)" and "Don't believe (act upon) P (CP)" certainly seem inescapable.'[16] There is indeed an air of inescapability about inferences of this type. Moreover, the type is unquestionably important for the theory of scientific critique. It may, however, be best to postpone discussion of it until it can be dealt with in a richer context than is provided by its isolated appearance here. For the present it may be enough to point out that the thesis that 'P is false' implies 'Don't believe P' lends no support to Bhaskar's central claim that 'P is false' entails a negative evaluation of the causal origins of P. It may be possible to pass securely from facts to values, though not from any point and by any route one chooses.

There is another aspect of Bhaskar's argument which has a general significance. The structure of the argument is not so clear as one might wish, but it seems reasonable to suppose that in it the positive evaluation of action is mediated by the negative evaluation of the sources of error. There is, to use a familiar idiom, a move from evaluation, as such, to prescription; more specifically, from criticism of the object to approval of action to change it. It should be said that Bhaskar's treatment of the issues involved here is more careful and restrained than is sometimes the case with exponents of scientific critique. Since an important version of the doctrine to be discussed later is vulnerable on this score, it may be well to ask why caution is needed. It should perhaps be conceded that there is something inherently practical about evaluation as such, in that it is necessarily connected with reasons for acting. There can, however, be no such connection with reasons for acting specifically to change what is being evaluated. This is transparently the case with historical objects which have now gone out of the reach of change. But the reforming urge may be out of place for all sorts of targets from the deplorable behaviour of fictional characters to disappointing sunsets. Criticism in such cases may be action-guiding for people interested in models of conduct or natural beauty, but it yields no imperatives to change its object. That Bhaskar is aware of the complications here is suggested by the constant invocation of *ceteris paribus* clauses, as in the passage cited above. This awareness is later made explicit: 'one can reason straight away to action directed at removing the sources of false consciousness, providing of course one has good grounds for supposing that it would do so, that no ill (or sufficiently overriding ill) effects would be forthcoming, that there is no better course of action which would achieve the same end'.[17]

With these provisions, Bhaskar's position is made secure against the more obvious objections. It still, however, seems to work with a view of the nature of evaluation that is, in a certain respect, too dynamic. There are, after all, well-established forms of evaluation that do not yield prescriptions for changing their object even under *ceteris paribus* conditions. A negative judgement on the merits of a painting does not give anyone, not even a Raphael, a reason for taking a brush, still less a knife, to the canvas. It is not that, as Bhaskar's qualified account might suggest, it provides a weak reason for doing so, one that is easily overridden by other, perhaps prudential, considerations. The truth is that no reason of this kind is generated at all, and to suppose otherwise is to misconceive the mode of evaluation involved. There are, admittedly, other spheres of judgement, and morality is usually taken to be the prime example, where *ceteris paribus* imperatives to change the object criticized do standardly arise. It seems worth asking why scientific critique should be assumed to belong to this respect with such spheres rather than with art criticism. A full account of the doctrine would no doubt have to resolve the issue. For Bhaskar's presentation, however, a more significant difficulty now arises.

It is that from a certain perspective his qualifications may be seen as conceding too much, as leaving evaluation not nearly dynamic enough. They will appear so, at any rate, for anyone seeking a model for understanding Marx's social theory. That Bhaskar himself has this ambition seems clear. His conception of scientific critique is from the start sharply differentiated from idealist notions and linked to 'historical materialism'.[18] *Capital* is later taken to be a paradigm of the kind of depth-explanation that is required, and its structure of argument is mapped on to the basic inference scheme: 'no value judgements other than those already bound up in the assessment of the cognitive power of Marx's theory are necessary for the derivation of a negative evaluation of the capitalist mode of production (CP)'.[19] Against this background it must be significant that acceptance of Bhaskar's qualified programme of critique need never commit anyone to approving of action to change society. For suppose it is agreed that contemporary society tends to generate illusions in its members. Attempts to alter this state of affairs may still be regarded as unjustified on the grounds that they are bound to fail, or can only partially succeed at the cost of enormous suffering (an overriding 'ill effect') or that complete success, if it is conceivable, must involve a totalitarian nightmare in which the absence of illusions is achieved only at the cost of everything else that makes human life in society worthwhile. Views of this kind are, of course, not mere theoretical possibilities, but represent important intellectual tendencies. They underlie Popper's opposition to large-scale 'social engineering' and that of some conservatives to all intentional projects of social reform. Such people may acknowledge the validity of Bhaskar's inference scheme while insisting that in human affairs other things never are equal in the way required for attacks on the roots of our illusions to be vindicated. Thus, one is left with a notion of social criticism that may never manage to provide rational grounds for radical practice. Without wishing to deploy detailed arguments at this stage, it should be said that this in itself makes it an unlikely model for conceptualizing Marx's method. It should also be said, however, that Bhaskar, although plainly anxious to remain in touch with the Marxist tradition, has a realistic conception of the actual closeness of the relationship.

An obvious way to characterize that conception is to say that while he regards Marx's social theory as giving substance to the programme of scientific critique, it is by no means the only way of achieving this. Other 'paradigms' are claimed to exist in the human sciences, for instance, in the tradition 'inaugurated' by Freud and in 'some of the work of the theorists of the life-world of social interaction'; that is, in psychoanalysis and social phenomenology.[20] The compatibility of scientific critique with a wide range of alternatives holds also for traditions of political practice. If the emancipation which is the object of the critique is to be 'of the human species', Bhaskar supposes that 'the powers of emancipated man must already exist ... in an unactualized state'. The 'key questions for substantive theory' then becomes, he continues, 'what are the conditions for the actualization of the powers?: are they stimulating (of the socialist tradition); or releasing (of the anarchic/liberal traditions)?; do they lie in social organization or individual attitudes, etc.?'[21] Thus, critique, the process of tracing false consciousness to its defective social origins, is indifferent as between, and hence unable to settle the rival claims of, socialist or anarchic/liberal approaches to the task of actualizing the emancipatory powers. This is a matter for 'substantive theory', an enterprise whose character is not further specified. So far as finding a model for Marx's theory is concerned, scientific critique must now appear somewhat underdetermined.

This impression is reinforced if one notes that in principle its basic pattern of inference 'applies equally to beliefs *about* natural, as well as social, objects'. Hence, it may be concluded:

> in as much as the natural sciences are also concerned in their own substantive critical discourse not just to isolate and criticize, but to comprehend and causally explain, illusory or inadequate beliefs about the natural world, then they too ... may come to explain false consciousness of nature at least partially in terms of human causes (e.g. faulty instruments, inadequate funds, superstition, the power of the church, state or corporations). In virtue of their explanatory charter, and in as much as they are in a position to give well-grounded explanations of false consciousness, then, the human sciences *must* and the natural sciences *may* (mediately, via the natural sociology of belief), arrive at value judgements on the causes, as well as the contents, of consciousness.[22]

It seems that the natural sciences may function as social criticism under the same warrant as the human sciences. In allowing this, Bhaskar is being strictly faithful to the logic of his position. More significantly, he is demonstrating a tendency that may be presumed to be built in to any form of critique founded on such categories as truth and falsity. The natural drift of this approach is, as Adorno's formulations on the matter suggest, to make the realm of criticism simply co-extensive with that of human cognition in general. Hence, it comes as no surprise to find that the dimension of social criticism is no more distinctive of Marx's project than of, say, Galileo's. Clearly, the specificity of the project is not to be captured along these lines.

There is an element in Bhaskar's discussion that may be taken as indicating a wish to secure a more substantial foothold in Marxist thought. The idea, familiar from Adorno, is that scientific critique may be founded on ascriptions not just of falsity but also of contradictoriness. Having reaffirmed that the human sciences must, in virtue of their explanatory charter, make judgements of truth and falsity which entail certain types of value-judgement. Bhaskar goes on '*Mutatis mutandis* similar considerations apply to judgements of rationality, consistence, coherence, etc.' He then proposes to generalize the basic inference scheme in a 'cognitive direction', in which the object of explanation is the 'contradictory character of some determinate set of beliefs'.[23] The suggestion is that the exposure of this character also licenses a negative evaluation of the sources of the beliefs and a positive evaluation of action rationally directed to removing them. A little later the locus of the contradictory relationships seems to shift from the level of beliefs to that of the sources themselves. What is under consideration at this point is the 'internal structure of a self-reproducing system' which 'generates and contains within itself' (i.e. the system) a 'functionally necessary mis-representation of itself'. In these cases, Bhaskar argues, it seems plausible to suppose that the structure 'must possess at least sufficient internal differentiation to justify attributing to it a "*Spaltung*" or *split*', and that if the system is 'to be capable of endogenous (essential) transformation' the split 'must constitute or be constituted by *antagonistic* (opposed) tendencies'. Bhaskar doubts, however, whether it is justified to apply a 'single unified category of "contradiction"' to such structures, and conjectures that a 'galaxy of concepts of contradiction' might be appropriate to them.[24]

The idea of a 'galaxy' is indicative, in another key area, of a certain caution on Bhaskar's part, specifically of a wish to be distanced from any simple monolithic viewpoint. But the idea is otherwise somewhat obscure, and its implications are left largely unspecified. Moreover, the possibility of generalizing the basic scheme is little more than asserted, and even if that scheme were free of the difficulties detailed above, the move would still need a separate justification. The significance of what appears to be a shift from truth to contradiction is dealt with no more explicitly by Bhaskar than it was by Adorno, and the interrelation of these categories is not further developed. Here, as elsewhere, much of the value of Bhaskar's discussion lies in the way it brings into sharp relief the major theoretical obstacles facing the project of scientific critique and raises fruitful lines of further inquiry. To this agenda one has now to add the implication that scientific critique is by its nature subject to a kind of universalizing drift that must tend to uproot it from any particular traditions of inquiry in the human sciences. There is also the suggestion that the most likely way to keep it focused specifically on Marx's social theory is by means of the category of contradiction. It should be added that Bhaskar's discussion usefully draws attention to the fact that the contradictions in question may have a dual location, in the beliefs that form the putative immediate object of scientific inquiry and in the social structures that underlie those beliefs. To explore these issues further, it may be best to turn to a writer whose influence on Bhaskar is evident and acknowledged, and whose work represents a sustained attempt to interpret Marx's social theory as scientific critique.[25] In an important series of writings, Roy Edgley has returned again and again to the project of a critical social science that relies entirely on 'cognitive or epistemological' or 'more generally', as he views it, 'rational values'.[26] At this point we may begin to consider those writings directly.

III

The foundation stone of the critical project for Edgley is, as he makes plain on many occasions, the category of contradiction. The category is said to be the 'key' to 'the critical nature of Marx's science'.[27] The 'essential critical category' of that science is 'contradiction in its dialectical form'.[28] This latter formulation is representative also in signalling a resolve, no less firm than that of the Frankfurt School, to preserve the dialectical character of Marx's theory, to exhibit it as essentially dialectical social science. The question to be asked is how precisely it is that the category of contradiction can sustain such a weight of significance. The easiest way into the complexities of Edgley's position is by considering his most direct and ambitious line of response. This is the claim that the connection between 'characterizing something as contradictory' and 'criticizing it' is 'internal and conceptual'. Hence it is that 'to characterize something as a contradiction, where that concept is a category of logic, is at least by implication, to criticize it'.[29] What is offered here is, on the face of it, a quite general conceptual thesis. The category of contradiction is held to be itself evaluative and, as such, an instrument of 'negative' appraisal, wherever it is employed. Even when not explicitly invoked, this thesis seems to underlie a good deal of Edgley's thinking. Moreover, although seldom expressed with the same clarity, some such assumption seems presupposed in, or at any rate serves to make sense of, the views of many other writers in this area. It is not difficult to appreciate its appeal. If it could be sustained, it would at once dissolve many of the thorniest problems that confront the project of criticizing society 'without means other than rational ones'. Hence, the prospects for sustaining it need to be carefully assessed.

Since the thesis is couched in universalist terms, the obvious form for objections to take is that of assembling what purport to be counter-examples. It is important to be clear as to what they need to establish. It will not be sufficient to show that contradictions may be, in certain circumstances, incidentally or instrumentally valuable. Thus, many writers are prepared to concede that contradictions in scientific or philosophical theories may be 'useful' or 'fertile'. They are so in so far as they stimulate further inquiry leading to their own dissolution. This view is compatible with, and indeed seems to require, the assumption that the contradictions are in themselves marks of weakness, not to be tolerated. Such a stance is well exemplified by Popper.[30] It is exemplified also by a writer whose views are, as he acknowledges, close to, and influenced by, those of Edgley. Richard Norman accepts that 'theories which are logically self-contradictory may be significant and fruitful just in so far as they are self-contradictory'. Yet he also insists that 'the existence of the contradiction shows that there is *something wrong with the theory* – it cannot be correct as it stands'. The two claims are wholly compatible in the light of the recognition that 'the contradictions in a theory are fruit-ful just because a self-contradictory theory cannot be accepted as it stands'.[31] Genuine counter-examples to Edgley's thesis have to show not that contradictions may be fruitful in this sense but that they are not in and for themselves necessarily defects or blemishes.

A range of cases with obvious claims to be considered here is constituted by works of literature. It is by no means a paradox to suggest that contradictions in, say, a poem may, so far from being defects, serve to enhance its vitality and richness and thereby its grip on our sensibili-ties. Their availability for such purposes have been exploited by many writers, and the results have been comprehensively explored by literary critics. Thus, for instance, William Empson's discussion of the sixth and seventh of his 'types of ambiguity' is an extended commentary on the doctrine that 'contradiction is a powerful literary weapon'.[32] This doctrine, it may be noted, accords well with a persistent strain in Marxist aesthetics, its tendency to regard the major writers of bourgeois society as precisely those who most completely incorporate its contradictions into their work. The cases in question are not, it should be noted, ones in which the writer exposes the contradictions for purposes of satire or criticism. To have such ambitions is already to have transcended in some measure the bourgeois horizon. The cases are rather ones in which the contradictions are unselfconsciously re-enacted in the work, and its artistic success is held to depend directly on the transparency and comprehensiveness with which this is done. The classic instances are provided by the judgements of Engels on Balzac, of Lenin on Tolstoy and of Lukács on Scott and Cooper.[33] No one has formulated the general conception more trenchantly than Adorno, in this respect an orthodox Marxist: 'A successful work, according to immanent criticism, is not one which resolves objective contradictions in a spurious harmony, but one which expresses the idea of harmony negatively by embodying the contradictions, pure and uncompromised, in its innermost structure.'[34]

Adorno does not simply preach this doctrine: it is practised to considerable effect in his own work of artistic criticism.[35] In the light of this evidence of theory and practice, an insistence that contradictions in literary works must be defects would surely represent an empty and pointless brand of rationalism.

There is no difficulty in extending the range of objects to which similar remarks apply, and it may be worthwhile to do so briefly. Thus, to move to a more mundane level, it would not normally be taken as a defect in a joke that it should contain, or revolve around, a contradiction. Indeed, if theories connecting humour with incongruity have any merit, one might expect a kind of natural affinity here. Freud's book on jokes may be cited as a rich source of material to support such a view.[36] *The Interpretation of Dreams* is equally appropriate in this context so far as its distinctive subject-matter is concerned.[37] It recognizes the existence, indeed the prevalence, of dreams containing contradictions of what seem uncontentiously a logical kind. Wholly absent from the discussion however, is any hint that such dreams are thereby in some way vitiated or flawed. The idea would in any case be absurd, missing the point so comprehensively as to create the suspicion of being itself a feeble attempt at the humour of conceptual incongruity. Dreams, in contrast to dream interpretations, are simply not suitable candidates for appraisal in such terms. Mention of the contrast is, however, a reminder that contradictions do after all in certain circumstances figure quite routinely as defects. What this in turn suggests is the need to move from the level of abstract conceptual connections to attend instead to the specificity of different kinds of objects. The role of theory is to supply the principle of the discriminations it then becomes appropriate to make. It has to be asked, in cases where contradictions figure as defects, what makes them so and what precisely is wrong with them. To achieve any progress with such questions one will have to deal in considerations which are both more concrete and more fundamental than Edgley tackles in connection with the thesis we have been discussing. His own explanation is that he had 'argued elsewhere' for the internal and conceptual nature of the connection between ascribing contradictions and criticizing.[38] This can only be a reference to his book, *Reason in Theory and Practice.*[39] It should be said, to anticipate the discussion a little, that such a reference may do the book less than justice. It is not clear that its arguments are so readily available to support the simple conceptual thesis, and this incapacity is wholly to its credit.

The arguments are presented, as Edgley was later to affirm, 'in the style and method of analytical philosophy'.[40] The book is both an exemplary achievement of that school, showing, and not merely protesting, its vaunted clarity and rigour, and a systematic attempt to subvert it from within. This attempt is focused on the doctrines that characteristically attend the central concepts of reason and logic. It is the treatment of logical matters that chiefly concerns us here. It serves to clear ground on which any contemporary attempt to reconstruct dialectical social science would do well to build. Hence, it has a general significance for the present discussion. Edgley's most straightforward revision of received views is a simple extension of their scope. Within the analytical movement, and, indeed, modern philosophy of logic in general, the bearers of logical relations had standardly been taken to be linguistic items of one sort or another; propositions, statements or sentences. Edgley's first enlarging proposal is that the list should include beliefs. It is a move difficult to resist, except on dogmatic grounds, at least so far as the category of contradiction is concerned. For, to begin to unravel a relationship referred to earlier, the category has traditionally been explicated in terms of the notions of truth and falsity. Contradiction has been understood as a relation whose terms necessarily have opposite truth-values, or, more liberally, to embrace 'contraries' or simple inconsistencies as well, whose terms are such that only one may be true at once, though all may be false. Beliefs are eminently qualified to meet conditions of this sort, for the ability to bear truth-values is indispensably bound up with their reason for existence. Hence, it is not surprising that everyday conceptions in this area are quite willing to recognize that a person's beliefs may be self-contradictory or that the beliefs of one person may contradict those of another. This readiness is, it may be said, grounded in the basic logical facts of the situation.

At this point Edgley's second major revision of analytical theories of logic should be considered. It is constituted by a major theme of his book, the idea that 'matters of logic are themselves, explicitly or by implication, evaluative or normative'.[41] The normative aspect with which he is mainly concerned consists in the fact that logical principles are 'principles necessarily having a normative bearing on the pyschological states of people'.[42] It is against this theoretical background that one should set the now familiar claim that 'logical categories such as contradiction, validity, consistency, etc. are as such evaluative and critical'.[43] A great merit of the discussion in *Reason in Theory and Practice* is that it is not content merely to assert or assume claims of this kind, but seeks to establish them by detailed argument. A crucial factor in the argument is the recognition that where inconsistency is objectionable 'its being objectionable implies that there is something wrong with either or both of the two items – something wrong other than their being inconsistent'.[44] Putting the point another way, it is that 'logical appraisal of something, i.e. appraisal of its rationality, presupposes appraisal of another kind'.[45] It remains to be seen what these other kinds of appraisal may be. The immediate significance of Edgley's insight is that it impels the argument in the direction indicated earlier, away from conceptual generalities and towards a concern with the concrete reality of specific objects.

In the case of beliefs the character of the more basic kind of appraisal is not difficult to discern. It derives from their primary role as bearers of truth-values. In this perspective, the vital fact about incompatible beliefs is that they cannot be equally true: 'one at least must be false, and that one it must be a mistake, and therefore wrong, to believe'.[46] This rule of appraisal is repeatedly stressed: 'in the central cases of belief, the kind of wrongness involved in being inconsistent must be the kind involved in being *mistaken*'.[47] This explains what is wrong with believing inconsistent things, but it is not quite the end of the search for foundations. For Edgley takes seriously the question 'What is wrong with believing what is false?'[48] The answer is swift and, surely, decisive. It is given in the thesis that 'the following basic principle for appraising beliefs is analytic: If p, then it is right (correct) to think that p, and wrong (mistaken) to think that *not-p*'.[49] Here, in the case of beliefs, is the ultimate ground of the claim that logical principles are necessarily psychologically normative.[50] Bedrock in this structure of argument is reached in the assertion of an analytic connection between what is believed and the rightness or wrongness of believing it. This way of putting things may itself reflect too accurately for some tastes the 'style and methods' of analytical philosophy. Nevertheless, the substance of the claim seems pointless to contest. The process of belief evaluation has surely to accept the primitive status of Edgley's 'basic principle', whatever terminology is used to express it. The substantive question is how much progress towards delineating a critical and dialectical social science is possible from such a standpoint.

Even at this stage the argument will serve to license a considerable range of scientific critical activity. Thus, in exposing the inconsistencies, and thereby the element of falsity, in rival theories, scientific work, both natural and social, is necessarily involved in criticism. Moreover, its criticism of theories is to be understood 'as having, even in *natural* science, a *social* target, i.e. as the criticism of the acceptance of those theories by possible subjects, including social institutions (e.g., the Church as a target of Copernican criticism)'.[51] For Edgley, as for Bhaskar, natural science may, in holding true to its founding charter, be social criticism. Social science is, however, in his view, critical of society in a larger and richer sense. For one thing its criticism of rival theories is direct criticism of part of its real object, since these theories are themselves elements of social, as contrasted with natural, reality. More significantly, its primary objects of study, are 'peculiar as objects of science in being also subjects with their own theories, views, and ideas, about their social practices and institutions'.[52] These ideas may form an ideology whose contradictions are liable to exposure by social science. In exploring them, that science will be critical of a substantial part of its distinctive object, and will be so just in virtue of its commitment to purely cognitive and rational values. Clearly, all this suffices to give social science a significant critical dimension. But Edgley's case does not rest entirely, or primarily, on the possibilities so far revealed. To encompass it fully, one has to note another way in which he breaks with traditional views of the province of logic.

It consists in a proposal to extend the scope of logical relations beyond propositions and beliefs to include actions and practices also. Such a move might be attempted along various routes, but Edgley's has the merit of simplicity and directness.[53] Its starting-point is the recognition that 'logical relations are not simply truth-value relations but hold more generally in virtue of relations of meaning'. It follows that 'they encompass not only specifically mental acts and states ("theory") but also practice, physical actions and activities of that peculiarly human type that "distinguishes the worst architect from the best of bees" (Marx, *Capital,* Volume 1) by being (capable of being) meant, intended or planned'.[54] The suggestion is that the writ of logic runs through the entire realm of meaning, and that actions as things 'meant' or, as Edgley felicitously puts it elsewhere, 'materialized meanings', are native inhabitants of that realm.[55] A consequence is that 'the logical relation of contradiction, at least in its form as inconsistency, can be instantiated not only between people's thoughts but also between their actions and practices'.[56] The implication of particular concern here is that 'people can be *accused* of acting inconsistently. They can, e.g., be criticized for doing inconsistent things, no less than for thinking inconsistent things.'[57] To say this is to state a claim of considerable importance for the project of a scientific social critique, but there is a still more ambitious step to come.

This is the attempted incorporation of social structures into the argument. The procedure is, as before, simple and bold, even if not now carrying quite the same degree of conviction. Its working assumption is that 'social structure is a structure of human practices, i.e. sets of practices whose nature is a matter of their relation to one another'.[58] Still more generally formulated, it is that 'Society, the object of social scientific investigation and knowledge, is a structure of practices.' Since, as Edgley goes on to assert, 'thought' is involved 'more or less, in any practice, at whatever level, including the most material', it follows that it is 'part of the very nature of society including its most material levels'.[59] This offers the prospect that a critique that lives off the possibilities generated by relations of thought may be able to take society as a whole, the entire object of social scientific investigation and knowledge, as its target. It should be said that the final step to this conclusion has involved a fairly brisk treatment of one of the most contentious issues in contemporary social theory, that of the relationship of agency and structure. Edgley's claim that structures just are sets of practices will strike many, and not merely 'structuralists', as rather easy and unmediated.[60] It may seem in danger of simply dissolving structure into agency and so losing its appropriate degree of autonomy. It is not possible to resolve these complex matters here, and, in any case, the rewards of doing so, in terms of the present argument, would scarcely be commensurate with the effort. It may be enough to grant that with the assimilation of action and practices and, at least partially, of structures, Edgley has shown how a substantial part, and perhaps all, of the subject-matter of the social sciences may be treated as a field of logical relations. Some pressing questions have now to be asked about this achievement.

There is, to begin with, a question about its implications for the project of scientific critique. Given that one has an account of why contradictory beliefs are objectionable, what, it should be asked, is objectionable about contradictory actions, practices and structures? It must, on Edgley's own showing, be something other than their being contradictory, and the notion of falsity is, as he makes clear, of no use here.[61] Beyond this, the response his writings reveal is by no means as articulated as one might wish. Nevertheless, in one important respect it is satisfyingly explicit. This is the fact that he does not wish to invoke any version of the idea that the critical programme is grounded in causal relations of generation. It is not in virtue of underpinning forms of false consciousness that contradictory structures become liable for criticism: they are, as it were, so liable on their own account. Thus, interpreting Marx, but expressing also his own standpoint, he asserts: 'material conditions in society cause defects at the level of ideas because they are defective in their own material way'.[62] This thesis is consistently maintained:

What Marxism ... does is not merely to insist on theoretical defects of its opponent theories, and then trace them causally to aspects of the material social structure as if these aspects were otherwise neutral and innocent. More strongly, it imputes those theoretical defects to aspects of the material social structure that are themselves defective, in particular to contradictions in that structure.[63]

This puts the point at issue plainly enough. Moreover, it represents what is surely in principle a more satisfactory position than that of Bhaskar or any other advocate of the causal theory. It has, at any rate, the merit of not having to rely on wavering intuitions about the normative import of the generative relation, intuitions whose light tends to fade just when it is needed most. In a sense, however, this advantage serves to throw the original question into even sharper relief. If contradictory practices and structures are defective independently of their causal powers, how is the ascription of this character to be justified? What is the specifically 'material' mode of defect in such cases?

Edgley's work contains numerous signals of the general form of a reply to these questions. They are given in passages such as the following.

The general defect of which self-contradiction is a specific form is: irrationality. It is because contradictions within a unity, self-contradictions, are defects, specifically irrationalities, that they need, in the language of dialectic to be 'resolved', 'overcome' or 'reconciled' by what is therefore, from a rational point of view, an advance or progressive change.

Elsewhere this idea is spelled out in a way that draws together a number of threads in the present discussion. Edgley is speaking of Marx, but also, as often, for himself:

in accordance with his materialist conception of social science refusing to leave the cognitive defects of opposing ideas simply exposed as illusions or mistakes, he traces these defects to their explanatory conditions in material practice. But he does not represent those conditions as otherwise neutral causes of such cognitive defects. Rather, he characterizes these conditions themselves as defective; irrationalities of theory are due to irrationalities of practice. It is this common irrationality shared by both thought and practice that is categorized by the single dialectical conception of contradiction.[65]

The conclusion is that contradictions in thought and in practice are alike defective just as irrationalities. This is, however, one might suggest, by way of being a largely formal answer to our question, of value chiefly in indicating where a deeper search should take place. In probing further, it may be wise simply to acknowledge the evaluative force that standardly belongs to ascriptions of irrationality, and, hence, to accept that, if the contradictions are properly so characterized, there is indeed something wrong with them. Moreover, the characterization indicates in a general way what that is: it is with offences against the light of reason that we have to deal. A question that still has life in it, however, is the question of what justifies treating contradictions as defects of rationality. Edgley gives little sign of taking it seriously, and hence it would be unrewarding to pursue in the context of his work. That it is worth pursuing is suggested by the generally similar line of argument developed by Richard Norman. His book, *Hegel, Marx and Dialectic,* written jointly with Sean Sayers in the form of a debate, deserves attention in any case as a rich source of insights into the central problems in the area.

5

Scientific Critique: Rationality

The points at which Norman develops, or diverges from, Edgley's position owe something to the specific circumstances of the debate with Sayers. For one thing, he is systematically obliged in that context to seek to relate his views to the tradition of dialectical thought. In particular, he has to address the thesis, strongly urged by his interlocutor, that nothing in that tradition justifies the treatment of contradictions as, inherently, defects. On the face of it, no one has put the point more trenchantly than Hegel, in a passage which Norman cites: 'In general, our consideration of the nature of contradiction has shown that it is not, so to speak, a blemish, an imperfection or a defect in something if a contradiction can be pointed out in it'.[1] Faced with this, Norman has some distinctions to make if he wishes to vindicate a critical role for dialectical contradictions. To begin with, he marks out an area where he, with Edgley, takes the critical role of contradictions to be unproblematic, though, in his view, with nothing distinctively 'dialectical' about it. The area is indicated in the claim that 'To point to contradictions in a belief or theory is to criticise it, to show it to be defective.'[2] This claim is presented by Norman as simply an aspect, or elaboration, of the law of non-contradiction, 'the formal logical law which stipulates that a self-contradictory proposition cannot be true as it stands, or that two contradictory propositions cannot both be true'.[3] From this perspective it appears that the evaluative significance of the concept of contradiction derives, in a now familiar way, from the link with truth and falsity. This interpretation is borne out a little later for the specific case of a theory by a remark which was cited above in a different connection: 'the existence of the contradiction shows that there is *something wrong with the theory* – it cannot be correct as it stands'.[4] For Norman, as for Edgley, what gives such contradictions their critical force is their function as markers for cognitive failure.

He turns next to consider 'the distinctive uses of "contradiction" in dialectical thought'.[5] The fact that in two of them the category lacks any critical function is what, in his view, explains, and enables him to accommodate, Hegel's verdict as given above. These are its use 'to refer to the *interdependence of opposed concepts*' and its use to refer to conflicts where the conflicting forces are 'characterized' by such concepts. The third use, the crucial one for Norman's purposes in being both dialectical and critical, becomes appropriate when the conflict is 'an internal conflict within the purposive activity of a human individual or human society or social institution' and, hence, 'can be seen as a *self-contradiction*'.[6] It is impossible to grasp the significance Norman attaches to this unless one considers his concrete instances. The first is 'the case of a teacher who is continually urging his students to think for themselves, constantly trying to get them to state their own ideas, but who, as soon as they say anything, immediately jumps down their throats, producing a host of incisive critical remarks which are so intimidating that they effectively inhibit the students from ever stating any thoughts of their own'. An extension of this example is the case of a university 'dedicated to the encouragement of critical thought' which tends 'to stifle the very critical attitudes which it encourages, for example by rigid syllabuses, by examinations which have the effect of gearing students' work to the production of correct and safe exam answers'. This example provides in turn, Norman suggests, 'a model for the idea of "contradictions in capitalism"'. Thus, 'capitalism frustrates the very possibilities of material abundance which it is capable of making available. What it promises through the rational organization of production within the factory or the firm, it frustrates through the anarchy of the market.'[7]

This discussion raises issues of great interest which will have to be taken up later. For the present one may concentrate on the help it offers with the immediate question of what is wrong with contradictions in activities and practices. In general terms Norman is plainly faced in the same direction as Edgley on this question. His detailed account of the dialectical use of contradiction is given under the heading 'Contradiction as Irrationality', and in the examples the objects of criticism are all individually characterized as 'irrational'.[8] The merit of Norman's treatment, so far as our question is concerned, is that it offers some points of entry into this rather blank conceptualization. What is held to be contradictory is in every case, it will be recalled, an internal conflict within some human purposive activity. This dimension of purposiveness is, it may be suggested, the clue we are seeking. At any rate a determined attempt is made by Norman to sustain it throughout the discussion. Thus, the flaw in the teacher's behaviour is that, in being self-contradictory and irrational, it is 'self-defeating'.[9] The university, we are reminded, is a human institution, existing for the pursuit of certain aims which are frustrated by its actual mode of operation. It has to be admitted, and the point is a significant one for reasons that will shortly emerge, that the case of capitalism will not, for all Norman's efforts, fit so happily into the pattern. Nevertheless, his argumentative strategy seems clear enough. Contradictions are to be viewed as irrationalities in so far as they defeat the human purposes embodied in forms of activity and practice.

As a basis for a version of social critique, this idea seems promising. It is, at any rate, easy to support from general considerations. The master category of rationality is standardly thought of as having, in its application to action, an inescapably teleological character. This is reflected in, for instance, the tendency to seek a paradigm in the process of intelligently shaping means to ends. It is true, and a common source of complaint, that the model is often abused by being given too much to do. It has to be borne in mind that it cannot be straightforwardly applied to many quite ordinary activities, from having a conversation to improvising at the piano or going for a walk. These activities are not normally structured in terms of an end that may be identified independently of them. A familiar way of making the point is to say that they are not means to anything external but are pursued just for their own sakes. Recognition of this need not, however, make any significant difference so far as present interests are concerned. It will not matter greatly that some activities have to be regarded as ends in themselves rather than as instrumental means. As this formulation itself suggests, they may still be appraised in terms of criteria that have to do with notions of intentionality and purpose. It is these notions, one may suggest, that give substance to the possibility of the rational appraisal of human activities.

It may be helpful here to consider, or reconsider, some specific situations in the light of the teleological perspective. It seems, for instance, to work well enough when faced with the problem of conceptualizing those in which contradictions figure most unequivocally and uncontentiously as defects. The most extreme form of intolerance of them is, perhaps, that shown by orthodox formal logic. The usual explanation of this rests on the idea that from a contradiction any conclusion whatever may be derived.[10] Susan Haack puts the standard view of what precisely is objectionable about this when she remarks that a logic that admitted contradictions would 'be useless for the purpose of discriminating valid from invalid inferences'.[11] The trouble with contradictions from this standpoint is that their effect is to spread chaos everywhere. Formal logic is, of course, in one aspect, a social practice, something human beings sustain through co-operative effort. Hence, it is significant that the defence of its attitude to contradictions should be explicitly couched in terms of its 'purpose'. A similar picture is drawn by those analytical philosophers who have been interested in the 'informal logic' of everyday discourse. Here too is a form of life which protects itself, unselfconsciously but effectively, against the threat of contradictions running riot. P.F. Strawson expresses a widespread view of the situation when he writes: 'The point is that the standard purpose of speech, the intention to communicate something, is frustrated by self-contradiction. Contradicting oneself is like writing something down and then erasing it or putting a line through it. A contradiction cancels itself and leaves nothing.'[12]

Once again, it is not the substantive merit of the claim that is of interest here. It is rather the overtly purposive and intentional form it takes, a form that reveals the conceptual shape in which answers to our question are most naturally cast.

This line of thought may be tested further by returning to an important, indeed crucial, case where the defectiveness of contradictions is more controversial. The discussion has so far tended to go along with the Popperian assumption that contradictions in scientific theories are in themselves defects that are useful only in so far as they are resolutely treated as such. This assumption has not gone without challenge, however, from historians and philosophers of science. It marks one of the points at which the influential writings of Paul Feyerabend break with critical rationalism. A large part of Feyerabend's concern is to warn the practising scientist against the 'barren and illiterate' logician who preaches to him about the virtues of, among other things, consistency, and to urge that instead 'he imitate his predecessors in his own field who advanced by breaking most of the rules the logicians now want to lay on him'.[13] In particular, the rule that he should always strive to overcome inconsistency is to be repudiated: 'inconsistent theories may be fruitful and easy to handle, while the attempt to make them conform to the demands of consistency creates useless and unwieldy monsters'.[14] Feyerabend's overriding concern throughout is with the 'growth' and 'progress' of scientific knowledge. In his view what the philosopher of science should be 'most interested in' is 'picking out and analysing in detail those moves that are necessary for the *advancement* of science'.[15] It is in the light of this concern that he wishes to reject the methodological presumption that contradictions in theories count as defects. What is significant here is, once more, the form, rather than the content, of the argument, the fact that to make his point Feyerabend has to appeal to the ends to be kept in view. In this case too, where one is dealing with what is usually taken to be the paradigm of human rationality at work, the moral is that whether contradictions are defects depends on the point of the practice in which they are embedded.

These results may be generalized in the following way. Social practices, and the institutions they help to constitute, may be seen as permeated with intentionality by virtue of embodying various modes of human will and consciousness. A grasp of the mode should enable one to see in every case the *telos* of the practice, and in terms of that one can assess the rationality of details. Hence, to speak of irrationalities in connection with forms of social life is to speak of obstacles to the achievement of the purposes that are implicit in the forms and provide their human significance. It seems obvious that contradictions are likely to figure prominently as obstacles of this kind. Nevertheless, it remains the case that whether or not they count as defects of rationality depends on the constitution of the form of life in which they arise. It is a contingent question to which the answer will vary with circumstances. Thus, they will not be breaches of the form of rationality that belongs to the practices of joke-telling, writing lyric poetry or initiating novices into the mysteries of Zen Buddhism. Here is surely the sketch of a framework for a viable conception of critique. It remains to be seen what its value is for purposes of general social criticism, and beyond that for making sense of Marx's science.

For a starting-point in exploring these issues, one cannot do better than return to Norman's examples. What should be noted is the contrast between the ease with which the teleological perspective copes with the self-contradictory teacher and self-contradictory university and the friction it encounters in the case of capitalism. The difference is reflected in Norman's language. The capitalism example is developed by him through analogy with the university. Thus, 'the university is internally contradictory because it defeats its own aim of encouraging critical thought' and 'correspondingly', he tells us, 'capitalism frustrates the very possibilities it creates for material abundance'.[16] He does not say, as strictly he should to secure the correspondence, that capitalism frustrates its 'own aim' of material abundance. That he should refrain from any such claim is wholly understandable. While one may feel reasonably secure in specifying the 'aim' of a particular institution, such as the university, matters are far less straightforward when it comes to a general form of social organization, such as capitalism. That system has its defenders and those who claim to speak on its behalf, but they are by no means agreed on its characteristic 'aims'. Moreover, the material abundance for all postulated by Norman seldom receives any special emphasis in their accounts, while the idea of there being some distinctive affinity here would be emphatically rejected by the system's opponents. The problem is the familiar one of detailing the 'concept' of so massive and disputed a form of social reality as capitalism. The entire field is an ideological welter of claims and counter-claims in which the suspicion of arbitrariness is often hard to avoid. This is not to deny that it is a potential field of rational argument. It may well be that Norman could enter the struggle to deploy objective considerations on behalf of his own conception and against others. But it would involve a kind of theoretical intervention in which he shows no interest, nor any sense that it might be required. Moreover, it would surely form an odd and unsatisfactory climax to the programme of scientific critique. The need to engage in such argumentation must undermine the original appeal of the programme. It had held out the prospect of bypassing these complications by building directly and exclusively on purely 'rational' values as the most secure foundation a form of critique can possess.

The problems run somewhat deeper, however, than has so far been suggested. It is not simply that the 'aims' of capitalism are difficult to establish with confidence. This whole way of speaking itself suffers from a kind of conceptual oddity, as, for instance, Norman's reference to capitalism's 'possibilities' does not. Some light may be shed on the underlying difficulty if one makes explicit an aspect of Norman's, as of Edgley's, position, that has not hitherto been the subject of direct comment. For both, it is specifically *self-contradictions* that constitute irrationalities and so serve as vehicles for rational critique.[17] According to their shared conception of contradiction as opposition of meanings, however, such contradictions are not the only ones that may arise. It is possible for individuals and institutions to contradict, in their words and actions, one another as well as themselves. The opposing poles of the relationship may, as it were, be lodged in distinct centres of subjectivity. For convenience, one may speak of 'intersubjective' contradictions in such cases. This notion is not on the face of it a critical one, at least not in the sense that has emerged in the case of self-contradiction. For intersubjective contradictions cannot plausibly be regarded as in themselves defects of rationality. Thus, for instance, they occur whenever one scientist gainsays the views of another, and such situations, so far from being irrational, might well be taken as paradigms of rationality in action. This practice of criticism seems far more inescapable a factor in the progress of science than is any desire to purge theories of their inconsistencies. With these reminders as background, a question arises as to how the contradictions of capitalism should be classified. If the critical and dialectical form of self-contradiction is to be understood as, in Norman's phrase, internal conflict within purposive activity, does capitalism qualify as a suitable agent to be its bearer and victim? Is it, as it were, sufficiently self-like for that role?

An affirmative reply would surely have little credibility, indeed be scarcely intelligible, outside some special theoretical framework. In order to focus the issue, one may consider a contradiction of capitalism that is often, on good grounds, held to be fundamental for Marx and has generally been so regarded by Marxists. This is the contradiction of labour and capital, or, in its explicit class expression, of proletariat and bourgeoisie. The example has no difficulty meeting the requirement of being meaningful opposition, as Norman recognizes: 'The conflict between proletariat and bourgeoisie is in part a conflict of beliefs, values, intentions, etc., and it is in virtue of this that the two classes can be said to *contradict* one another.'[18] It seems natural to treat this case as, in the terms of the present discussion, an intersubjective contradiction, a view strongly suggested by the final part of Norman's own statement. Such an interpretation is wholly in keeping with the way the relationship is treated by Marx throughout his career. Some textual evidence with a direct bearing on the situation may be cited here. In the list of agents whose purposive activity may suffer from self-contradictions, Norman had included 'a human society'. Though not elaborated or defended, this is a substantial and contentious claim. Thus, it is striking how Marx consistently opposes all such suggestions, most characteristically through the denial that society may be regarded as itself a unitary subject.[19] It is significant also that the error in question is specifically identified by Marx as being of a 'speculative idealistic' kind. The emphasis may be seen as reflecting a more general hostility to the idealist tendency to assimilate all contradiction to self-contradiction. It is a tendency encouraged and underwritten by an ontology in which all forms of consciousness are ultimately to be seen as instruments of the Idea, and all purposive activity as an expression of a reality that is, Hegel insists, subject as well as substance. Apart from such perspectives, the autonomy of intersubjective contradictions is irreducible and must be respected. Indeed, the need to theorize it adequately, so as to vindicate the possibility of a dialectic that is not one of pure self-contradiction, is a vital one for materialist philosophy. For such a dialectic, class contradictions in particular must have a central place. It will not be able to solve the problems they pose by treating them as irrationalities in virtue of being internal conflicts within the purposive activity of class society. For it will not view that society as a purposive actor in the sense required.

The search for what is wrong with contradictions in actions and practices seems now to have ended in a blind alley. Their defectiveness has, it was suggested, to be conceived specifically as irrationality, as a self-defeating tendency in whatever they inhabit. The contradictions of capitalism and, more generally, of class society, are, however, not fully intelligible in those terms for a non-idealist social theory. At this point a possibility may be considered that retains something of the essential thrust of the Edgley–Norman approach without so obviously leading away from Marx and materialism. The essential element is what was earlier called the teleological perspective, the idea that contradictions may mark infirmities of purpose, obstacles to the attainment of ends. The chief difficulty for this view arose in connection with the move from individual institutions, such as the university, to comprehensive social forms, such as capitalism and, beyond them, to society itself. Yet the larger realities too may be assessable for success or failure in being expressive of purposes. These will not be of the limited type of 'encouraging critical thought', but of a general character, being grounded in human nature and in their realization the fulfilment of that character. Just as individual institutions serve specific ends people have, so, it may be suggested, society itself answers to the ends of humanity as such, as the indispensable matrix of the good life. There are complex theoretical tasks involved in working out this suggestion, most notably in the formulation of a detailed theory of human nature, a 'philosophical anthropology'. Such a theory may be expected to answer the questions of how we are to conceive of ourselves as human beings, of what is distinctive about our existence, of what its well-being consists in, and of what purposes are compatible with, or components of, that condition. Given a set of answers to these questions, even the largest social forms will be liable to criticism for failure to meet the standards they represent.

This is a sketch of a version of critique which, for all the problems it raises, is at least not obviously incoherent or unviable. Indeed, it may be that, if foundational questions are pressed hard enough, the idea of social critique is always likely to end up in some such position. It is, at any rate, a terminus towards which the proposal to rely on 'rational' values alone seems naturally drawn. For, as the discussion has shown, it is hard to see how else the key critical notion of irrationality is finally to be understood. The same tendency may be traced in Frankfurt School theory, and is, as we have noted, at its most explicit in the work of Marcuse. The conclusion that philosophical anthropology is the 'truth' of social critique has, however, a particular irony in the scientific case. Even more drastically than the attempt to specify the aims of capitalism, its effect is to undercut the considerations favouring the proposal in the first place. So far from offering a safe passage avoiding theoretical complexities, it turns out to lead into one of the most tangled and daunting of philosophical debates, that which surrounds the project of a theory of human nature. Thus, the original impulse dissolves in the course of being articulated and grounded.

Even if the tangles could be unwound one may well doubt whether the results would serve to reconstruct Marx's programme. The issues involved here have a wide significance, and will recur in the discussion. It may suffice for the present to note some general considerations which tell against the possibility. The first is a difficulty similar to that faced by

Habermas's search for foundations. It is one of seeing how the critical standards could be immanent in relation to any determinate social forms. They must surely be insensitive to the pressure of particular circumstances, but stand over against them, rebuking and offering guidance in the name of humanity. This will scarcely yield the concrete, mediated, historical immanence required for a dialectical theory. The claims of anthropological critique to constitute such a theory are problematic on other grounds. An important factor in them must presumably be the distinctive use made in the critique of the category of contradiction. At this point a line of thought is available which figures with varying degrees of explicitness in the literature. The category has indeed, it may be said, a crucial role. Its primary locus is not, however, the internal structure of the social forms themselves, but rather the contrast between the level of achievement they represent and the truly human conditions postulated in the anthropology. This contrast is what grounds the dialectical critique of the forms. The problem is, however, that the notion of contradiction is now getting dangerously extended. Indeed, it becomes hard to see how any version of critique could fail to be depictable as contradiction-exposing and so as dialectical. The contradiction is simply the gap between the critical standards and the criticized reality, a gap that must, one might suppose, always obtain if a space is to open for negative evaluation. The tendency at work here is one to which the notion of contradiction is peculiarly liable, that of expanding to absorb every kind of hiatus or misalignment within, and between, consciousness and society. The tendency has surely to be held in check if contradiction is to remain the central category of a distinctively dialectical approach to social theory.

I

The discussion has so far been largely concerned with the articulation and grounding of the idea of scientific critique. It should now be possible to stand back a little in order to situate it theoretically within a larger framework. In particular, it needs, in keeping with the aspirations of its sponsors, to be related more systematically to the themes of a socialist critique of society and of the status of Marx's social theory. The chief source of misgivings here has already been noted in connection with Bhaskar's version of the idea. It is that the whole conception may suffer from a kind of abstract rationalism that makes it impossible to focus on the specificity of socialist, still more of Marxist, theory. The difficulty arises, it may be alleged, in virtue of its essential character, its constitution through universal values of reason. Its prospects for keeping an anchorage in the tradition of dialectical thought, and thereby of Marxism, are based on the significance attached to the category of contradiction. It is natural to take the critical view of contradictions as implying a commitment to the idea of a society from which they are wholly absent. Yet it is precisely the dialectical tradition that has insisted most firmly on their pervasive and inescapable role in human life. The moral of this situation has been forcefully drawn by Sean Sayers in the course of the debate with Norman:

> If capitalism must be criticized merely on the grounds that it is self-contradictory, then so too must socialism and all other concrete and historical forms of society. The only non-contradictory society would be an abstract utopia, and nothing could be more foreign to Marx's idea than to make this the basis of his social criticism.[20]

This verdict is difficult to resist. There are no grounds, and exponents of scientific critique have not tried to adduce any, for attributing to Marx a generalized hostility to contradictions in society as such, nor what is therein implied, the fantastic ideal of a society from which they have been eliminated. At most he may be credited with a critical attitude towards the contradictions specific to class society and, hence, with the ideal of a society free of them. If one wishes to insist on the theoretical significance of this point, some grounds would have to be given for the discrimination it involves within the domain of social contradictions. It would have to be shown what is wrong with the self-contradictions of capitalist society as contrasted with the self-contradictions of socialist society. It must be something other than their status as self-contradictions; that is, in Norman's terms, internal conflicts within purposive activity. The point may be put by saying that contradiction is not enough: other values will have to be enlisted to carry through the programme of critique.

This point has been developed at some length by a critic of Edgley's work. Russell Keat argues, in line with Sayers, that the realization of the value of reason involved in critical social science would be 'the elimination of contradictions'. His objection is not that this achievement is theoretically or practically impossible but that it would not, so far as he can see, 'be necessarily accompanied by the realization of specifically socialist values such as the socialization of the means of production, distribution according to need, abolition of the state, and democratic control of social processes'. The charge that the way Edgley characterizes his critical social science 'is not distinctively *socialist*' extends to methodology as well as final goals, for 'criticism of contradictions does not exhaust the meaning of socialist criticism', at least in the sense

Edgley gives to contradictions.[21] In a later contribution to the debate, Keat spells out what he has in mind here. He accepts Edgley's view 'that, in the social sciences, there's a legitimate sense (absent in the natural sciences) in which there can be "contradictions in reality", and that a social theory, in identifying these, is at least implicitly critical of them'. What he rejects is the belief that 'the concept of "contradictions" can encompass the range of criticisms that have traditionally (and correctly) been made by socialist opponents of capitalism'. As examples of such criticism, Keat suggests 'the alienated character of work, the competitive and individualistic nature of social relationships, the division between mental and manual labour, the absence of genuine democratic forms of control, and so on'.[22] Keat's objection is, however, not merely an objection to treating all socialist criticism as criticism of contradictions: more generally, it is to treating it as essentially scientific in character. He, quite reasonably, reads Edgley as claiming that 'a *socialist* critique' can 'be founded exclusively on a *science* of society'. He thinks 'both that this is mistaken and that it impoverishes the character of socialist theory and practice'. In opposition to such a view, he holds that there is much that is socialist that falls outside the set of judgements 'establishable by a social science'. Hence it is that 'any position which restricts socialist critique in this way, and dubs non-scientific "moralistic" critiques as (in pejorative senses) "ethical", "utopian", or "reformist", may easily obliterate essential areas of moral and political discourse in the name of socialist *science*'.[23] The argument is that socialist critique is deformed and diminished by being conceived as exclusively scientific in character, and still more by being conceived as specifically the scientific critique of social contradictions. This is a formidable case which strikes near the heart of the whole enterprise, and deserves serious attention.

Edgley's response to Keat's initial criticism is, however, somewhat terse and unhelpful. It does little more than affirm that 'a science that takes objective social contradictions as its target *must* be socialist', and that although such criticism does not exhaust the meaning of socialist criticism 'explicitly', it does so 'implicitly'.[24] The basis for Edgley's confidence on these matters, the chief point at issue, is left unclear. Elsewhere, though not in direct response to Keat, a more concrete and fruitful line of thought is developed. Its premise is that the category or contradiction is 'basic to and presupposed by all the other critical concepts that Marx's science generates'.[25] In another paper Edgley addresses himself in detail to these other concepts, and the examples chosen coincide, at least in part, with the list suggested by Keat. The chief ones are exploitation, alienation and commodity fetishism. These, it is claimed, 'instantiate' and are 'integrated into' Marx's science by their connection with the 'essential critical category' of 'contradiction in its dialectical form'. The 'specific critical categories' have, Edgley claims, 'two characteristics that mark them as special forms of this general dialectical category of contradiction': 'On the one hand they are relational, and the general form of the relation they denote is that of practical contradiction within a unity. On the other they bear critically on both thought and practice, involving both illusion and subjection.'[26]

Something has undeniably to be conceded to this argument. Putting the point in a preliminary way, it is that the 'other critical concepts' may indeed be said to 'presuppose' the category of contradiction, in that the category supplies an ingredient in their meaning. Nevertheless, it is misleading to represent the position by the claim that they 'instantiate' or are 'special forms' of it. It may also be noted that the achievement of showing that they have something of the character of contradictions is hardly surprising. This is so partly because of the ease and fertility with which contradictions are liable to arise in human affairs on a conception of them as oppositions of meanings. In class-divided societies situations of this kind seem bound to be ubiquitous and inescapable. Hence, any concepts capable of getting an explanatory grip on such societies are highly likely to exhibit the contradictory pattern. To see this, is, however, to grasp little of their specificity and, in particular, their distinctive evaluative thrust. At this point the discussion can advance only by looking at concrete cases.

The concept that, for Edgley, 'occupies the commanding position in Marx's science', is 'the critical category of exploitation'.[27] This seems to be undeniably relational in form and to involve typically relations of meaningful opposition, that is of contradiction. If, however, one wishes to theorize it as essentially a critical category, one needs to say significantly more than this. It may, for instance, have to be added that it denotes specifically an oppositional relation of inequality and, of the unfair, unjust or otherwise illegitimate use of its advantage by the dominant side. Edgley's own term 'subjection' usefully conveys something of what seems required here. Similarly, though less immediately, 'alienation' may be seen as presupposing some kind of contradictory structure. To capture the evaluative significance of the category, however, one has surely to note that it involves the 'making strange' of what is conceived as properly the subject's own. As with the successor category of exploitation, the core idea is of wrongful dispossession, whether of products of labour or aspects of being. It is in this dimension that the peculiar evaluative force of the categories is exerted. Yet it is a dimension whose presence is in no way guaranteed by the description of the relationships concerned as contradictory, and which in turn draws nothing of significance from that description. Thus, it is as if Edgley's 'two characteristics' fall apart on inspection, and turn out to have no inner unity. The critical bearing of the categories derives from sources not given in, or implied by, the specification of their contradictory aspects; that is, from independent sources of value.

This conclusion is wholly in line with the usual treatment of the topic by commentators, including those most anxious to stress the evaluative character of the categories of exploitation and alienation. It does not generally seem to occur to them to suppose that much is to be gained by subsuming the categories under the rubric of contradiction, still less that they may be adequately theorized through doing so. Even a writer as close to Edgley's position as is Norman is unable to follow him here. Norman accepts that '"contradiction" cannot be the *only* critical concept to be employed by socialist science'. As he immediately makes clear, the other concepts required are not to be regarded as simply special forms of contradiction, but have their separate identities: 'It is equally important for a socialist critique to assert that capitalism is exploitative and oppressive, that it turns work into drudgery, that it destroys relations of co-operation and solidarity between human beings.'[28] Thus, Edgley is isolated in his attempt to maintain the absolute centrality and sufficiency of the critical category of contradiction. It is now difficult to view the attempt as a success within its own terms of reference. What this discussion suggests is that Keat is basically correct in holding that quite other values are necessary for the enterprise of socialist critique. He is surely justified also in drawing the implication that the insistence on the exclusively scientific character of that critique must impoverish socialism. This verdict seems inescapable if, as both he and Edgley assume, socialist theory is essentially a critical theory of society. From such a perspective, the purely scientific focus must ultimately appear as an irksome and unnecessary restriction. Indeed, it may be suggested that Keat is expressing the true spirit of socialist critique, and claiming the freedom that properly belongs to it, when he asserts the right to be 'moralistic', 'ethical' and 'utopian'. At any rate, in the light of a whole-hearted commitment to the enterprise, Edgley's dependence on the scientific handling of contradictions may well seem unacceptably reductionist. Thus, if socialist theory is critique, Keat's case seems in the end unanswerable. Moreover, Edgley's attempt to answer it is crippled by sharing this fundamental premise. The premise is not itself, however, unchallengeable, and to challenge it may be the only way to preserve what is valuable in Edgley's work.

His problem is that he is unable to integrate his two main intellectual commitments. They are, on the one hand, to the idea of dialectical social theory and, hence, to the centrality of social contradiction, and, on the other, to the conception of social theory as social critique. The possibility that now asks to be taken seriously is that it is the second of these that should be abandoned. The suggestion seems plausible enough on general grounds. It may well be that while contradiction can never be central to, and constitutive of, social criticism, it does have precisely this status in the movement of social reality itself and, hence, for the thought that seeks to encompass that movement. Its significance for theory may, as it were, be best understood as more narrowly cognitive rather than as also evaluative. Moreover, this, it may be suggested, is after all the crucial insight and pillar of dialectical tradition in such matters. From this standpoint it will appear that it is not only, or primarily, the project of socialist critique that is impoverished through Edgley's attempt to merge two distinct problematics. More significantly for our purposes, the idea of a dialectical social science suffers a loss of identity in the process.

II

For the present, however, it is necessary to remain with the concrete expression of the merger strategy, the idea of a critique of contradictions, as the questioning of it is still incomplete. In particular, there are implications to be considered of the argument concerning what might be called the critical inertness of the category of contradiction in situations of exploitation and alienation. For the difficulty that arose there may be generalized to the primary oppositions of belief and action which are basic to Edgley's theory. Even in these cases, the natural home, as it were, of the category, it may be thought to bear no actual critical weight. This is borne rather by the concepts which supervene upon it, in Edgley's account, of falsity and irrationality. To suggest this is in a sense merely to restate in sharper terms a point he had himself made in earlier fundamental work on theoretical and practical reason. It is that where contradictory situations are objectionable there must be something wrong with them other than simply their contradictoriness. The significance of the point should now be allowed to cast its light over the later project of the critique of social contradictions. In this light the category of contradiction begins to seem suspiciously like an idle cog in the critical mechanism. It is, to vary the metaphor a little, like a translucent screen laid over it which gives way at a touch to expose directly the working parts. These parts consist of notions of truth and rationality which have a life independent of the category and are in no sense mere forms or instantiations of it. That category may now be seen as at best a heuristic device whose function is to signal, albeit in the right circumstances infallibly, the presence of some kind of defect. Once thus revealed, however, the specific character of the defect has to be conceptualized by other means. From this standpoint Keat may in his turn be accused of conceding too much to Edgley's position, thereby illustrating once more the basic similarity of their views. For he accepts that contradiction is a genuine working tool of criticism, though of limited usefulness. To accept this is itself, it now appears, to misconceive the true situation.

The theme of contradiction as a critical category is, however, by no means exhausted. For it has not yet been traced to its deepest roots in Edgley's work. To omit to do so is to miss both some exemplary achievements of that work and the fundamental reason for its failure to yield an appropriate model for understanding Marx's science. At this point one has to return to the origins of the whole enterprise, the extension of the scope of logic from propositions to beliefs. In *Reason in Theory and Practice*, Edgley offers a 'schematic outline' of 'the logic of belief', an outline which displays the analytical method in philosophy to powerful effect. In the course of it he introduces the 'key notion of a point of view', a notion which is such that 'the point of view of a person sets a limit on the questions that logically can arise from this point of view'.[29] The crucial implication for the logic of belief is contained in the fact that: 'I may say and mean "It is right to think that p but he doesn't think that p" but not "It is right to think that p but I don't think that p"; there is no first-person present-tense counterpart of the assertion "he mistakenly thinks that p"'.[30] Edgley's development of this logical point is wholly in keeping with the general spirit of his work in insisting on the intimate connection between matters of truth and of consistency. For the conclusion established here in the case of falsity is later explicitly made to embrace inconsistency also:

> in central cases of belief it is logically possible to believe what is inconsistent only if it is not known or believed to be inconsistent: i.e. it is possible both for someone to believe that p and that q and for the propositions that p and that q to be inconsistent, but not for someone to believe that p and that q believing or knowing the propositions that p and that q to be inconsistent. For to believe or know that 'p' is inconsistent with 'q' is to believe or know that one of them at least is false, and it is logically impossible for anyone to think or know that what he thinks is false.[31]

This is a trenchant and convincing account of the logic of belief. Its insights have, moreover, an indispensable part to play in the theory of dialectical social science. Nevertheless, it contains the seeds of disaster for Edgley's own conception of that science as critique. What it shows is that, so far from being paradigmatic terms of appraisal for beliefs, 'false' and 'inconsistent' have, in the crucial first-person cases, no appraising role whatever. For such locutions as 'I mistakenly think that p' or 'I inconsistently think that p and that q' have no normal uses. Edgley has demonstrated that I cannot, logically cannot, criticize my own beliefs as false or inconsistent, since whatever is open to criticism by me in those terms will not count among my beliefs. With regard to whatever is properly so accounted, I cannot say, and mean, that they are false or inconsistent. The discovery of falsity or inconsistency in one's own beliefs is not, so to speak, an unfortunate event in their lives but rather the termination of their lives. In such cases the would-be objects of appraisal do not sustain their identities long enough to be the bearers of the critical predicates. It is for this reason that there can be no first-person critical uses of the concepts of falsity and inconsistency.

If one asks how Edgley could suppose that his view of the logic of belief is compatible with, indeed belongs to the foundations of, his doctrine of social critique, only one answer seems possible. It is that he simply takes for granted that the critique is conceived and formulated from a third-person point of view. Moreover, such an assumption needs to be invoked if one is to make sense of scientific critique in general. Thus, it is characteristic of Norman's approach that he should present the basic insight in the following terms: 'It is, of course, when we come to speak of a person's beliefs as in conflict with one another, and there-fore self-contradictory, that the concept of "contradiction" becomes a *critical* concept.'[32] The point to note is that it is 'we' who criticize 'a person'. This pattern is maintained throughout Norman's discussion: self-criticism never figures on the agenda.[33] At the level of social theory, the governing principle that emerges is that such theory is constructed from the viewpoint of the observer, not the historical subject. The principle is, as other elements in Edgley's work at least can testify, singularly inappropriate as a basis for understanding Marx. It could, however, to anticipate the further course of the argument, serve as the defining principle that underlies all the more superficial features of the movement known as 'Western Marxism'. The significance of Edgley's analysis of the 'point of view' is that it enables one to provide micro-foundations for such a judgement. It permits an entire historical move-ment to be, as it were, condensed into a drop of grammar, an achievement of the kind to which analytical philosophy perpetually, and usually in vain, aspires. Yet in his own thought this potential marks the site of a structural tension, a tension that here, as so often, stands wholly to the credit of the thinker who preserves it intact without any facile 'resolution'. To see what is involved it is necessary to examine the elements of resistance to the third-person model that were referred to earlier.

The issues are best approached in terms of an objection raised by

Keat. It is directed to the fact that Edgley '*apparently* takes belief in the revolutionary potential of the proletariat as either *the* or *a* defining characteristic of socialist critique'. This, in Keat's view, 'removes the main emphasis, in articulating a socialist standpoint, from where it should be – namely in the distinctive nature both of what it takes to be objectionable, oppressive, etc. about capitalism, and of its conception of an alternative form of society that is historically realizable'.[34] It is entirely proper, as we shall see, to take the theoretical significance of the proletariat as crucial in Edgley's scheme. Yet in complaining of the distorting effects of this assumption Keat is once again speaking with the true voice of the critical project. Such an assumption must indeed remove the emphasis from what is vital to that project, its targets and its alternative vision, towards what is merely contingent for it, the identification of those who will be guided by its prescriptions. Keat is here following the unrestricted logic of his theme, a logic for which Edgleys stress on the defining role of a particular class can only be an irrational obstruction. In a general way the position resembles that which arose from Keat's strictures on the critical role of contradictions. To summarize it, one might say that what he has seen is that the constituents of Edgley's position; the centrality of contradictions, the conception of theory as critique and the theoretical uniqueness of the proletariat, do not form a coherent package. His solution, justified in its own terms, is to insist on the critique idea while allowing the others to lapse. Edgley cannot take this way out for reasons which are also entirely commendable, having to do in large part with his sense of what is most authentic in the Marxist tradition. It is his conviction of the peculiar closeness of the link between Marxist theory and the working-class movement that concerns us now.

This conviction is based on an attachment to certain canonical formulations of Marx. Typical of them is the following, cited more than once by Edgley:

> Just as the *economists* are the scientific representatives of the bourgeois class, so the *socialists* and the *Communists* are the theoreticians of the proletarian class ... in the measure that history moves forward, and with it the struggle of the proletariat assumes clearer outlines, they no longer need to seek science in their minds; they have only to take note of what is happening before their eyes and to become its mouthpiece.

In a comment on this passage, Edgley notes that Marx's science 'aligns itself with the working class by theoretically supporting the working-class movement, as its theoretical mouthpiece actually calling for ... revolutionary change'.[35] Elsewhere, the passage is taken in conjunction with the claim in the *Communist Manifesto* that 'The theoretical conclusions of the Communists ... merely express in general terms, actual relations springing from an existing class struggle.' Edgley's gloss once again stresses the idea of a relationship 'according to which social scientific theory may *express* or be the *mouthpiece* of a social movement ... not simply as speaking *of* it but as speaking *for* it'.[36] In similar vein, he refers to Marxism as 'the voice' of the working-class movement.[37] This dimension is so important for him that he employs it as a crucial test for other commentators. It is a test that is failed by, for instance, Louis Althusser in view of the 'continuing theoreticist tendency in his understanding of Marxist science'. This is a bourgeois survival 'due to his failure to appreciate the full philosophical depth of Marx's *theoretical* revolution and thus the way in which Marxist science, without deserting its scientific standpoint, constitutes itself theoretically as the mouthpiece of the workers' movement and their *political* revolution'.[38] Clearly, there is an emphatic consistency about the terms Edgley focuses on for the relationship of Marxist theory and working-class movement: it is always the language of 'expressing', 'voicing' and 'being the mouthpiece of'. The doubts to which the present discussion has given rise do not concern the appropriateness of this language. They are whether the intimacy of the relationship it celebrates can ever be conceptualized on the critique model, and whether, if it cannot, Edgley may not himself be a victim, in a refined form, of the 'theoreticist tendency' he condemns in Althusser.

The tension here shows itself in matters of detail, especially in conceptual gaps that Edgley would surely not pass over in silence were he not in the grip of a heterogeneous theory. There is, for instance, a tendency to represent the process of criticism as considerably more dynamic than is reasonable. In the passages cited above, and elsewhere, one finds the suggestion that to criticize something simply *is* to call for it to be changed. At times this suggestion is wholly explicit: 'To criticize something is to appraise or evaluate it, usually negatively, that is to object to it, reject it, to oppose or attack it, generally in words, and thus in those words to call for it to be changed.'[39] Even on an activist view of the nature of criticism, however, it emerges only as necessarily generating reasons for acting of some sort. As our earlier discussion shows, it cannot seriously be maintained that these must always be reasons for acting to change the object of criticism, for counter-examples spring all too readily to mind. A similar elision of ideas occurs in the formula also cited above; 'its theoretical mouthpiece, actually calling for revolutionary change'. Such calling for change is not the obvious or primary task of a theoretical mouthpiece. These calls may, and do, occur without any significant backing from theory. A theoretical mouthpiece does, on the other hand, have a genuinely indispensable task, that of articulating the world-view of its possessor, of making manifest whatever cognitive grip that subject has managed to achieve on its situation. In class society, one may add, the concept of contradiction will slot naturally into a pivotal role in the enterprise, a responsibility in which it is, as we have seen, profoundly uneasy where the business in hand is social criticism.

The hasty transitions in Edgley's argument are symptoms of a general predicament to which one should now directly turn. What is at issue are the prospects for reconciling his vision of the proletariat with his commitment to critique. The issue is not resolved simply by including the proletariat within the audience for the critical message, even as a specially receptive part of it. It will not suffice to acknowledge that members of that class are more likely, as a matter of fact, to feel the force of Marxist critical reasoning. This could only be a contingency which is quite inadequate to redeem the internal character of the relationships involved. The theory must, as Edgley insists, speak *for* the class, not merely *of* it, and, one may now add, not merely *to* it either. The question is whether critique can, on his conception, reflect or embody the required categorial distinctions in the way different groups are related to it. It may be helpful to work towards the answer by considering how other forms of the doctrine would fare on this test.

Ideological critique can, it must be admitted, accept, implicitly at any rate, the existence of significant variations within its constituency and a distinction between that constituency and the world at large. For, as was shown earlier, it has force only for those prepared to accept in some degree the standards of judgement represented by whatever ideology is in question. The Frankfurt School's own version is, it was suggested, best understood as a form of bourgeois self-criticism. Hence, there is a sense in which it may be said to speak 'for' a specific group, the liberal bourgeoisie. More generally, it might be said to speak for all who subscribe in some degree to bourgeois ideology; that is, for everyone outside the ranks of the only radical opposition to bourgeois society, the revolutionary working class as conceived by Marx. Such a critique can offer little help in seeking to theorize the practical significance of his own social theory. In moving to the School's moral critique, however, one begins to lose the ability to enforce or assume any differentations of the kind that is required. The considerations it deals in of freedom and justice have to be understood as binding on all in so far as they are rational. Their authority is such as to provide every individual agent equally with a reason for seeking to realize them.

With scientific critique, the universalizing process is taken still further. Now the foundational value of reason does not even require to be articulated through such social forms as freedom or justice. Its demands impose themselves immediately in virtue of the nature of thought and inquiry as such. The critique doctrine attains at this point its purest level of abstraction, a level at which it is quite unable to accommodate strategic distinctions of status between different groups in relation to its procedures and findings. It is a conception in which the specificity of the link between a class and its theory has become wholly dissolved. If scientific critique is a mouthpiece at all, it can only be for the universe of rational beings in general. But in speaking for all, it speaks for no one in particular. As Edgley sees, and has shown, Marx's theory cannot be grasped in such terms. It demands to be conceived as formulated from, and expressive of, the point of view of a quite determinate element in society, the class of the revolutionary proletariat. Once again it is the abstract rationalism built into the critique model that proves to be the stumbling block. Yet this discussion also engenders a suspicion that any version of critical theory is likely to find it difficult to enter into the kind of internal relation with a historical subject that would constitute it as an integral part of the movement of social reality; that is, as genuinely dialectical theory. This suspicion will recur when one comes to engage more directly with the requirements for such a theory as laid down within the classical tradition.

III

Edgley's position has turned out to be an unstable mixture of elements, some of which it is, however, necessary to preserve. Chief among these, so far as giving a philosophical account of Marx's social science is concerned, is the emphasis on the definitional importance of the working-class movement. This has, as Edgley has shown, too firm a textual base and, it may be added, too much hermeneutic vitality to be abandoned. The account will also need to build on his path-breaking work in establishing what might be called the human dimension of logic and specifically in bringing belief and practice under its sway. This achievement is significant for enabling a robust and straightforward sense to be given to the crucial idea of social contradiction. The way forward from here is best indicated in the contribution which was made to the discussion by Sayers. A starting-point is offered by a series of striking comments directed against Norman's view of reason and against what follows from it, his ' "critical" or "evaluative" concept of contradiction':

> Reason for him is not only theoretical but also practical. In either case, however, the law of non-contradiction is its constitutive principle. For, as

Norman explains it, reason is consistency and conformity to the law of non-contradiction....

The world, then, is to be 'criticized' – things ought not to be as they are. And if we ask: what is the basis of this 'criticism'? – the answer is: the requirements of pure abstract reason, and ultimately the requirements of formal logic and the law of non-contradiction.

This is neither Hegel's philosophy nor Marx's: it is pure Kant. . . .

Both Hegel and Marx reject this abstract, moral, Kantian perspective in all its forms.[40]

This identification of the intellectual provenance of Norman's view of reason is surely persuasive. As he is in this respect fully representative of scientific critique we have here an important element in the background of the tendency as a whole. In providing it, Sayers also sheds light on the issue raised earlier of the relationship with Frankfurt School theory. The answer that begins to emerge is that in so far as the link is thought to be constituted by the concept of reason, it is more apparent than real. Some decisive shift in this regard has occurred between the two forms of social critique doctrine. It may be characterized as a shift from Hegel back to Kant or, slightly less opaquely, from an objective to a subjective concept of reason. But such descriptions have to be filled out carefully, and this is best attempted at a later stage of the discussion.

For the present we should return to Sayers's treatment of the 'critical' or 'evaluative' concept of contradiction and of his preferred alternative:

Dialectical philosophy does not seek to 'criticize' the world in this fashion; rather, it seeks to understand the reality of things in an objective and *scientific* way....

The 'critical' concept of contradiction, the idea that contradiction is something 'irrational' that ought not to be, is a negation of the fundamental principle of dialectical thought, according to which contradiction and conflict are the essential nature of all concrete things.[41]

In these remarks, one may suggest, Sayers succeeds in confronting scientific critique from the heart of the dialectical tradition. It would not be too much to say that the task of theorizing social science in accordance with that tradition is essentially one of resolutely maintaining and systematically elaborating these insights. He does not himself, it must be admitted, take one far in this direction. In large part this is no doubt due to the circumstances of the debate with Norman. Such a specialized development of the dialectic could not fail to exceed its limits. But one has also to acknowledge the signs that he does not always hold fast to the truths he has so strikingly expressed, and in the face of Norman's hostility is at times inclined to draw back from their implications.

Norman interprets passages of the kind just cited in the most natural way when he takes them as a denial that 'Marxist theory is a critical theory'.[42] Yet, as he gratefully notes, Sayers subsequently seems to qualify this stance. For he goes on to make the, to Norman, 'much more acceptable' assertion that 'Marxism does criticize capitalist social institutions'.[43] To deal adequately with the issues that arise at this point requires distinctions whose presentation is best reserved for a later stage of the argument. For the present it may be enough to note that it is one thing to provide, in the course of a massive and varied body of work, instances of negative evaluation, and another to conceive of that work as a whole as essentially critique. To grant, as cannot credibly be denied, that Marx does the one is not to accuse, still less convict, him of the other. In this context it should, however, be remarked that Sayers appears to hold not merely that Marx sometimes criticizes capitalist institutions, but also that his theory is properly characterized as a 'critique of capitalism'.[44] Sayers's concern on these occasions is to rebut Norman's conception of critique as an abstract utopian opposition to social contradictions as such. He does not attempt to spell out in any detail what a more adequate conception might be. As Norman notes, the chief point he makes in this connection is that Marx criticizes capitalism 'not merely by judging it to be something bad which ought not to be, on purely formal and *a priori* grounds, but by providing the substantial basis of a scientific analysis of the laws actually governing it'.[45] It is not immediately clear, and Sayers does not explain, how such an analysis could count as a *critical* achievement. To leave matters in this state is to be vulnerable to the charge of seeing Marx's science as merely descriptive and explanatory in the manner of bourgeois theory. This line of thought is vigorously pressed by Norman. He characterizes Sayers's denial of critical theory as 'a denial of the primary impulse behind all socialist thought and action'. 'One might almost attribute to Sayers', he goes on, 'the view that "philosophers so far have tried to change the world; the point, however, is to understand it"'.[46] This is a serious charge which must be met by any socialist who wishes to reject the critique doctrine. Indeed, it is now clear that both Norman and Sayers are basically correct in much of what they affirm, as of what they deny. Thus, Sayers is correct in denying that Marx's theory is a social critique founded on an evaluative concept of contradiction and in affirming its essentially scientific character. Norman is correct in denying that it is merely a means of understanding the world and in affirming that it is also a socialist theory, a means of changing it. What remains to be established is that all of these insights may be retained and reconciled in a comprehensive vision for which the theory is socialist precisely in virtue of being scientific. At this point we return once more to our central problem of interpretation, but now as the outcome of a discussion which has put us in a position to tackle it decisively.

The lessons of scientific critique and, more especially, of the work of Edgley and Sayers have much to contribute to that task. In the most general terms the moral of the discussion is that their grasp of, and loyalty to, the fundamentals of classical Marxism cannot be accommodated within the theoretical framework they assume or seek to impose. In particular, they cannot be integrated with the characteristic Western Marxist assumption that radical theory must be social critique. By quite different routes Edgley and Sayers may be said to have arrived at the outer limits of this tradition of thought and to point beyond to the need for its supersession. The delineation of the concrete forms of what should supersede it may be said to comprise the main agenda of contemporary Marxist thought. Dealing with it must involve reaching across the long interlude of Western Marxism to recover the original forms of the classical period. An engagement with those forms in their own terms can no longer be postponed.

PART II

Marx's Social Science

6

The Standpoint of Evaluation

It may be advisable to preface this discussion by remarking once again on the specificity of the central question with which it deals. For failure to bear this in mind has resulted in much confusion and wasted effort in the literature. The question is one of what may be termed the logical status of Marx's social science. The nub of the problem it presents is how to conceive of the science's practical dimension, its claim to be socialist science. The first point to note is that the matter is not to be settled simply by pointing to the presence in Marx's writings of denunciations of the social conditions of his time. That such denunciations, often framed with great vigour and inventiveness, may be found there is undeniable. Their presence does not of itself establish, however, that he conceived of his science as essentially a critique of social conditions, nor of such critique as a significant aspect of its responsibility to its object. There are, as we shall see, compelling reasons for refusing to attribute any such conclusions to him. Moreover, they have in this case been much too easily won. Social scientists have not in general been notably successful in keeping their writings free from animadversions on the subject matter. Almost any reasonably large-scale body of work will qualify as critique on the grounds being considered here, and so as having the same kind of practicality as Marx's science. The point at issue is a simple one concerning the limits of what may be established by a certain range of evidence. Yet the use made of Marx's animadversions by commentators suggests that it is easily overlooked. These remarks are all too often given a larger significance than they can bear in that they are taken to be decisive for our central question; that is, as showing that Marx conceived of his basic role as that of social critic.

A second preliminary point concerns the need to distinguish our question from the larger one of the historical role and effectivity of intellectual factors in general. The importance of bearing this distinction in mind can, however, scarcely be gainsaid once attention has been drawn to it. More tempting, and equally to be avoided, is the tendency to assimilate the question to the more specific issue of the forms of consciousness required to enable and mediate the development of the socialist movement. Marx should not be taken to have assumed that work of the kind to which he devoted himself, still less his own individual achievement, is simply co-extensive with, or exhaustive of, those shaping forces. He should not be taken to have assumed that a mass socialist consciousness requires for its constitution only such findings as his science yields, or some development of them, that social science is all-sufficient in this respect. It would also, of course, be unwise to doubt his conviction of the crucial importance of scientific insight. It is reasonable to suppose that he regarded it as the most difficult to attain, and replace, of all the ingredients of revolutionary consciousness. There are no grounds for ascribing to him either megalomania or false modesty concerning these matters. Putting the point in another way, one may note that to deny that he thinks of his scientific work as essentially normative in character is not to imply that he regards normative beliefs and judgements as of no historical significance. Neither will it follow that, if he can be shown to have acknowledged their significance, he must have viewed his social science as in some measure constituted by, or as a repository of, such beliefs and judgements.

I

These are somewhat abstract considerations. It may help to crystallize them if one takes a preliminary look at the character of the textual evidence. Some references with a bearing on our concerns have already been cited and more will be found at various points in the pages that follow. This bearing is quite consistent and unequivocal in its nature, and one has, it may be supposed, only to attend to the texts to register it. A passage in *The German Ideology* serves to set the scene. It is concerned with the unity which the proletarians require in order 'to put a summary end to the entire hitherto existing world order'. In reality, Marx insists, they 'arrive at this unity only through a long process of development' in which, he judiciously remarks, 'the appeal to their right also plays a part'. The appeal is, he adds, 'only a means of making them take shape as "they" as a revolutionary, united mass'.[1] This process of 'taking shape' is, one might suggest, the fixed centre of Marx's interests and endeavours throughout his career. That the appeal to the proletarians' right is acknowledged as playing a part in it is undeniably significant. The acknowledgement has, however, a supplemental, concessionary tone which hardly suggests that the part is taken to be a major one. Moreover, it has to be noted that, in spite of it, Marx consistently sets his face against any personal involvement in such appeals. This is so not merely in his scientific work but also in more directly 'political' contexts. His characteristic stance is captured in the complaints to Engels about being obliged against his wishes 'to insert two phrases about "duty" and "right" into the Preamble to the Rules [of the First International], ditto about "truth, morality and justice"', and his satisfaction at their being placed 'in such a way that they can do no harm'.[2] The tendency to be scornful of any reliance by socialists on such phrases is strongly marked in his writings after the earliest period. It is in this spirit that he refers to the 'ideological nonsense about right and other trash so common among the democrats and French Socialists'.[3] His concern that his own branch of the socialist movement should not fall victim to the language of values sometimes finds what may seem extreme forms of expression. In a letter of 1877 he protests at the 'rotten spirit' which 'is making itself felt in our Party in Germany', a spirit he associates with 'a whole gang of half-mature students and super-wise diplomaed doctors who want to give socialism a "higher, idealistic" orientation, that is to say, to replace its materialistic basis (which demands serious objective study from anyone who tries to use it) by modern mythology with its goddesses of Justice, Liberty, Equality and Fraternity'.[4] The tension suggested here between the normative orientation and the cognitive grasp which is the fruit of 'serious objective study' is deeply rooted in Marx's thinking about these matters and forces itself on one's attention again and again. For the present we may conclude this overview of the evidence by noting another passage in *The German Ideology* which rehearses the theme of the rejection of the normative and points towards an alternative. 'Communism is for us not a *state of affairs* which is to be established, an *ideal* to which reality [will] have to adjust itself. We call communism the *real* movement which abolishes the present state of things.'[5]

If communist theory is not to be the systematic organization of the ideal, the issue of its role in the real movement becomes pressing. What part does it play in the taking shape of the 'revolutionary, united mass' which is at the heart of that movement? The question is what intellectual weapons the proletarians need to be equipped with in their formation as a revolutionary subject. To ask this is, in the idiom suggested earlier in the present study, to ask what is the essential content of proletarian ideology.

The answer provided by Marx's writings is, once again, in its general outlines consistent and unmistakable. It is hinted at in the contrast drawn in the letter to Sorge between wanting to give socialism a 'higher, idealistic' orientation and the 'serious objective study' of its 'materialistic basis'. The emphasis throughout is on cognitive achievement of a certain kind, not as normative insight but as a grasp of the historical situation of the revolutionary class. Whenever, as is rather frequently the case, he takes an optimistic view of the state of proletarian consciousness it is to the acquisition of such a grasp that he refers. In one of his earliest pieces of writing he remarks of the Silesian weavers: 'The Silesian rebellion *starts* where the French and English workers *finish*, namely with an understanding of the nature of the proletariat.'[6] A similar judgement is given on the workers of the Paris Commune:

> The working class did not expect miracles from the Commune. They have no ready-made utopias to introduce *par décret du peuple*. They know that in order to work out their own emancipation, and along with it that higher form towards which present society is irresistibly tending by its own economic agencies, they will have to pass through long struggles, through a series of historic processes, transforming circumstances and men.

This knowledge constitutes their 'full consciousness of their historic mission'.[7] The same emphasis, transposed to a different level, is found when *The Communist Manifesto* explains what distinguishes the communists theoretically from 'the great mass of the proletariat': it is 'the advantage of clearly understanding the line of march, the conditions, and the ultimate general results of the proletarian movement'.[8] The underlying conception has not altered when towards the end of Marx's life he advises a correspondent:

> The doctrinaire and necessarily fantastic anticipation of the programme of action for a revolution of the future only diverts one from the struggle of the present.... Scientific insight into the inevitable disintegration of the dominant order of society continually proceeding before our eyes and the ever-growing fury into which the masses are lashed by the old ghostly governments, while at the same time the positive development of the means of production advances with gigantic strides – all this is a sufficient guarantee that the moment a real proletarian revolution breaks out the conditions (though these are certain not to be idyllic) of its immediately next *modus operandi* will be in existence.[9]

This letter has a general interest for its summary of the factors comprising the 'sufficient guarantee'; scientific insight, the 'lash' of material circumstances and, accompanying both, the development of the means of production. The wider issues involved will be taken up later. For the present, one may simply note the conclusion that so far as consciousness is concerned the vital need of the revolutionary proletariat is a scientific grasp of the dynamics of capitalist society.

II

The discussion should move at this point from a general survey of the role of the normative in the texts to consider their dealings with the specific theme of critique. These dealings are on a substantial scale and extend throughout Marx's career. There is, it must be conceded, an element of difference to be registered between the earliest writings and all that comes later. A shift of focus occurs, a change in the kind of objects that characteristically become liable to critical attention. The shift seems too organic, too much a reflection of the process of finding one's individual voice, to be called a 'break' in development, even if its theoretical weight could warrant such language. Moreover, it serves to counter claims of a 'break' where this is conceived in terms of a Hegelian youth and non-Hegelian maturity. The movement in question is better understood as one towards Hegel, and away from what in this context appears as the distortions of the intellectual companions of the young Marx, the Left Hegelians.

In the earlier writings the critical net is cast very widely indeed, encompassing at its widest 'the ruthless criticism of everything that exists' (*alles Bestehenden*). At the same period one finds support for, in roughly descending order of generality, 'criticism of religion' as 'in *embryo* the *criticism of that vale of tears* of which religion is the *halo*'; the subjection to criticism of '*modern* socio-political reality itself'; the treatment of 'conditions in Germany' as 'an object of criticism', a criticism which has '*indignation*' as the 'essential force that moves it' and '*denunciation*' as 'its essential task'. [10] Clearly, social criticism is taken to be a legitimate activity in these texts. Moreover, it should be acknowledged that social objects are not simply identified as legitimate targets; their criticism is presented as a major, perhaps the primary, task of the radical theorist. A quite different situation obtains in the later writings. It is true that, as noted earlier, animadversions on social conditions do occur in them. These are generally, however, in the nature of asides, wrung from the writer by pity and anger, against the grain, as it were, of his main preoccupation. If one chooses to connect them, they might be seen as forming a peripheral theme in these writings. Even then they could carry little suggestion that anything of theoretical importance is at stake, nor that in making them a social scientist might be discharging a major responsibility. They would not, in short, convey any sense of amounting to an intellectual programme which had much personal significance for Marx. Moreover, an ascription to him of such a programme must run up against his constant strictures on attempts to cast socialist theory in a normative mould. These suffice of themselves to make 'criticism of society' an unlikely rubric for his own mature work.

Although readily available for that purpose, he chose never to employ it.[11] What has to be recorded is rather an absence or silence on this score, a fact that should be allowed its own weight of significance. At the very least it gives those who assume that the work is essentially a critical social theory something to explain, a task which, however, they rarely show any sign of acknowledging.

The need to do so is, perhaps, obscured in some measure by the continuous noise generated in the texts by the idea of critique. It always remains of great importance there, and, indeed, as a central organizing category. The focus, however, comes to be 'the critique of political economy' in virtual exclusion of all else.[12] This project supplies the title or subtitle of all Marx's major scientific writings and has a strong claim to represent the favoured and, as it were, official self-description of his work. Hence, its significance for the present inquiry can scarcely be exaggerated. No attempt to reconstruct Marx's concept of social theory can hope to succeed without doing it full justice. Yet here again one has to insist on the specificity of the project. What has to be done justice to under this self-description is the enterprise of criticizing an element, albeit a central one, of bourgeois ideology. This is not to be identified with that of criticizing bourgeois social relations and structures in any general way. The differences of scope and methodology should surely be attended to in serious exegetical work.

An explanation of the development of Marx's attitude to criticism would have to be set in the context of his changing relationship with the Young Hegelians. Their entire programme, as Marx conceived it, had a critical character, and in the process of disengaging from it he sometimes gives the impression of repudiating criticism as such.[13] The process cannot be charted in detail here. What should be noted is the extent to which, even in the earliest period, his dealings with criticism strike a distinctive note, untypical of Young Hegelianism in general. It is partly that the language he uses has a more radical edge, a feature which carries a recognition of the limitations of mere criticism: 'the weapon of criticism cannot replace the criticism of weapons'.[14] More significant is the fact that from the beginning he identifies with a quite specific strand in the work of those he was to label the 'German ideologists'. The identification expresses itself as a marked hostility to criticism as simply negative appraisal, and particularly, it should be said, as negative appraisal founded in the detection of contradictions. This is characterized in the *Critique of Hegel's Doctrine of the State* as 'vulgar criticism':

> it criticizes the constitution. It points to the existence of antagonistic powers, etc. It discovers contradictions (*Widersprüche*) everywhere. A criticism that still *struggles* with its object remains dogmatic. For example, it was dogmatic

to attack the doctrine of the Holy Trinity by pointing out the contradiction of the three that were one. True criticism shows the inner genesis of the Holy Trinity in the brain of man. It describes its birth. Similarly, a truly philosophical criticism of the present constitution does not content itself with showing that it contains contradictions: it *explains* them, comprehends their genesis, their necessity.[15]

This passage is of particular interest for its indications of the grounds for Marx's hostility to the idea of criticism as the exposure of contradictions. Such criticism 'still struggles with its object' and in doing so 'remains dogmatic'. Here Marx is, it may be suggested, pointing to a general difficulty for criticism that professes to be immanent. The principle of all such criticism is the laying bare of the kind of internal opposition or incoherence of which contradiction is the paradigm. For the standards by which the object is condemned must not be external but rather emergent within the object itself. The peculiar defect to which immanent criticism points is the failure of the object to satisfy what are in some sense its own standards. The difficulty indicated by Marx in the passage just cited is the closeness with which this criticism must remain tied to its object and to the conceptual world in which that object is at home. It can never yield a truly radical approach, one which takes up the object by the roots. Hence, it must always be 'dogmatic' in the familiar sense of imposing an arbitrary closure on questions that legitimately arise, questions addressed to the fundamentals of the matter in hand. Frankfurt School ideological critique will serve to illustrate these limitations. It rests on exhibiting the failure of bourgeois society to realize its own aspirations to freedom and justice. Hence, it accepts, into its very soul, as it were, the constraints of the bourgeois horizon. Marx by contrast, as we have seen, steadfastly refuses to accord even these highest bourgeois aspirations a norm-setting, foundational role for socialist theory.

The nature of the dilemma that confronts any attempt at a Marxist version of social critique is now clear. Unless it achieves immanence it must forfeit the claim to be dialectical, and hence integrally linked to Marx's thought. To succeed in being immanent, however, it must sustain a degree of involvement with its object that will set limits to its radicalism. It will not be able to speak authentically for the social transformation of capitalist society and so sacrifices the link with Marx in another way. There are, as we have already seen, critics who effectively opt for one or other horn of this dilemma. Against the ideological critique which fails to be radical one may set the transcendental enterprise of Kantian rationalism which fails to be dialectical. Marx's own position involves a rejection of the terms of the dilemma and thereby the entire programme of a dialectical and socialist critique of society. The position is fully developed only in the mature critique of political economy, but is adumbrated in the passage quoted above. He is writing there, as the choice of illustrations suggests, under the influence of Feuerbach and specifically of the idea of a 'genetico-critical' approach to the object.[16] Yet the sense that comprehending and finding fault are antithetical activities is already strongly marked, and this was to endure and become dominant. It surfaces in, for instance, the treatment in the first volume of *Capital* of 'the kind of criticism which knows how to judge and condemn the present, but not how to comprehend it'.[17] By this stage scientific inquiry is, of course, no longer conceived under Feuerbachian auspices. Where forms of social reality are concerned the genetico-explanatory interest has come to overwhelm the critical. It was suggested earlier that the development may be understood as a move towards Hegel, based on a deeper grasp of his dialectic. The process of showing this in detail may start by considering the Hegelian echoes in the reference in *Capital.*

III

There are numerous texts which might be cited as the source. An obvious candidate is the Preface to the *Phenomenology*, a work whose significance for Marx has already been noted. Near the beginning Hegel outlines the correct attitude to take towards the subject matter of a philosophical work, and warns:

> exertions concerning the aim, the results, the differences that may exist in this respect, or the critical judgements of aim and results, are . . . easier work than they may seem to be. . . . To judge (*beurteilen*) that which has contents and workmanship is the easiest thing; to grasp it is more difficult; and what is most difficult is to combine both by producing an account of it.[18]

Later in the Preface more details are given of the ways in which 'the argumentative manner' (*das räsonierende Verhalten*) is opposed to 'the thinking that comprehends' (*das begreifende Denken*). The first is that 'such reasoning adopts a negative attitude against its content and knows how to refute and destroy it', a form of 'insight' that is, for Hegel, mere 'vanity'.[19]

It seems reasonable to conclude that Marx's sense of the negatively judgemental as inimical to comprehension is shared by, and may be assumed to be in some measure formed under the influence of, Hegel. In the case of both thinkers questions of intellectual temperament may have some significance here. An aspect of them is caught in Hegel's use of the term 'vanity' (*Eitelkeit*). This puts one in touch with an enduring tendency in dialectical thought, its scorn of the empty subjectivity of merely individual opposition.[20] In another aspect one has to deal with a quasi-aesthetic distaste for the kind of reasoning involved in being judgemental, a form of calculation that mimics thought processes central to the life of bourgeois civil society. From this standpoint Hegel and Marx appear as precursors of Nietzsche rather than as successors to Kant.[21] What should be insisted on at present, however, is that we are concerned not with surface phenomena but with features whose roots go deep in the Hegelian and Marxist systems of thought. The thesis to be explored is that dialectical processes have no need of negative evaluations and that where such evaluations are integral parts of the process there is no dialectic.

To begin with, one may note that the main text of the *Phenomenology* offers no support for any suggestion that negative judgements on the successive moments are required to mediate the transitions between them. Hegel's own methodological comments assign no role to any such layer of mediation and it would be wholly superfluous in the light of them. Their keynote is an insistence on the peculiar directness and immediacy of the transitions as the work of the contradictions themselves:

> The necessary progression and interconnection of the forms of the unreal consciousness will by itself bring to pass the *completion* of the series ... [when] the result is conceived as it is in truth, namely, as a *determinate* negation, a new form has thereby immediately arisen, and in the negation the transition is made through which the progress through the complete series of forms comes about of itself.[22]

If one combines such general comments as these with the testimony of the concrete instances, a certain picture of the nature of dialectical movement emerges without undue strain, a picture that would be widely endorsed by commentators on the text.[23] It will be set out here in a preliminary way, and grounded and refined in the course of subsequent discussion.

The basic dialectic in the *Phenomenology* is a dialectic of consciousness: it is 'the detailed history of the *education* of consciousness itself to the standpoint of Science'.[24] Consciousness must, according to Hegel, have an object: it is consciousness *of* something.[25] The general form of the contradictions is that of a conflict between the idea of the object with which the subject consciousness is initially possessed and the object as it is actually encountered in experience. The source of movement is the discovery by the subject consciousness, not that the forms are as such undesirable or contain flaws, but that they are contradictory. This discovery has, one must assume, some immediately practical significance for a subject meeting minimal conditions of rationality. Such a consciousness cannot simply rest in the awareness of its own contradictions. The awareness is of itself destructive of existing forms, and drives the subject towards a determinate resolution of the crisis and a fresh stage in the education of its consciousness. This force exerts itself in a modality which is neither that of practical judgement as normally understood nor that of a psychological mechanism. It is rather that of conceptual necessity, 'necessary progression'. Its effectivity constitutes at least a part of the substance of the attribution of rationality to the subject in the first place. For a subject which failed to meet this condition could hardly begin to play a role in the movement of reason which is dialectic.

This preliminary sketch has been couched in somewhat abstract and, indeed, metaphorical terms. Before spelling it out in concrete and liberal ones it may be well to confirm that we have not lost contact with Marx, that he has in fact a deep appreciation of the procedure sketched above. His most explicit treatment of the matter occurs in the course of examining the 'modifications' to which Proudhon 'subjects Hegel's dialectics when he applies it to political economy'.[26] Marx begins by explaining Proudhon's basic strategy:

> For him, M. Proudhon, every economic category has two sides – one good, the other bad.... The *good side* and the *bad side*, the *advantages* and the *drawbacks*, taken together form for M. Proudhon the *contradiction* in every economic category. The problem to be solved: to keep the good side, while eliminating the bad.[27]

This method of working by means of evaluations is sharply contrasted with that of Hegel, the thinker who is for both Marx and Proudhon the founder of modern dialectic: 'Hegel has no problems to formulate. He has only dialectics. M. Proudhon has nothing of Hegel's dialectics but the language. For him the dialectic movement is the dogmatic distinction between good and bad.' The focus then narrows to consider the chief difficulty which Proudhon's strategy encounters:

> If he has the advantage over Hegel of setting problems which he reserves the right of solving for the greater good of humanity, he has the drawback of being stricken with sterility when it is a question of engendering a new category by dialectical birth-throes. What constitutes dialectical movement is the coexistence of two contradictory sides, their conflict and their fusion into a new category. The very setting of the problem of eliminating the bad side cuts

short the dialectic movement ... from the moment the process of the dialectic movement is reduced to the simple process of opposing good to bad, of posing problems tending to eliminate the bad, and of administering one category as an antidote to another, the categories are deprived of all spontaneity; the idea 'ceases to *function*'; there is no life left in it.[28]

The sense that the evaluative perspective has no part in, and indeed is profoundly antipathetic to, dialectical thought could scarcely be more forcefully expressed. There is a particular significance in what Marx identifies as the chief difficulty, its fatal impact on the dimension of 'life', 'movement' and 'spontaneity'. What constitutes that dimension is the action of the 'contradictory sides' themselves; the very setting of the evaluative problem destroys it. This emphasis is important and we shall have to return to it. For the present one may be content with the general assurance that the understanding of dialectical movement being canvassed here is fully in line with that of Marx.

IV

The phenomenological process is, it appears, one in which preconceptions are overturned by coming into contradiction with comprehended experience. Hence, it may be regarded from one standpoint as a dialectic of the formation and transformation of beliefs. It now seems natural to inquire whether Edgley's analysis of the logic of beliefs, as endorsed in the previous chapter, may not be helpful in rendering the conception more precise. There is after all no reason in principle why the exploration of a dialectical theme should not be able to draw on such analytical achievements. The implication of Edgley's analysis that is crucial for present purposes is that to discover a contradiction in one's own beliefs is not in any standard sense to arrive at a negative judgement on them, nor is it properly described in terms of being provided with reasons for changing them. It is already itself a form of such change: the beliefs can no longer be enumerated as they were before the discovery. As Edgley insists, one logically cannot say, and mean, 'I inconsistently think that p and that q.' Coming to realize that p and q are inconsistent may be taken to be a primitive kind of dialectical discovery. It is an insight which does not simply add incrementally to the existing belief structure but is, to some greater or lesser extent, directly transformative of it. The mechanism responsible is a purely conceptual one, not a matter of bringing normative or psychological pressures to bear. Herein, it may be suggested, lies the basic model of how the practical significance of the discoveries of dialectical social science is to be conceived. It is a model that will, of course, have to be considerably enriched and extended before it can hope to do all that is required.

An aspect which should be developed immediately is hinted at in Edgley's stress on the distinction between first- and third-person points of view. The issue this raises is one of what is involved in being and remaining a unitary subject. As Edgley has shown, the outcome of the discovery of the self-contradiction may be characterized as a case of inconsistently thinking that p and that q only by someone else: it is not a characterization available to the maker of the discovery. It is, of course, perfectly possible, and in fact commonplace, for people to believe inconsistent things. Moreover, these inconsistent beliefs may be consciously held and readily available to introspection or questioning by others. Such possibilities seem to presuppose, however, that the inconsistent items are in some sense normally held apart, entertained in different contexts for different purposes on different sorts of occasion. The closer they are to direct juxtaposition, the greater is the conceptual strain, and part of what comes under strain is our sense of the stability and coherence of the believing subject. The limiting case is represented by the schematic example given above in which they are made to form the components of a single propositional claim. At this point the putative believer seems to be in danger of bifurcating by trying to enact, as it were, the situation of distinct centres of subjectivity caught in a meaningful opposition. What is dynamic, it may be suggested, about the contradiction discovery is that it transforms the belief situation under the threat of reconstituting the possessor of the beliefs as a split personality. Thus, the bringing to light of the contradiction derives at least part of its practical force from its destructive potential for the integrity of the subject. On the assumption of a unitary subject enduring in time, the process of discovery is in and of itself a process of self-transformation.

It should be noted that this conclusion allows at least partial agnosticism on the vexed question of the possibility of 'contradictions in reality'. At any rate the argument for the transformative power of the discovery of self-contradictions does not depend on any general prohibition, on logical or ontological grounds, of such a possibility. Some preliminary clarification may be in order here. It is plain that the present discussion is in one significant sense committed to the existence of contradictions in reality. For it is committed to the view that social life contains elements, such as the beliefs, intentions and practices of individuals and groups, which may stand in relations of subjective and intersubjective contradiction. Using the term in a straightforwardly referential way, one may try to capture such situations by speaking of contradictions in social reality. To put the matter in this form is not, however, to imply that adequate descriptions of that reality must themselves be contradictory. The assumption that it is, though common enough in the literature, signals a confusion which everyday uses of the relevant concepts have no difficulty in avoiding. It is a familiar enough occurrence for people to believe inconsistent things and for others to take it on themselves to point this out. It is not usually supposed that whoever undertakes the task must themselves be guilty of inconsistency. This simple case serves well enough to establish in principle the feasibility of a science that makes contradictions in society the topic of its own coherent discourse. The inference that its propositions must themselves be contradictory has as much merit as the textbook example of drivers of fat oxen being required to be fat. It quite overlooks the significance of a shift from the object level to a meta-level of discourse.

This does not, however, dispose of the issue. For some friends of dialectic insist that one should also recognize the existence of contradictions in reality in precisely the strong sense of situations describable only by means of contradictory locutions. Moreover, they argue, our logic, if it is to be adequate to the needs of our ontology, must be able to accommodate such locutions. Hence it is that they are led to construct the systems of dialectical logic already referred to which dispense with the principle of non-contradiction in its classic, Aristotelian form. The merits of these systems are controversial and it would fall well outside the scope of the present discussion to try to adjudicate them. There are, however, some points to be made here on the general issue. It may be worth noting, to begin with, that the position of the founders of dialectical tradition is by no means clear. It is obvious enough that some of Hegel's statements suggest a radical stance, an outright rejection of the Aristotelian principle of non-contradiction. Nevertheless, many commentators have been concerned to argue that, properly understood, they may after all be accommodated within it. The writings of Engels contain, as is well known, some even more strikingly radical formulations. There is, however, nothing comparable in the work of Marx who is in this respect, as in others, orthodoxly Aristotelian. These circumstances have given rise to a complex, wide-ranging and, it seems fair to say, hitherto inconclusive debate.[29] Once again there is no need to try to settle matters here. We are not required to take a stance on the general question of whether contradictory propositions may have application to reality. What is certain is that we are committed to holding that, whatever the overall status of the principle of non-contradiction, it is, as Adorno recognized, the principle of subjective thought.[30] That is to say, it embodies a condition which the thinking subject must meet if it is to maintain its identity. Whether it is equally constitutive on the side of the object is a question that may be left open so far as the present inquiry is concerned. A partial closure is, however, required in order to make the project of phenomenological dialectic intelligible. Universal tolerance of contradictions would be fatal to rendering the life and movement of that dialectic. 'Without Contraries is no Progression', but if consciousness can rest in the contemplation of its own Contraries, the springs of Progression must dry up and all rational dynamism is lost. It has been shown above that dialectical discovery is directly practical on the condition that contradiction cannot simply be assimilated by existing structures of consciousness but serves to dissolve them. This dialectic works, one might say, by driving its material towards the limiting case, the ever-receding horizon of contradictions in subjective reality that demand to be described by breaching the principle of non-contradiction. That the horizon does eternally recede is the precondition of the entire process.

V

The discussion should now turn to reconsider the features of dialectic which, according to Marx, are particularly at risk in Proudhon's evaluative reading. In stressing them he is surely speaking with the true inwardness of Hegel's thought. It is almost impossible to exaggerate the stress that is laid there on the vital and dynamic character of dialectic. A particularly eloquent, yet still representative, passage occurs in the *Encyclopaedia Logic*. The passage is concerned with various misunderstandings of dialectic, including, in a formulation that seems to foreshadow Marx's critique of Proudhon, the tendency to treat it as 'nothing more than a subjective see-saw of arguments *pro* and *con*'. As against all this, Hegel insists that in its 'true and proper character' dialectic is an 'indwelling tendency outwards' which arises because 'For anything to be finite is just to suppress itself and put itself aside', or, as the addition to the section remarks more expansively, 'the finite, being radically self-contradictory, involves its own self-suppression'. Thus understood, the dialectical principle 'constitutes the life and soul of scientific progress, the dynamic which alone gives immanent connection and necessity to the body of science'. Once again the addition offers a striking comment in terms strongly echoed by Marx: 'Wherever there is movement, wherever there is life, wherever anything is carried into effect in the actual world, there Dialectic is at work.'[31] The negative assessment of individual elements is plainly not essential to this process. The transitions have rather to be conceived as in some sense the work of the contradictions themselves, as they go under and are replaced in virtue of the law of their own finite nature.

The challenge posed by the *Encyclopaedia* passage to the science as social critique thesis may be spelled out in more concrete terms. In the first place there is Hegel's insistence here, as on innumerable other occasions, on the 'immanent connection and necessity' proper to the body of science.[32] If this is essentially a body of social criticism it is not easy to see how the requirement can be met. The basic assumptions of the critique thesis serve to demarcate a realm of practical judgement involving the conscientious weighing of diverse sorts of considerations. It cannot be denied that the series of such judgements may possess a rational unity and coherence. This is, however, more naturally thought of as the unity of a static structure than of a dynamic process. It is a matter of the conformity of the individual judgements to the standards of judgement and perhaps also of their mutual compatibility when universalized in thought-experiment. It does not depend on the effectivity of the immanent connections between the judgements themselves. Yet such effectivity seems indispensable if one is to be justified in speaking of the science as a necessary progress. This idea of the essential directionality of the series is in turn at least partly constitutive of its status as a dialectic. The critique doctrine now appears in a perspective that will be familiar from an earlier point in our discussion. As an interpretative theory it too may be said to operate in the wrong modality, a modality too weak to capture the idea of dialectical progress.

A second, and related, difficulty arising from the *Encyclopaedia* passage is suggested by Marx's use of the term 'spontaneity' in connection with the dialectical categories. The issue is posed squarely by Hegel himself in referring to dialectic as an 'indwelling tendency outwards' and a constant 'self-suppression'. The idea is that dialectical movement is essentially, as Hegel makes clear on many occasions, 'self-movement'.[33] To see what underlies his confidence in this property, and the problems it presents for the critique thesis, it may be helpful to approach his dialectic from another direction.

A passage which reaches an unusual level of explicitness runs as follows:

> this dialectic is not an activity of subjective thinking applied to some matter externally, but is rather the matter's very soul putting forth its branches and fruit organically.... To consider a thing rationally means not to bring reason to bear on the object from the outside and so to tamper with it, but to find that the object is rational on its own account; here it is mind in its freedom, the culmination of self-conscious reason, which gives itself actuality and engenders itself as an existing world. The sole task of philosophic science is to bring into consciousness this proper work of the reason of the thing itself.[34]

The hallmark of dialectic is, once more, self-activity; 'the matter's very soul putting forth its branches and fruit organically'. The helpful addition in the passage is its conceptualizing of the theme through the category of reason. The self-activity is, it appears, the work of reason in and through the object itself. Hence, a rational approach to it, on the dialectical conception, is one that finds it to be 'rational on its own account'. This represents a challenge which the versions of critical social theory which have been considered here must find difficult to meet.

Those which have their roots in the analytical movement seem simply unaware of any requirement to meet it.[35] They are protected by the third-person point of view which pervades them. From that viewpoint what is necessary to constitute the rationality of inquiry is that the inquirer be rational. All that is required of the object is that it be rationally intelligible and assessable, amenable to the categories of theoretical and practical reason. This is in Hegel's terms precisely a bringing to bear of reason on the object from the outside. It involves no suggestion that the object is itself not merely accessible to reason but, as it were, an embodiment of it, a participant with the critic in its life. In this as in other respects analytical versions of critical theory are content with a concept of reason which is that of Kant rather than Hegel.[36] Hence it is that criticism informed by this concept retains all its validity as 'a jewel shining in darkness', even though the world should utterly fail to 'strive towards' it.[37] It is not at all dependent, as dialectic is, on the assumption of the basic concurrence of thought and reality.

The Frankfurt School has a much deeper sense of the demands of dialectical tradition in this area. This gives its failure to meet them a self-conscious, even tragic, quality absent from the analytical writers. The nature of the failure has been sufficiently documented in previous chapters. Here it suffices to be reminded that the rationality of social reality on its own account, its striving towards thought, is the theme prefigured in the title of Marcuse's *Reason and Revolution* and worked out in the body of the text. It is, as we have seen, a theme that in later years he found difficult, and in the end impossible, to sustain. The School's most systematic attempt to theorize the 'indwelling tendency outwards' succeeds only in exhibiting it as a 'dialectic of enlightenment'. The reason at work in the object turns out to be a harbinger of damnation and terror rather than human freedom. It is, moreover, a form of reason, 'instrumental' and not 'substantive', which divides the object sharply from the critical subject, instead of being, as in Hegel's conception, the vehicle of their inner unity.

The element of tragic failure here has a further aspect. It does not ultimately consist in the fact that these thinkers see the need for a certain kind of intellectual foundation which they are unable to provide. It is rather that there is an incongruity between foundations of that kind and the structures they seek to erect. For whatever could count as providing the foundation would serve to make the structures redundant. To put it another way, it is not simply a contingent fact about these thinkers that their socialist critiques lack roots in dialectical tradition. They are critics just by virtue of their inability to share the rational optimism that pervades the classic texts. The criticism of existing society then represents the only option available to them as social theorists for keeping a link with the socialist project. To suggest this is not itself to criticize the critics. They, like everyone else, are of course children of their time and their situation calls for historical understanding, not condemnation. An attempt to provide what is needed will be made in a later chapter when these remarks can be reviewed in a larger setting.

7

The Dialectic of Classes

For the present the point to note is simply that if the object is rational on its own account, the role which the theorist is characteristically required to play is not that of critic. It is one not of judging the present but of disclosing its potentiality, of making manifest what is latent and bringing to the surface what is active only in a subterranean way. The primary task is what Hegel says it is, that of bringing into consciousness the 'proper work of the reason of the thing itself'. Formulations couched in this spirit abound in the work of Marx, even in the writings most subject to the influence of Young Hegelian 'distortions'. Their presence there testifies to a conception of the relationship between social theory and social reality that constitutes the deepest layer of continuity with Hegel and gives substance to the claim that in certain fundamental respects he was a Hegelian all his life. It is a conception that separates Marx and Hegel from the Kantian tradition and from many of their own pupils and followers, then and now. Thus, the aim of giving voice to what is dumbly implicit is what underlies the demand that 'petrified conditions must be made to dance by having their own tune sung to them'.[1] Less metaphorically, it finds expression in such claims as these:

The reform of consciousness consists *entirely* in making the world aware of its own consciousness, in arousing it from its dream of itself, in *explaining* its own actions to it.... It will then become plain that the world has long dreamed of something of which it needs only to become conscious for it to possess it in reality.[2]

There is much more in the same vein:

it is our task to drag the old world into the full light of day and to give positive shape to the new one. The more time history allows thinking mankind to reflect and suffering mankind to collect its strength the more perfect will be the fruit which the present now bears within its womb.[3]

Images of pregnancy and birth seem almost inescapable in this context and are persistently resorted to in Marx's mature writings. A well-known instance occurs in the Preface to the first edition of *Capital.* A society which 'has begun to track down the natural laws of its movement' can, we are assured, 'shorten and lessen the birth-pangs' of its development.[4] At times the pregnancy metaphor is invoked to mark an explicit contrast with the model of normative striving. Thus, in *The Civil War in France* the workers are said to 'have no ideals to realize, but to set free the elements of the new society with which old collapsing bourgeois society itself is pregnant'.[5] In this situation theory is an obstetrical aid and the proper title for the theorist is not critic but midwife. This is, of course, a time-worn metaphor which goes back to the Platonic dialogues; that is, to the thinker whom Hegel accepts as the 'inventor of dialectic', the first one to give it 'the free scientific, and thus at the same time the objective, form'.[6] The metaphor is, however, time-worn only because it fits so well.

Some additional light may be shed on this conceptual field by considering the scope allowed within it to radical thinkers opposed to the social order. It is not easy to make consistent or persuasive sense of Hegel's views on the matter. It seems clear, however, that in principle he does concede a legitimate role for such thinkers. In practice it is generally the 'world-historical' figures, such as Socrates, who benefit from the concession. The activities of such individuals can be reconciled with the doctrine that the proper task of theory is to bring into consciousness the work of reason within existing reality. Their achievement is to enlarge their society's awareness of what reason is working at within it. In doing this they should be seen not so much as opposing the old order, rather as pointing to, or representing, the elements of that order which are bringing about its dissolution. In the case of Socrates it is the principle of subjective freedom which is destined to overthrow the immediate harmony of the *polis.* Socrates is the vocal instrument of the forces embodying this principle who advances their action by making them conscious of themselves and their situation. Hence it is that even the *Republic* which 'passes proverbially as an empty ideal' is 'in essence nothing but an interpretation of the nature of Greek ethical life'. It is an interpretation focused on a 'deeper principle' which was 'breaking into that life', a principle which is 'the pivot on which the impending world revolution turned at that time'.[7] There is, no doubt, much in Hegel's handling of this theme that draws on his personal conservatism. This functions here as a distorting factor of subjectivity which contributes to the impression of incoherence.[8] Nevertheless, the basic assumption is clear, impeccably orthodox and, in appropriate circumstances, revolutionary in its implications. It is that dialectical social thought must be in harmony with the underlying movement of social reality of which it is the expression. This assumption is fully shared by Marx.

The evidence of its being shared is dispersed with varying degrees of explicitness throughout Marx's writings. Many passages with a bearing on the question have been, or will be, cited in this discussion. For the moment it may be instructive to pursue a particular aspect of the situation. This is Marx's distaste, which is quite as strong as Hegel's, for the vanity and empty subjectivity of merely individual protest. It shows itself in, for instance, the verdict in *The Communist Manifesto* on the founders of the systems of 'critical-utopian socialism and communism':

> Historical action is to yield to their personal inventive action, historically created conditions of emancipation to fantastic ones, and the gradual, spontaneous class organization of the proletariat to an organization of society specially contrived by these inventors. Future history resolves itself, in their eyes, into the propaganda and the practical carrying out of their social plans.

The ideas of these 'inventors' are, as one might expect, firmly linked by Marx to the 'then undeveloped state of the proletariat':

> the proletariat, as yet in its infancy, offers to them the spectacle of a class without any historical initiative or any independent political movement . . . the economic situation, as they find it, does not as yet offer them the material conditions for the emancipation of the proletariat. They therefore search after a new social science, after new social laws, that are to create these conditions.[9]

The Poverty of Philosophy gives a similar treatment of the theme, with a clearer indication of how it is resolved. There too the socialists and communists who are 'the theoreticians of the proletarian class' are, in the undeveloped state of the class, 'merely utopians' who 'improvise systems and go in search of a regenerating science'. It is only later 'in the measure that history moves forward, and with it the struggle of the proletariat assumes clearer outlines' that they 'no longer need to seek science in their minds', but have only 'to take note of what is happening before their eyes and to become its mouthpiece'. What this involves is spelled out precisely in terms of insight into the hidden potentialities of the present: 'So long as they look for science and merely make systems, so long as they are at the beginning of the struggle, they see in poverty nothing but poverty, without seeing in it the revolutionary, subversive side, which will overthrow the old society.' It is from the moment they acquire this insight that their science ceases to be 'doctrinaire' and 'has become revolutionary'.[10] Thus, revolutionary science is the disclosure of the emergent reality of the old society. This is the proper characterization of Marx's social theory in its own self-conception.

The characterization is fully appropriate only to the work of Marx's maturity. Yet it is not difficult to see in it the realization of the project announced in his earliest sketch of an intellectual position. This is the letter to his father in which he declared that he had left behind the idealism of Kant and Fichte and had come 'to seek the idea in the real itself'.[11] He connects the decision with his first serious engagement with Hegel's philosophy, a connection that seems wholly fitting. For the phrase he uses would, as we have tried to show, serve equally for the programme of that philosophy. The saying which perhaps best encapsulates the entire region of intellectual history is, however, provided by Hegel himself. It is the notorious claim: 'What is rational is actual (*wirklich*) and what is actual is rational.'[12] In recognizing the central significance of this saying for dialectical thought in general, one has, of course, to read it as Marx would have done and as Hegel intended. In particular, one should attend to Hegel's warning to his critics:

> existence is in part mere appearance, and only in part actuality (*Wirklichkeit*).... In a detailed *Logic* I had treated among other things of actuality, and accurately distinguished it not only from the fortuitous, which, after all, has existence, but even from the cognate categories of existence and the other modifications of being.[13]

Thus, 'actual' (*wirklich*) is in Hegel's work a 'technical term' best taken as opposed to 'potential' rather than to 'unreal' or 'non-existent'.[14] Understood in this way, Hegel's slogan may be said to capture the fundamental tenet of Marx's system also.[15] That system can mean little to anyone for whom the slogan has become empty, opaque or incredible. In Marx's case what it specifically signifies is the commitment to theorizing socialism as the inner truth and disguised destiny of capitalism, its potentiality on the way to being actualized. This commitment pervades the entire structure of thought and has constantly to be borne in mind if one is to comprehend its distinctive details, from the role of the proletariat as the 'grave-digger' the bourgeoisie has prepared for itself to the, otherwise curious, significance attached to the development of the joint-stock company as a concrete manifestation of capitalism's self-suppression.

Considered as attempts to bridge the existent and the actual in bourgeois society, Marx's social theory may well be said to be both more inclusive and more consistent than Hegel's. To say this is to follow the lines of Marx's own early critique of the *Philosophy of Right*. That work aspired to 'recognize reason as the rose in the cross of the present'.[16] Yet, as Marx shows, in a striking use of the category of contradiction as a weapon of criticism, the attempt founders again and again in incoherence and inconsequentiality.[17] More significantly still, it proves unable to accommodate a fundamental aspect of bourgeois reality, the 'direct producers' of wealth: 'the *absence of property* and the *class of immediate labour*, of concrete labour, do not so much constitute a class of civil society as provide the ground on which the circles of civil society move and have their being'.[18] Thus, the working class is the 'invisible worm' in Hegel's rose, the dark secret which destroys its life. It is true, of course, that he is aware of the contradictions here, particularly as they manifest themselves in intractable problems of poverty and unemployment. The 'solution' he proposes, 'colonizing activity' in search of new markets, is, however, merely gestured at, without any serious attempt at integration into the theory as a whole.[19] In truth, it is radically subversive of that theory in that it implies that Hegelian civil society is not an independent, self-sustaining system. Its viability depends on success in an enterprise which by its nature surely cannot be pursued indefinitely. Colonial expansion must, it would seem, have a finite end in view as the supply of potential colonies becomes exhausted.

It might be suggested that the uncharacteristic lack of depth and thoroughness in Hegel's thinking in this area owes something to his historical situation. Like the utopian socialist critics, he was faced with the spectacle of a proletariat 'in its infancy ... without any historical initiative or any independent political movement'. This is not to imply that the proletariat might ever have figured for him, as it was to do for Marx, as the 'universal class', the self-conscious solution to the riddle of contemporary history. Hegel is not a Marxist 'without the proletariat', nor, indeed, a socialist of any kind.[20] The point to note is simply the absence from his field of vision of a necessary condition for posing in a truly comprehensive and fruitful way problems of which he was in some measure aware. This condition was to be met for Marx, coming on the scene at a later stage of the dialectic of bourgeois society. The existence of a developed proletariat did not simply permit a clearer grasp of the contradictions of that society; it provided a solution in the form of a collective subject which could embody rational prospects of actualizing social existence. To locate Marx's work historically in this way is to raise a question that haunts later Marxist theory and forms the essential background of the current 'crisis of Marxism'. It is whether the solution he found corresponds to a unique historical conjuncture which is now irrevocably lost. At any rate the solution quite soon ceased, it may be argued, to be available in anything like the same form to his successors who were accordingly driven back on what were in essence pre-Marxist, 'critical-utopian' positions. An attempt to theorize these developments must be made later. Before doing so it will be necessary to obtain a more detailed grasp of the character of Marx's appropriation of the dialectical theme.

The proposal to be filled out in this chapter is that what underlies Marx's conception of the practical significance of his social theory is his allegiance to an idea of method derived ultimately from Hegel. As the earlier discussion suggested, it is the phenomenological dialectic which should be taken as the appropriate model. It has of all the varieties of dialectic in Hegel's work the most obvious claims on our attention. These are partly a matter of internal affinity. The present task is to show how a theoretical understanding of society can have a dialectical character. It is, as it were, the possibility of an 'epistemological' dialectic that has to be demonstrated. The *Phenomenology of Spirit* is centrally concerned with forms of cognition, with 'the path of the natural consciousness which presses forward to true knowledge'.[21] On general grounds it is, in any case, a key text of the Hegel–Marx nexus, constituting for Marx 'the true point of origin and the secret of the Hegelian philosophy'.[22] Thus, there is at least a strong *prima facie* case for regarding it as crucial for present purposes. Whether the case is established has in the end, of course, to depend on the fertility and explanatory power of the proposal. The first step seems at any rate obvious enough. It is the assumption that in Marx's appropriation of the theme the phenomenological subject is the social class and the dialectic of consciousness becomes a dialectic of class consciousness. As in any phenomenological dialectic the source of movement will be the progressive unfolding of self-contradictions, and the practical status of social theory has to be achieved through its part in this process.

I

The basic account of phenomenological transitions that was given earlier must now be enriched in certain respects. The strategy used by Edgley for extending the realm of the logical involved a movement from propositions to beliefs to actions to social structures. What needs to be inserted formally into this picture are intentions and purposes, the volitional dimension of action. It should not be hard to achieve in so far as one is primarily concerned to identify potential bearers of the distinctive logical relation of contradiction. The natural way to explain how beliefs qualify for this role is to note their capacity to be true or false, where contradictions are assumed to be essentially oppositions of truth-values. Recent philosophy of logic has frequently been willing to build on this idea by entertaining the possibility of logical relations between items which can sustain values analogous to truth and falsity.[23] Intentions as such cannot, of course, possess truth-values, but they can succeed or fail in being realized. This creates the space for the kind of binary operation that allows the idea of contradiction to take root. It is at least a necessary condition for intentions to be realized that their objects, that which is intended, should come to obtain in the world. They are, it may be suggested, contradictory when those objects are conceived of in ways that make them incapable on logical grounds of being realized jointly. This would normally be thought to be the case where the objects are states of affairs that fall under such headings as 'capitalism' and 'the classless society' or 'the dictatorship of the proletariat' and 'liberal democracy'. It may be added that the recognition that the achievement of some goals may logically rule out the achievement of others is solidly entrenched in that logic of natural language which it is among the tasks of formal logic to capture and articulate.

These claims may be tested by inquiring whether there is an argument on the volitional side analogous to that given earlier for beliefs. The critical case arises when someone has goals which they become convinced are incompatible. The will is set on states of affairs conceived of under descriptions such as 'getting rich' and 'winning salvation' which the person comes to see, perhaps through reading the New Testament, are not capable of being satisfied together. It might be supposed that what is being envisaged is a situation describable from a first-person standpoint by a locution of the form 'I inconsistently will that R and that S'. This is, however, quite as impossible to say and mean as is the parallel locution for beliefs. The discovery of self-contradiction is equally transformative here by virtue of the conceptual network in which it is located, a network composed of the concepts of various volitional states and of what is involved in being a unitary subject of volition. What is being envisaged is once again a contradiction in subjective reality whose logical absurdity serves to dissolve existing forms of consciousness. It may, perhaps, be objected that there are volitional states which can perfectly well survive the discovery that their objects are incompatible, as, for instance, those which fall under the rubrics of 'hoping' and 'wishing'. There is, however, an important distinction to be preserved by insisting that there are others of which this is not true, a side of things which the present discussion tries to represent by the language of 'intending', 'willing' and 'having goals and purposes'. It is possible to entertain known incompatibilities in the modes of daydreaming or wishful thinking. But this cannot occur where the will is seriously fixed on determinate states of affairs conceived as appropriate ends of action.

These are the significant cases here, since they are what give rise to the possibility that states of consciousness may figure as constitutive elements of actions and, hence, they must carry the hopes of making sense of the project of a dialectic of practice. It will scarcely matter if the exposure of contradictions has nothing directly practical about it where the connection with action is merely adventitious.

The introduction of intentions does not substantially alter the original picture. It may, however, enable one to give a somewhat more mediated account of the place of actions within it. Edgley and Norman rely on a general notion of logic as coterminous with meaning, and of actions as meaningful events, to carry the argument. It should now be possible to spell this out a little more. Thus, if intentions as well as beliefs are admitted within the scope of logic, the further step to embrace actions as well is not a large one, at least if contemporary philosophy of action is taken as a guide. Indeed, it will then appear rather as a continuous movement borne on the internal links that bind the key concepts. The stress on this internality serves various functions related to a question which has haunted the literature: 'What is left over if I subtract the fact that my arm goes up from the fact that I raise my arm?'[24] For it indicates the general area in which solutions should be sought to the problem of distinguishing human actions from pieces of behaviour and other events in the natural order. It has seemed obvious to many that they must involve reference to such modifications of consciousness as belief and intention. The stress on internality has the further advantage of seeming to provide the most straightforward way of individuating particular actions. These may be thought to derive their identity from the specific elements of belief and intention which they express. The underlying assumption is that ultimately actions cannot be adequately characterized independently of the way they are conceived of by the agent and that to specify this is, typically, to say what was believed and intended in performing them. From this standpoint, beliefs and intentions may be said to be partly constitutive of the actions in which they are embodied.

Actions as such cannot have truth or falsity predicated of them in the sense that is important for logic, and it is hard to see how they could be the bearers of values that are in any significant way analogous. It seems to follow, on the account given earlier, that they cannot be terms in such relations as contradiction. But now it appears that they have integral parts that do meet the required conditions. This opens up the possibility of speaking of what are at least quasi-logical relations between them that hold in virtue of full-strength logical relations between their corresponding ingredients of belief and intention. Thus, one is led to suggest that they stand in a relation of contradiction to one another when their cognitive and volitional elements are opposed in the manner sketched above. This would be to use the category of contradiction in an extended sense. The general justification must be that it involves a rational development of the primitive idea, not an arbitrary wrenching of it. Moreover, it preserves what is essential in that starting-point so far as the dialectic is concerned. This is the conception of a relation whose terms confront one another in an opposition that cannot be understood as merely contingent or external and whose explication accordingly leads one to draw on logical categories.

The awareness that there may be conceptual and, in a broad sense, logical relations between actions is reflected clearly enough in ordinary usage. An individual's actions are commonly appraised as inconsistent where what seems to be involved is that they are explicable only as the outcome of contradictory beliefs and intentions. Moreover, such actions are recognized within everyday conceptions of these matters as being in a special way self-stultifying, a way that partakes of the character of logical, and not simply factual, error. To complete this part of the discussion, it should be noted that if the claim that the category of contradiction is applicable to actions is granted, there are no theoretical obstacles in the way of assimilating those sustained modes of action or sets of actions that are called 'activities' and 'practices'. It is then a straightforward matter for the argument to take in what may be thought of as the petrified practices that constitute social institutions and structures. At this point we return to Edgley's thesis that the field of logical relations incorporates virtually the entire subject matter of the social sciences. Moreover, the detour we have taken may be regarded as a way of giving substance to the basic insight that human social life is so saturated with language and meaning as to be a natural extension of the scope of logic, however the heartland is conceived. Among the logical relations instantiated there, contradiction is likely to have a prominent place.

There are some other general remarks to be made in order to complete this stage of the argument. The source of inspiration here is a phenomenology. This would, however, be a wholly inadequate model for Marx's dialectic if its subject were to be conceived of as pure intellect. The emphasis on purpose and action should help to reduce this risk. The subject has to be a centre not just of cognition but also of will and agency, a desirer and doer as well as a knower. Hence, its consciousness is both theoretical and practical and, moreover, is necessarily embodied in some determinate locus of activity in the world. A dialectical social theory must, after all, be specifically concerned with factors of social change and, for that and other reasons, with forms of human practice. It is in the light of these concerns that consciousness as such becomes significant. Thus, purpose is involved in the dialectic in so far as it finds expression in, and shapes, action. Belief is relevant as the all-pervasive medium of the formation of purpose. Hence, if one may still speak of a dialectic of consciousness, it has to be understood as that of a practical, embodied consciousness. It should still be possible, as we shall hope to show, to think of cognitive discovery as the leading edge of the dialectical process. The unity of belief, purpose and action in the subject has, however, to be constantly borne in mind.

It should be conceded at this point that dialectic cannot achieve the same frictionless ease of transition in the realm of action as in that of consciousness alone. For actions do have the extra dimension of being pieces of behaviour, events in the natural world. In this dimension the workings of reason are always liable to encounter some measure of inertia or recalcitrance. When dealing with activities and practices one has also to allow for the momentum that may carry them as forms of behaviour through the decay of their initiating purpose. On the other hand, one should bear in mind that Marx's dialectic presupposes from the start a subject meeting minimal conditions of rationality and capable of developing through the dialectical process so as to meet more exacting ones. In the case of such a subject it may justifiably be expected that modes of behaviour will sooner or later reflect alterations of thought and purpose. What has to be recognized, on the other hand, is that this dialectic has a temporal aspect which is not significant in the same way in the dialectic of pure consciousness. The fact that its effectivity is unfolded in time need not deprive us of the advantages of speaking of dialectical movement, for it preserves the essential point of such language. It leaves open the possibility that what we are confronted with is a rationally intelligible development with its own immanent logic, not the blank externality of a causal sequence. Of course, a great deal remains to be done before one could claim to have vindicated the idea of a materialist historical dialectic, but there seems no reason to doubt that the first steps may legitimately be taken.

II

It was suggested above that in Marx's use of the phenomenological model consciousness is assumed to be embodied in those distinctive social actors which are social classes. Such assumptions are sometimes thought, particularly by critics with 'methodological individualist' sympathies, to give rise to difficulties of an ontological kind. It is not possible to deal comprehensively with the issues here, but something may be done to draw their sting so far as our argument is concerned. Firstly, it should be noted that a commitment to the existential legitimacy of collective social actors is by no means confined to Marxism but is widely shared across the main reaches of orthodox, 'bourgeois' social science.[25] Hence, if the philosophy of science is to be responsive to the actual practices and achievements of its subject matter rather than a source of *a priori* legislation about them, there is a presumption that any difficulties are so many challenges for it to overcome. The philosophical debate has all too often, however, had a remote and factitious character that fails to engage with the living concerns of practitioners of the social sciences. The second point to make is that many of the keenest advocates of methodological individualism, whenever they do attempt to spell out the concrete implications of their position or relate it to any substantial body of social scientific work, seem obliged to license just the same kinds of explanation as their supposed opposites, the methodological collectivists. This tendency is, of course, just what our first point would lead one to expect. It may be illustrated in a way directly relevant to present concerns from the work of a writer who was earlier discussed in a different connection.

There is no school of thought in recent years which has taken greater pride in its attachment to methodological individualism than the new 'rational choice', 'game-theoretic' or 'analytical' Marxism. The best guide and compendium for the movement is, without doubt, Elster's *Making Sense of Marx.* This work takes its subject frequently to task for his offences against individualist canons of explanation. Yet its treatment of those canons has elements of ambiguity which are curiously symptomatic of the debate in general. Thus, it contains almost as many warnings of the dangers of rigidly insisting on them 'at the current stage'. To do so may be a 'premature reductionism' yielding only 'sterile and arbitrary explanations'.[26] Elster's individualism has, it seems, a utopian tinge: it is a *desideratum* whose full achievement is postponed to an indefinite future. Moreover, it is by no means plain sailing even where he is not consciously waiving, but may be assumed to suppose he is applying, the principle. For it is unclear what are the limits of what may properly be predicated of the social actors in such cases. Thus, Elster asserts that in modern capitalist societies 'the main classes have become strategic actors in the full sense'.[27] Given his understanding of what the strategic mode involves, this is to equip them with substantial and extensive capacities. It is not at all surprising to learn that collective actors may be credited with policies and purposes and the ability to shape a process towards its end.[28] The difficulty is to see what more a social scientist committed to methodological collectivism might require. The puzzle is not made easier by moving to a lower level of abstraction to consider Elster's treatment of particular topics. Thus, he recognizes that if the bourgeoisie of mid-nineteenth-century France had been 'a fully class-conscious collective actor', they might well have behaved in the way postulated by Marx and so have redeemed the 'teleological tendency' of his views.[29] Here the disagreement with Marx has plainly come to rest not on theoretical divergences but on a different reading of the historical situation. It seems reasonable to conclude that, if one looks behind the more general programmatic statements to what Elster is in practice prepared to allow, no significant constraints on our project need be feared. Indeed, his class-conscious, strategic actors seem eminently suited to figure in key roles at advanced stages of the dialectic which is its chief concern.

The subjects of this dialectic are classes. A class may be thought of as equipped with a view of its social world which has to cope with the demands of everyday existence in that world. For a subordinate class, at least in the earlier stages of the dialectic, the essential content of this world view is supplied by the ruling ideas which are, Marx tells us, the ideas of the ruling class. In his distinctive idiom, the subordinate class may be said to be subject to the ruling ideology; that is, to the set of ideas and beliefs which serve the interests of the ruling class by legitimating its rule. This ideology, like any other, involves cognitive claims. It purports to embody a correct picture of social reality. It is these claims which, according to our model, will come in conflict with, and be refuted by, experience. Such experience is not, of course, unmediated. It is human social experience and as such highly conceptualized, not a registering of raw data. The dialectic of class consciousness is the process through which the way it is conceptualized comes increasingly to be informed by scientific insight. Thus, in Marx's version, the phenomenological dialectic is fuelled by the opposition of ruling ideas and comprehended experience. In the central case with which he was concerned this, it turns out, is equivalent to the opposition of bourgeois ideology and proletarian science. It should now be possible to appreciate the exactness of the self-description of his work as a 'critique of political economy'. That is to say, it is a critique of the central, most intellectually formidable version of the bourgeois ideology of his time. Marx saw the significance of his life-work as bound up with the destruction of the cognitive core of that ideology. This is intelligible in the light of the scheme presented here, in that such a work of destruction helps to break the grip of the ruling ideas by exploring the gap between what they project and the reality. In doing so, it exposes and activates the primary contradiction of the dialectic of class consciousness.

Marx's work seeks also, of course, to develop a scientific understanding of capitalist society. As Engels remarks, it is at the same time 'a criticism of the whole of economic literature' and 'a systematic integration of the whole complex of economic science', an 'inter-

connected development of the laws of bourgeois production and bourgeois exchange'.[30] In scientific work in general the criticism of existing
views and the presentation of alternatives are activities that go hand in
hand; that are, indeed, but two sides of one coin. In the present instance
the intimacy of the link is best captured through the central dialectical
notion of contradiction. Marx observed two main tendencies in the
relationship of the political economists to the contradictions of the capitalist system. These correspond more or less to the distinction between
'classical' and 'vulgar' economy. The hallmark of the classical writers,
such as Ricardo and Sismondi, is that they acknowledge the existence of
contradictions. The bourgeois character of their work derives from the
tendency to take them as natural, eternally valid features of human
society as such. In the work of the vulgar economists the contradictions
are generally concealed or ignored, either through stark insensibility or
as a part of a programme of apologetics. The overall result is to constitute political economy as bourgeois ideology in virtue of its conceptual
underpinning of bourgeois social arrangements as an ideal or, at any
rate, an inescapable reality.[31] In either case the remedy is supplied by a
dialectical inquiry which exhibits the contradictions not as static and
timeless forms, but as historical phenomena subject to the 'laws of
motion' of the society. The inquiry must 'at the same time' be a critique
of political economy for it is by its very nature the assertion of what that
ideology lives to deny. In being such a critique it strikes at the ruling
ideas in a critical area of their legitimating activity. Thus, it serves as a
trigger of the dialectic of the class subject by exposing for that subject
the fundamental contradiction of preconceptions and experience. The
preconceptions posit a world of natural harmony or immutable division,
while the science reveals a structure of contradictions in a movement
towards resolution.

The practical role of science needs to be further specified. The term
'science' itself may be somewhat misleading here. For it tends to be
associated in English usage with the natural sciences, and even, in
particular, with what are supposedly the most successful and advanced
of them, such as physics and astronomy. These disciplines are all too
frequently taken as paradigms of what 'science' truly is. The term
Wissenschaft involves no such partiality, signifying quite generally the
organized pursuit and achievement of knowledge. English usage tends
also to suggest a somewhat rarefied activity that is the prerogative of a
specialized group of professionals, the 'scientists'. Such a conception will
not suit the needs of a model which postulates that scientific understanding may come to permeate the world view of class subjects. It is
plainly foreign to the spirit of Marx's thinking in this area. The possibility of science arises for him whenever the appearances of things fail to

correspond to their reality. His basic image of scientific activity is the going behind such appearances to find what they conceal. In the case of social science the possibility of this unmasking arises for subordinate classes just in virtue of their role in social production. For the ruling ideology is never entirely successful in imposing its version of reality, or at any rate, its success is inherently precarious. Thus, it is a persistent theme in Marx's writings from early to late that subordinate classes are in a privileged position so far as grasping the truth about their society is concerned: they are best placed to penetrate the fog of its phenomenal forms.[32]

This thesis is by no means confined to the proletariat, but is intended quite generally. Hence it is that the bourgeoisie in its heroic period had access to important insights into the nature of the society it was seeking to dominate, insights which received their most complete expression in classical political economy. Its ideology began to degenerate into 'the bad conscience and evil intent of apologetics' only after the conquest of political power.[33] The insights themselves, together with those later available to the proletariat, are significant as both the historical basis and conceptual model for all further elaboration of social science. In this elaboration Marx recognizes a role for specialized intellectuals, and he thought of himself as playing that role for the working-class movement. Such contributions are possible, however, only in so far as the theorists adopt the standpoint of the epistemologically privileged class and become its mouthpiece. Social scientific understanding is in the first instance the birthright of such classes. This view of their cognitive capacity fits, of course, with Marx's sense of their historical significance. In particular the potential of proletarian science fits with his view of the revolutionary mission of the class, with the insistence that 'the emancipation of the working classes must be conquered by the working classes themselves'.[34] For such a conquest to occur, the dissemination of forms of scientific understanding among the workers is indispensable.

III

The discussion should now begin to move to more concrete levels. The task of self-conscious theory is, it appears, to articulate in scientific form insights that arise as it were 'spontaneously' for subject classes. In Marx's case the central concepts form a tightly knit group whose function may be characterized in general terms as that of theorizing the role of labour in commodity production. The group includes the concepts of class and class struggle, of value and surplus value, and of labour power and exploitation. As Marx freely acknowledges, he had for the most part taken over elements in the work of bourgeois historians and economists. So far as the central stock of ideas is concerned he made the firmest claim for his own originality in the case of labour power and of the distinction between abstract and concrete labour, ideas which in his view provide the 'pivot' (*Springpunkt*) on which an understanding of political economy turns.[35] The implication of our argument is that these concepts should be seen both as the scientific precipitates of the development of class struggle and as serving in turn to intensify it by raising it to higher levels of self-consciousness. They are vital factors in the ideological process through which 'men become conscious of the conflict and fight it out'.

The explanatory field for which Marx's central theoretical concepts are intended is class society and, specifically, capitalist society. Hence, it is not surprising that, as noted earlier, they should characteristically denote situations of contradiction in the sense of meaningful opposition, conflicts of beliefs, aspirations and practices. These constitute, in our suggested terminology, 'intersubjective' contradictions. It may now be supposed that, in addition to the dialectic of class consciousness, the discussion has to accommodate one of contradictory relations between classes, an intersubjective as well as a subjective dialectic. For it seems reasonable to hold that class struggle must be paradigmatically, within a Marxist framework, a sphere of dialectical operations. The accounts Marx gives of the development of that struggle in modern society should therefore be fitted within the terms of the argument.

The clearest view of the process may be obtained from its point of culmination. It is natural to represent the final stage of the class struggle, in Marx's conception of it, as structured around the proletariat's acquisition of a grasp of the network of intersubjective contradictions in which it is caught. From its origin as a class 'in itself', a group constituted by a given location in the productive process, it ultimately succeeds in acquiring a full awareness of the reality of the situation, of the fact that its perspectives and aspirations as a class are comprehensively opposed by those of the capitalist class embodied in the existing social order. This has in large part the character of a long-term piecemeal process, a progressive accumulation of detail. It is obvious, however, that Marx's interest is focused primarily on certain developmental stages, points at which a shift occurs from one level of consciousness and practice to another. Such transitions also have a special interest for the present discussion. For they serve to crystallize the question of the distinctive contribution of theory and do so in what may be thought of as specifically 'dialectical' terms.

The first of these stages is the initial transition from the class 'in itself' to the class 'for itself', the acquisition by a group, whose members have the same relation to the mode of production, of a sense of the reality of its common interests and of a will to pursue them. A characteristic way in which Marx signals the importance of this development is by saying that with it the movement takes on a 'political' form:

> Economic conditions had first transformed the mass of the people of the country into workers. The combination of capital has created for this mass a common situation, common interests. This mass is thus already a class as against capital, but not yet for itself. In the struggle ... this mass becomes united and constitutes itself as a class for itself. The interests it defends become class interests. But the struggle of class against class is a political struggle.[36]

> Every movement in which the working class comes out as a *class* against the ruling classes and tries to coerce them by pressure from without is a political movement ... the movement to force through an eight-hour, etc., *law* is a *political* movement. And in this way, out of the separate economic movements of the workers there grows up everywhere a *political* movement, that is to say, a movement of the *class*.[37]

The stage at which the workers seek to secure an eight-hour day by political action does not, of course, correspond to the highest level of their class consciousness as envisaged by Marx. There is a further stage which is marked by the realization that the contradictions are systematically interconnected and cannot be overcome without the destruction of the system. With it there is the emergence not merely of a 'political' but of a truly 'revolutionary' consciousness, a 'realization that communism is totally opposed to the existing world order'.[38]

The theory of class struggle is intended to have a general application. Hence one finds that the two great stages in the development of the proletariat are closely paralleled in the historical struggles of the bourgeoisie: 'In the bourgeoisie we have two phases to distinguish: that in which it constituted itself as a class under the regime of feudalism and absolute monarchy, and that in which, already constituted as a class, it overthrew feudalism and monarchy to make society into a bourgeois society.'[39] Thus, there are, it appears, at least two points where one has to acknowledge, not a piecemeal accumulation of detailed insights but rather a great leap forward; the formation of the class for itself as a political force and its formation as a revolutionary agent which is the prelude to its reshaping society. These are points at which it seems particularly appropriate to speak of a transformation of consciousness and action, and they are therefore of the greatest interest in the context of the present discussion.

The dialectical tradition contains resources which seem expressly suited to deal with cases of this kind. Thus, for instance, it may be said that they exemplify the law of 'the transformation of quantity into quality': 'quantitative difference suddenly passes at certain points into qualitative change'.[40] The specific change with which we have been concerned is an intellectual one from a growing collection of detailed insights to a synoptic grasp of the unity of the whole. The importance attached in the tradition to the category of 'totality' may also be taken as reflecting the requirements of theorizing processes of this kind. Among those who have engaged with Marx's work from a dialectical perspective, it is Lukács who has most firmly insisted on its crucial significance: 'The whole system of Marxism stands and falls with the principle that revolution is the product of a point of view in which the category of totality is dominant.'[41] Elsewhere in *History and Class Consciousness* there are formulations even more finely tuned to present concerns: 'The primacy of the category of totality is the bearer of the principle of revolution in science.'[42] It seems entirely correct to suggest that what we are centrally concerned with is indeed the adoption by certain historical subjects of the point of view of totality. This way of speaking, together with that of a law of quantity and quality may, however, still strike one as unacceptably abstract or, at best, descriptive. It should now be possible to vindicate their explanatory power by giving them a more concrete expression.

The possibility of such expression arises from a recognition of the role of theoretical concepts in science. The suggestion to be made is that the qualitative change and shift to a totalizing vision are mediated through the development at the crucial moments of appropriate scientific concepts. Thus, the intelligibility of the dialectical scheme depends at least in part on the unifying and synthetizing power of these concepts.[43] 'Class struggle' may be taken as the archetype here. Its formulation was, Marx insists, the achievement of bourgeois thinkers in the creative period of their class. The basis and, as it were, raw material for the achievement lay in the sense of common interests and a common enemy that was borne upon a subject group struggling to assert its place in society. This pattern was to be re-enacted by the working class. Hence, it seems reasonable to associate the scientific concept of class struggle with the first of the qualitative changes referred to earlier. It is the key theoretical mediation from the 'in itself' to the 'for itself'. A rational reconstruction of the concept would locate its genesis in the first stirrings of awareness of the contradictory purposes and perspectives in which the subordinate class is enmeshed. In its turn it serves to crystallize and systematize this awareness, and to direct in full self-consciousness the identification of further instances.

A similar picture unfolds when one turns to the theoretical advances which Marx regarded as accessible only from the class standpoint of the proletariat and in respect of which he was inclined to stake a claim for his own originality as the thinker who first fully articulated that standpoint. These are primarily the advances associated with the proletariat's awareness of its own status as a commodity. The scientific precipitates of this situation are the pivotal concepts of political economy that were referred to earlier. They may be accorded a similar pivotal role in mediating the second of the major qualitative changes, the transition to the revolutionary class consciousness of the proletariat. A grasp of the nature of labour as a commodity is the essential clue to the structure of the commodity world and signifies for the proletariat that its emancipation as a class is inextricably bound up with the fate of that structure as a whole. It is the last, vital step towards the adoption of the standpoint of totality so far as the system of commodity production is concerned. Among the commentators it is once more Lukács who has shown the deepest insight into the significance of this element in Marx's thought and has given the most illuminating account of how and why it is that 'the process by which a man's achievement is split off from his total personality and becomes a commodity leads to a revolutionary consciousness'.[44] What should be particularly noted is that in this case too it seems proper to speak of theoretical achievements which are the result of insights spontaneously given in the nature of the objective situation and which serve in turn to organize the further exploration of social reality in all its ramified contradictoriness. This kind of spiralling interaction is, of course, often thought of as being 'dialectical' in one sense of that protean term.

The preceding argument may be summarized as follows. The immediate object of dialectical social science is provided by social contradictions, specifically the intersubjective contradictions of class society. For capitalism, and hence for Marx's science, the fundamental contradiction is that of labour and capital. Through the development of social scientific insight, subject classes achieve a grasp of the true nature of their situation. This process includes qualitative leaps made possible by the universalizing power of theoretical concepts. The whole development may be seen as activating the contradiction of the preconceptions derived from the ruling ideology and reality as it is experienced and understood. Thus, it serves as the driving force of the dialectic of class consciousness. Viewing these relationships from the other end, as it were, it may be said that the intersubjective dialectic of classes is worked out in its later stages through the subjective dialectic of class consciousness. More specifically, the conflict between classes can be superseded in a transition to a new society only if the historical process becomes conscious for one of its participants, the proletariat. This class has to attain a high level of consciousness and scientific understanding in order to become in the full sense the subject of history. In that role the subjective and intersubjective dialectics of class society come together and complete their course. It is against this background that one must interpret the claim that dialectical social science is practical and revolutionary. It is so in so far as it forms and transforms the consciousness, and thereby the practice, of the subjects who make history. The process is not to be understood as requiring the mediation of criticism of the successive moments. It is ultimately to be explicated in terms of the directly transformative power of the discovery of self-contradictions by the dialectical subject. This is the substance of the traditional idea that dialectical thought is by its nature a dynamic element in human affairs. It is not a means for securing a basis for ratiocination about the desirability of social change but is already itself a form of such change.

8

Reason in History

The discussion has so far been concerned to reveal the basic structure of Marx's position and to fill in the more important details. Something vital is, however, missing from this picture. The attempt to supply it takes one to the heart of the problems bequeathed with Marx's intellectual legacy and thus to the sources in that legacy of the contemporary 'crisis of Marxism'. Speaking roughly, and in terms previously proposed, one may say that what is missing is an explanation of where the spirit of rational optimism that pervades and animates the structure is derived. But this formulation needs to be refined considerably before it can serve as a guide. The view that Marx's social theory has the status of a critique of its object has been rejected here in favour of the view that its essential task is to discover and express the rational potentiality of that object. This conclusion accords with the midwife role of theory in dialectical tradition. What is required to make such a role viable is the assumption that the present really is pregnant with a more rational future, that, in Hegelian terminology, the rational is the actual. A large part of our remaining task may be captured by noting that this assumption stands in pressing need of justification. It was suggested earlier that Hegel does not succeed in carrying through his dialectical programme in social theory: it founders on some intractable features of bourgeois society. This gives our present concerns an even sharper edge. The question is what vindicates the claim that Marx succeeds where Hegel fails, in exhibiting the inherent rationality of the bourgeois order. This is in substance the question of what vindicates the central proposition of Marx's social theory, that socialism is the hidden truth and emergent reality of capitalism. The question may be posed more concretely still, and in a way that directs attention to the area where Hegel comes to grief. How, one may ask, is it possible to justify the identification of the proletariat as the historical subject through which the rational potentiality of capitalist society is realized?

It may be helpful to begin by considering Hegel's answer to the question of how the rational optimism of the dialectic is to be grounded. This should throw light on the nature of the intellectual resources needed to deal with the same question addressed to Marx. It will help to keep the issues focused if we take our bearings from Marx's understanding of Hegel's position, an understanding that is, perhaps surprisingly, broadly in line with the bulk of orthodox opinion. It leaves little room for doubt either as to the general character of Hegel's view or as to what Marx finds unacceptable in it. In contrasting the two versions of dialectic he writes:

> My dialectical method is, in its foundations, not only different from the Hegelian, but exactly opposite to it. For Hegel, the process of thinking, which he even transforms into an independent subject, under the name of 'the Idea', is the creator of the real world, and the real world is only the external appearance of the idea. With me the reverse is true: the ideal is nothing but the material world reflected in the mind of man, and translated into forms of thought.[1]

The theme of the Idea as independent subject is the pivot on which Marx's break with Hegelianism turns.[2] It is in essence an ontological break, a rejection of the ontological foundations of Hegelian method. Marx's reading of this ontology, though often expressed in heightened language, is in general agreement with that of generations of commentators. It can, moreover, draw on strong support in Hegel's writings. Here one may, for instance, cite such dramatic pronouncements on the motive force of the historical dialectic as the following:

> the only thought which philosophy brings with it is the simple idea of *reason* – the idea that reason governs the world, and that world history is therefore a rational process. From the point of view of history as such, this conviction and insight is a *presupposition*. Within philosophy, however, it is not a presupposition; for it is proved in philosophy by speculative cognition that reason . . . is *substance* and *infinite power*.[3]

History is, it appears, rational because reason is present in it as substance and subject. It is plain that a doctrine which presupposes rational subjectivity in this form is not available to Marx. He is in this respect by no means alone. In the various litanies from Croce onwards of what is living and what is dead in Hegel, it is the ontological vision, conceived along the lines sketched here, that is most readily assigned to the philosophical graveyard. The claims of reason as an autonomous creative subject raise few echoes in the contemporary world, even among 'Hegelians'.[4] At present, however, our concern is with the form of Hegel's solution rather than its substantive merits. The intellectual resources it employs may be roughly identified as being drawn from two closely related areas of thought. These are social ontology and the philosophy of history. It is not to be expected that one will find an explicit and integrated doctrine using such resources in Marx. Nevertheless, the two areas in question are represented by important elements in his work. These are scarcely ever related explicitly to one another, nor are they brought to bear individually in any systematic way on our present concerns. They are still a substantial presence and, once the issue has been raised, their significance for these concerns can scarcely be doubted. It remains to be seen how successfully they may be drawn together to provide the framework of a general theory.

The philosophy of history is an obvious direction in which to look. For in one aspect the basic problem is how to conceive of the project of a materialist historical dialectic. The argument so far may reasonably claim to have laid the foundations of such a conception. It has shown how, in principle, theory may be a 'material force' through the transformative power of the discovery of self-contradictions by historical subjects. Such discoveries may intelligibly be granted a strategic role in history more generally. Yet all this serves at best to establish the formal possibility of a historical dialectic. For it to be concretely realized it is not enough that there should be contradictions coming into view and being replaced. There must be some immanent, progressive logic to the sequence of changes. What is required is not simply an indefinite series of randomly resolving contradictions but an essentially directed movement. This is required in order to provide an assurance of an overall shape to the story and, more especially, of the determinate outcome envisaged by Marx. It seems that one must be able to speak, as Hegel does, of reason as being in some sense at work in history and that sense will have to be articulated without the rich backing of idealist metaphysics.

The attempt to reconstruct Marx's thinking in this area is attended by peculiar difficulties. They arise in large part because of the high level of abstraction at which it has to operate, a level where his own work is notoriously inexplicit and unsystematic. In consequence, the attempt is forced to proceed in somewhat greater freedom from the texts than one might wish. This in turn makes the task of interpretation, and of assessing the result, more complex than usual. The level of abstraction itself creates difficulties of assessment in that it leaves it unclear what would count, and how decisively, for and against whatever is proposed. Moreover, the enterprise is subject at the outset to doubts as to whether it is feasible at all. The student of Marx may well have ringing in her ears such warnings as that against 'using as one's master key a general historico-philosophical theory, the supreme virtue of which consists in being super-historical'.[5] This must have a sobering influence, and yet it is by no means fatal to our project. Marx is chiefly concerned here, as on similar occasions, to make a methodological point. The passage as a whole does not seek to deny the value of a 'clue' to the 'forms of evolution' in history. The intention is to warn against efforts to derive it by *a priori* theorizing or lazy extrapolation from a single case rather than the detailed study of the separate forms. It is entirely reasonable to conclude that Marx does wish to reject the idea that philosophy can supply history with a ready-made framework of meaning. Hence, he may be said to reject the Hegelian project of a philosophy of history.[6] Yet he is far from disowning the need for any general framework for historical inquiry and indeed his writings reveal a commitment to a certain view of its character. What is important, it may be surmised, is that this view should arise and function in some active and, one may say, dialectical interrelation with empirical study. In what is usually regarded as its canonical expression in his writings it is presented in just those terms, as developing from, and in turn becoming the 'guiding principle' of, such study.[7] Though not the outcome of speculative cognition, the findings which comprise the guiding principle have sufficient theoretical weight for present purposes. For they offer a general characterization of the historical process which will serve to ground expectations of a directionality in it. All that commentary can hope to disclose here is, in view of the considerations we have been sketching, merely a thin thread of argument. This must not be asked to do more than its nature permits. Yet a thin thread is a great deal better than no argument at all and, used with discretion, can play a significant role in the discussion. It should also be noted that the canonical passage has an unusual evidential status. It is given what appears to be special prominence by Marx, and has been taken in that spirit by generations of readers. The issues it raises cannot be overlooked in this inquiry. Moreover, the process of dealing with them yields a vital perspective on its central themes.

The most general way in which history may be characterized for Marx is that it reflects the development of the capacity of human beings to interact with the natural world. The 'guiding principle' is a vision of the growth of human productive power bringing in its wake successive transformations of society: 'At a certain stage of development, the material productive forces of society come into conflict (*Widerspruch*) with the existing relations of production. . . . From forms of development of the productive forces these relations turn into their fetters. Then begins the era of social revolution.'[8]

Whatever may be obscure in this passage, it plainly throws up yet another domain of contradictions in progressive movement. It seems that one has accordingly to acknowledge another level of dialectic, a level where the terms are the forces and relations of production. It is convenient, in spite of a disagreeable neatness, to refer to this as the 'objective' dialectic to distinguish it from the levels of subjective and intersubjective dialectics identified earlier.

Some implications of the passage for our argument may readily be drawn out in a preliminary way. Contradictions in the objective dialectic are, it appears, characteristically resolved through the replacement of outworn relations of production by ones which are better suited to the movement of the forces. The 'fetters' are broken and replaced by fresh 'forms of development'. This story is for the most part enacted in class society. The role of classes within it is to be seen, one may suppose, as that of agents or representatives of tendencies within the forces and, hence, as primary instruments of its enactment.[9] This is to say, in the terms of our discussion, that transitions in the objective dialectic are accomplished through the mediation of the intersubjective dialectic of classes. The overthrow of existing relations of production is the work of a hitherto subject class which proceeds to impose new social forms stamped in its own image. Thus, the replacement of feudalism by capitalism was achieved through the bourgeois revolution and the replacement of capitalism by socialism will be achieved through the proletarian revolution. Such transformations require certain levels of consciousness on the part of the social actors. Hence, at this point one may introduce the subjective dialectic. The final transition to socialism presupposes that this dialectic has reached an advanced stage, marked by a relatively high level of social scientific understanding on the part of the proletariat. Thus, proletarian revolutionary consciousness is necessary for socialism to be achieved and socialism is necessary for the full development of the productive forces. That these forces have some immanent tendency to develop in history now begins to appear as the basis of the entire structure of ideas.

The difficulties to which this account gives rise may be said, for present purposes, to be of two kinds. In discussing them one soon encounters in varying degrees the constraints imposed by Marx's silences at the relevant level of theory. Nevertheless, there is something useful to be said in both cases. The first question is that of how to justify or defend the claim alleged to form the basis of the structure. There is, secondly, the question of the logical form of explanations in which the claim figures: how precisely is it that the development of the forces may explain changes in the relations. A line of thought is available here which offers help with both questions at once. The key notion to be invoked is a form of the central dialectical category of reason. It is the

form which Hegel has in mind in the *Phenomenology* when he declares
that 'reason is purposive activity' and goes on to allege that self-moving
purposiveness is to be identified with being a subject.[10] Such purposive
subjectivity is at the heart of the cluster of ideas that have now to be
explored.

It is in this region that Marx finds the specific identifying feature of
human activity: 'what distinguishes the worst architect from the best of
bees is that the architect builds the cell in his mind before he constructs
it in wax'. As the choice of illustration suggests, the primary arena in
which the feature is displayed is the labour process. The passage
continues: 'At the end of every labour process, a result emerges which
had already been conceived by the worker at the beginning, hence
already existed ideally. Man not only effects a change of form in the
materials of nature; he also realizes [*verwirklicht*] his own purpose in
those materials.'[11]

The task of showing the relevance of these ideas to our first question
has to take initially a schematic form. The labour process is inherently
purposive and the workers may be thought of as exercising reason in the
choice of means to realize their purposes in it. They have an incentive to
realize them with a minimum of effort and, hence, efficiently. Their
exercise of reason is liable to suggest, at least occasionally, changes in
the means which are from that point of view improvements. Such
changes are from another point of view so many ways of enhancing the
productive capacity of the workers. In a context which allows for
communication between them, others will be able to see the point of
innovations and to adopt them in their own practice. So it may be
supposed that they will have some tendency to catch on and be
preserved in the community. At this point it begins to be possible to
speak of a development of the productive forces. Thus, the dynamism of
the forces may be thought of as internally related to the operation of a
distinctively human form of purposiveness in the labour process. The
relation has been sketched here in abstract terms and the story begins to
run into difficulties precisely when one seeks to render it more concrete.
Nevertheless, it may still be regarded as a way of specifying a theme that
is undeniably of great importance to Marx and to dialectical tradition. In
his view the 'outstanding achievement' of the *Phenomenology* is that in
it Hegel 'conceives the self-creation of man as a process' and, crucial for
this achievement, he 'grasps the essence of *labour* and comprehends
objective man – true, because real man – as the outcome of man's *own
labour*'.[12] The rationality which is a defining feature of human labour
must have a central place in this process of self-creation. At least part of
its significance lies in the internal connection with the development of
the human capacity to cope with the external world. This development

is, for both Marx and Hegel, an integral part of humanity's self-creation, and, in another aspect, simply is the growth of the productive forces.

The difficulties with our reconstruction chiefly arise, it was suggested, when one begins to make it less schematic. Before doing so, it will be useful to consider what it may be thought to achieve. Its merits are apparent at the level of the initial statement and have to do with the conceptual light it sheds over various aspects of Marx's position. Thus, it suggests that a problem sometimes associated with the linkages between the theory of history, 'historical materialism', and that of class and class struggle is wholly imaginary. It is supposed that there are two orders of reality involved, class consciousness and the productive forces, which are so disparate as to make interaction, or integration within a single totality, scarcely intelligible. It should now be clear that there is no ontological gulf here. In invoking the forces one is not appealing to what is radically other than consciousness. The invocation can have explanatory force only in so far as it is ultimately an appeal to the efficacy of human desiring and projecting. This efficacy rests, it appears, on our ability to shape means to ends and to learn from one another. Thus, it rests in part on what is often termed 'instrumental rationality' and this circumstance gives rise to the second point that should be made. Instrumental thinking is of the essence of the purposive character of the labour process and, hence, plays a vital part in a materialist interpretation of the role of reason in history. Hence, our scheme serves to call in question, at least in terms of fidelity to the spirit of Marx, the tendency in the Western Marxist tradition to hold such rationality cheap and to place its exercise in sharp contrast to the world of authentic human communication.

The positive aspects of the scheme may be illustrated further by considering the help it offers with the second question posed above, that of the form of explanation involved in Marx's theory of history. The question has been the subject of much debate, centred usually on the rival claims of 'causal', 'functional' and 'teleological' interpretations, with the last two alternatives often thought to be suspect or, at any rate, mysterious.[13] If one had to choose from this list, it is clear that the emphasis on purposiveness must suggest the teleological option. The development of the forces has been represented here as ultimately grounded in the teleology of labour. Moreover, whatever other types of explanation may be involved, a teleological model is crucial in explaining the influence of the productive forces on the relations of production and, specifically, in rendering it intelligible that the directionality of the forces should be transmitted to the changing forms of society. There need, however, be nothing disreputable in this way of conceptualizing the situation. It may be elaborated and justified in terms that the discussion has now made available.

It may be useful to bear in mind that there is nothing unusual or recondite about purposive explanation as such. On the contrary, it is, as has been widely remarked, the primary mode of explanation in everyday life. There we seek to understand the behaviour of others on the presumption that it is goal-directed. People sometimes achieve their goals, or reasonable approximations to them, and their holding of those goals will then figure in the explanation of the coming to be of the end states. Explanations of this kind are equally indispensable if one seeks to understand the role of powerful and successful individuals in history. If one's ontology allows social groups as historical actors, the pattern of explanation has a still wider scope. Thus, the ability of fully class-conscious collective actors to impose their ends on the flux of events will be bound to have explanatory significance. The resort to teleology here is in principle no more dubious than it is in everyday life, being similarly grounded in the aspirations and actions of determinate subjects. This is all the more obvious where the subjects succeed in, as it were, concretizing their wills in such potent institutional forms as armies, trade unions, parties and states. Attempts at purposive explanation in social theory are most likely to come under suspicion where they seem to be dealing in purposes without a purposer. The possibility of this kind of obscurantism should not, however, be allowed to cast doubt on the validity of the form of explanation. Neither, as we shall see, is it in the least typical of Marx's practice.

It may also be noted, without attempting a detailed treatment of the issues, that our classification of forms of explanation is by no means watertight. Purposive explanation is a species of rational explanation in the most literal sense of explanation in terms of reasons for acting. Such reasons may well be said to operate as 'causes' in a proper sense of that commodious term. For they may be identifiable as what effectively, amid a welter of background conditions, brings it about that certain states of affairs come to obtain. It should be added that purposive explanation is often particularly appropriate in contexts which also lend themselves to 'functionalist' interpretations. Where purposive activity is successful the results are likely to accord with the interests of the actors, for instance, by being supportive of social arrangements that constitute those interests. In the case of established and powerful groups this may create an impression of effective adaptation over large areas of social life. The language of function may then be difficult to avoid, and Marx does not always manage to do so. Its use may, however, carry no commitment to functionalism as an explanatory paradigm. It need not involve the genuinely problematic assumption that invoking the functional benefits of the arrangements is in itself of value in explaining them. In all cases the mediations linking the explanation and what it explains have to be specified. For a wide range of cases with which Marx was particularly concerned, doing so typically involves reference to the sustained and determined exertions of ruling classes and their agents. The functional character of the existing arrangements may then be important in showing their eligibility to serve as appropriate ends of action for such actors. It is, however, this role, and not adaptive convenience as such, that carries the explanatory weight.

The discussion may be given a more concrete turn by means of an illustration from Marx's writings. A representative example of his practice is provided by the account in Volume 1 of *Capital* of the process through which the agricultural population was expropriated from the land, a key episode in the development of capitalism in Britain:

> The prelude to the revolution that laid the foundation of the capitalist mode of production was played out in the last third of the fifteenth century and the first few decades of the sixteenth. A mass of 'free' and unattached proletarians was hurled onto the labour-market by the dissolution of the bands of feudal retainers, who as Sir James Steuart correctly remarked, 'everywhere uselessly filled house and castle'. Although the royal power, itself a product of bourgeois development, forcibly hastened the dissolution of these bands of retainers in its striving for absolute sovereignty, it was by no means the sole cause of it. It was rather that the great feudal lords, in their defiant opposition to the king and Parliament, created an incomparably larger proletariat by forcibly driving the peasantry from the land, to which the latter had the same feudal title as the lords themselves, and by usurpation of the common lands. The rapid expansion of wool manufacture in Flanders and the corresponding rise in the price of wool in England provided the direct impulse for these evictions. The old nobility had been devoured by the great feudal wars. The new nobility was the child of its time, for which money was the power of all powers. Transformation of arable land into sheep-walks was therefore its slogan.[14]

The process was later facilitated when the expropriators gained effective control of the state and used it to serve their ends. By this stage, at least, it is surely legitimate to speak for analytical purposes of these proto-capitalists as constituting a collective social actor:

> After the restoration of the Stuarts, the landed proprietors carried out, by legal means, an act of usurpation which was effected everywhere on the Continent without any legal formality. They abolished the feudal tenure of land, i.e. they got rid of all its obligations to the state, 'indemnified' the state by imposing taxes on the peasantry and the rest of the people, established for themselves the rights of modern private property in estates to which they had only a feudal title, and, finally, passed those laws of settlement which had the same effect on the English agricultural labourer, *mutatis mutandis,* as the edict of the Tartar Boris Godunov had on the Russian peasantry.[15]

In the aftermath of the 'glorious Revolution' the process was extended still further by the appropriation of state lands:

> The bourgeois capitalists favoured the operation with the intention, among other things, of converting the land into a merely commercial commodity, extending the area of large-scale agricultural production, and increasing the supply of free and rightless proletarians driven from their land.[16]

Marx is engaged here in concrete historical analysis which is not explicitly linked to meta-theoretical considerations. Nevertheless, it seems entirely natural to regard the analysis as conforming to, and indeed as showing the fertility of, the 'general principle' of his studies. The overall significance of the developments traced in it is that they represent the installation of vital elements of capitalist relations of production. In the course of them feudal rights in land are replaced by the rights of bourgeois private property, and peasants and agricultural labourers are transformed into formally free proletarians compelled to sell their labour-power. A link between those changes and the development of the productive forces is implicitly assumed throughout the discussion. The assumption may reasonably be thought to approach the surface in such references as that to the importance of the 'rapid expansion of wool manufacture in Flanders'. Moreover, in introducing the historical analysis Marx had related its themes to the dimension of class and class conflict. The 'epoch-making' character of the revolution on the land was said to consist in the way it acted as a lever 'for the capitalist class in the course of its formation'.[17] Thus, one may anticipate that all the levels of dialectic distinguished earlier will be found reflected with varying degrees of sharpness in the analysis.

The analysis, as the cited passages show, is pervaded by the language of intentionality. This is occasioned not by any mysteriously autonomous teleological, or functional, tendencies but by the strivings of specific historical actors. The changes which are the subject of the analysis come about directly through their pursuit of self-interest. Though not, in the relevant stages of the historical dialectic, based on a truly scientific understanding of their situation, the pursuit is nevertheless endowed with sufficient awareness to be intelligent and effective. Moreover, as the passages also show, the level of consciousness rises in the course of historical time. In consequence, one has at a certain point to acknowledge a shift from uncoordinated individual action to the emergence of the class as a collective actor in the full sense. This is, of course, the crucial step in the process of class formation referred to by Marx in his introductory comments. The replacement of existing relations of production by ones better suited to the exploitation of the forces is the work of human actors, individual and collective, who perceive that they stand to benefit from such changes. Their purposes and practices comprise the key mediations between forces and relations. Thus, the analysis may also be said, in the terminology suggested earlier, to illustrate the way in which the objective dialectic moves forward through the subjective and intersubjective dialectics of classes. Indeed, the illustration may be thought to proceed on lines that are in a certain respect too clear-cut and undeviating. The will of historical actors does not always succeed in finding so faithful an expression in social reality. Elsewhere one has to allow for more significant resistance from the wills of others and from structural constraints inherited from the past. There must also be room for all the paradoxes of rational action, involving the achievement of suboptimal or counterfinal results by intentional agents. These circumstances lead purposes to miscarry or be deflected, and the actual course of events has to be understood as the outcome of a complex of interacting forces. The recognition of complexity here does nothing to impugn the validity of purposive explanation, nor its strategic role in Marx's system. It is rather a reminder of the formidable difficulty which may attend such explaining in social scientific practice.

Even when viewed in this light the significance of the point should not be exaggerated. In a certain range of cases, central to Marx's intellectual interests, it may be entirely reasonable to expect a simpler pattern to prevail. The manner in which the teleology of labour promotes the development of the forces may well be thought to belong to this range, at least so long as the presentation remains at the schematic level so far attained. For it may be presumed that, at the decisive moments, an overwhelming mass of human aspirations will be found to incline in the same direction, towards the goal of the technical alleviation of toil. A somewhat analogous weakness of countervailing forces may be thought characteristic of major episodes in the evolution of the forces–relations nexus. A rising class representing the deepest tendencies of its time is in the nature of the case likely to be able to impose its will in all essentials. This is the possibility exemplified by the expropriation of the agricultural population and one of primary importance for Marx's conception of history in general. It should also be emphasized that even in the most complex cases the main intellectual challenge is not one of grasping the logical form of explanation that is required. It is rather one of providing convincing explanations of the appropriate form. The focus of attention deserves to be not the often barren and weightless puzzles of the philosophers but the rich and concrete predicaments of historians and social scientists.

I

At this point the discussion should turn to consider the difficulties raised by the answer provided to the first of the major questions posed earlier; that is, by the explanation of the developmental tendency of the productive forces. They arise most acutely when one tries to give the basic argument a less abstract interpretation. An obvious way to set about this is to assign specific social roles to the actors so that, for instance, the direct producers became designated as slaves, serfs or proletarians. It then becomes plain that the difficulties stem from the social mediations needed to link the rationality inherent in the labour process with the actual development of the forces in particular historical circumstances. Thus, for instance, it is quite implausible to suppose that slaves must have an interest in innovation as a means of ameliorating their conditions of work. What Marx stresses in this connection is rather their tendency to misuse beasts and implements as the only available form of expression, however distorted, of their humanity.[18] Neither is it plausible to suppose that slave owners have any general interest in promoting technical change. Referring to 'the ancient mode of production which depended on slavery', Marx writes:

> the ancients never thought of transforming the surplus-product into capital. Or at least only to a very limited extent.... They used a large part of the surplus-product for unproductive expenditure on art, religious works and public works. Still less was their production directed to the release and development of the material productive forces – division of labour, machinery, the application of the powers of nature and science to private production.[19]

The failure to transform the surplus-product into capital is the cornerstone of this reasoning. Marx followed classical political economy in assuming that the continuous creation and investment of a surplus was the key to economic development. The energies of slave owners, however, and perhaps of all pre-capitalist ruling classes, are chiefly expended in consumption rather than investment.[20] In these circumstances no strong or sustained development of the forces is to be expected. It is now clear that such an expectation has to rest not merely on the assurance of a formal rationality but on the specific presence of a body of favourable social conditions. The nub of the matter, forcing itself on one's attention at this point, is that the conditions are adequately provided only under capitalism. The capitalist class obtains control of the labour process as the outcome of historical struggles which encompass the transformation of peasants into proletarians. The process is then harnessed to those ends of profit seeking and capital accumulation which are, for Marx, at least partly constitutive of the capitalist system. The pursuit of them leads naturally in his view to technical progress, as capitalists seek to improve the productivity of labour.[21] Thus, the rational adaptation of means to ends in the labour process is geared to the development of the forces by becoming part of the institutionalized logic of capitalism. Marx has a keen sense of the distinctiveness of capitalism in this respect. It receives a particularly strong expression in the first volume of *Capital*: 'Modern industry never views or treats the existing form of a production process as the definitive one. Its technical basis is therefore revolutionary, whereas all earlier modes of production were essentially conservative.' A footnote at this point refers to a passage in *The Communist Manifesto*:

> The bourgeoisie cannot exist without constantly revolutionizing the instruments of production, and thereby the relations of production, and with them the whole relations of society. Conservation of the old modes of production in unaltered form, was, on the contrary, the first condition of existence for all earlier industrial classes.[22]

The theme of the distinctiveness of capitalism has a solid presence in Marx's work, and our argument will undoubtedly have to be able to accommodate it. Some care is needed, however, in spelling out the content of the theme. Even in the strongest formulations Marx is not concerned to deny, as some commentators have supposed, that any technical change occurs in pre-capitalist societies.[23] The point is that by comparison with capitalism such societies are 'essentially conservative': only under capitalism is change ontologically guaranteed, as it were, by being grounded in the nature of the system. In more concrete terms the contrast lies, one might suggest, in the fact that only under capitalism is its pursuit fully self-conscious and institutionally embodied. Its occurrence elsewhere must, to the extent that it lacks such grounding, be casual and contingent and, hence, limited in scope, irregular and precarious. Capitalism alone is dynamic through and through by virtue of its very constitution.[24] At the very least one has now to concede that only with the advent of capitalism is the progressive logic of labour given anything like a free rein and allowed to project its image with some degree of fidelity on to the actual movement of events. Elsewhere its expression is blocked, more especially, it would seem from Marx's comments, by ruling classes who benefit thereby and have the power to arrange matters accordingly. It should still be possible to conceive of the development of the forces as an inclination buried deeply in the processes of production that must sustain all human societies and capable of energizing and shaping such societies provided that the obstacles in its path are removed. It will have to be what a contemporary writer has called a 'weak impulse'.[25] It will be an impulse liable to be overborne and even to lack all apparent effectivity for vast stretches of historical time. A materialist dialectic has to be as accustomed to the idea of the sleep of reason as of its cunning. Yet, of course, to sustain the metaphor for a moment, sleep is not death, nor perpetual absence and still less sheer non-existence. Between the view that history is intelligible as the workings of a rational process, however muted and fractured, and, hence, as a meaningful totality, and the view that it presents only sequences of causal externality without any overall determinacy, there is, one might say, all the difference in the world. It is a qualitative difference if anything is.

Disagreements at this level of generality have, moreover, as Marx and Hegel were well aware, implications for the entire conceptual field.[26] They involve theoretical assumptions which cause the light to fall on it from one direction rather than another, affecting the apprehension of all objects within its boundaries. Less metaphorically, it may be said that these assumptions help to determine what expectations it is proper to have and, hence, what in the actual outcome counts as problematic or anomalous. It is only in the light of them that decisions can be made as to what is normal and what is exceptional, and these decisions are independent of how empirically striking the exceptions happen to be. Thus, it is not the frequency with which the weak impulse is drowned out that is significant here, but the theoretical grounds for speaking of such an impulse in the first place. This situation may readily be paralleled from other areas of intellectual inquiry, including Marx's scientific study of capitalism. The thesis concerning the developmental tendency of the productive forces has an analogy that suffices for present purposes in the 'law of the tendency of the rate of profit to fall'. Whatever the technical soundness of the arguments for the law, its form is conceptually in good order, and it is not open to easy empirical refutation. Marx explicitly allows for 'counteracting influences' which 'cross and annul the effect of the general law'.[27] Anyone who wished to maintain the position today would, no doubt, have to allow for many other influences which he could not have envisaged. Nevertheless, when all allowances are made, the law retains an explanatory point. It indicates what is in general terms to be expected if the special factors fail to operate. More concretely, it suggests, among other things, what the capitalist class has to do while it rules, and the likely direction of events in the absence of its sustained and effective efforts. A commitment to a dialectical view of history founded in the teleology of labour may be expected to have a similar shaping influence in its appropriate domain. Even a weak impulse will be strong enough to be felt throughout this region.

There is striking and unimpeachable textual evidence that Marx held a certain view of the course of human history as a whole and of the dynamics of its progress along that course. The task of reconstructing his view and the pattern of argument underlying it is, for reasons already referred to, unusually sensitive and hazardous. Nevertheless, in any serious interpretative study it has to be attempted, and the results, as we have also seen, are likely to have profound implications for a wide range of substantive issues. They have a bearing, though perhaps not so powerful as one could wish, on the chief question with which this part of our study is concerned. In its most concrete form this was presented as the question of what could justify a rational confidence in the proletariat as the historical subject which brings to an end the era of capitalism. The theory of history provides the indispensable framework within which alone the question can intelligibly arise. It may also serve to provide the encouragement needed to tackle it energetically. Yet it cannot of itself be made to yield a range of considerations rich and specific enough to constitute an answer. It will help to bring this out sharply if one notes that in a certain respect the discussion of the theory may even be thought to have enhanced the difficulty of answering. The prospect arises from the emphasis that was laid on the distinctiveness of capitalism. On the face of things this is a positive factor in the situation. It suggests solid grounds for acknowledging the directionality of the productive forces in the current period of world history, grounds which are substantially independent of any contentious thesis about the overall shape of that history. Under capitalism at any rate, it may be supposed, there is a strong impulse at work in this area. The way in which the strength of the impulse has to be theorized may well, however, be a source of concern.

What happens to the impulse under capitalism, it was argued, is that it comes into conscious operation in harmony with the basic logic of the system. It is as if the dialectic which had been stumbling forward in darkness now emerges into at least partial light and begins to move with appropriate assurance and directness. A motto for the process is suggested by an aphorism of the young Marx: 'Reason has always existed, but not always in a rational form.'[28] The assumption of such a form under capitalism is a historical development with the most profound and ramified significance. It finds a reflection in, for instance, the achievement by representatives of the rising capitalist class of the first genuinely scientific understanding of society, with its highest expression in classical political economy. The proletariat is a beneficiary of the development and, in turn, takes it substantially forward. Marx insists, as we have seen, that the socialist revolution requires an advanced level of consciousness, incorporating forms of scientific insight, on the part of the workers. It now seems possible to characterize in a general way the answer that must be given to the chief question which has been concerning us, the question of what justifies the identification of the proletariat as revolutionary subject. In terms of the present discussion, the question is how to conceive of a crucial transition in the materialist dialectic, the moment at which the proletariat sets itself in opposition to the 'hitherto existing world order' and seeks its overthrow. The lesson emerging from our consideration of Marx is that it is at any rate to be viewed as the decision of a free, self-conscious actor. This conception is strongly echoed in later Marxist thought.[29] Yet a difficulty arises when one tries to accommodate it within the argument we have drawn from the general theory of history.

That argument attempted to integrate the various levels of the materialist dialectic. The forces of production were taken as supplying the source of energy and direction at the objective level. This shaping power is to be thought of as working downwards to the intersubjective dialectic, given that classes are the immediate agents of the changes ultimately determined by the movement of the forces. Shifts of consciousness within the subjective dialectic may then be regarded as occurring within a structuring and constraining framework. It becomes possible to conceive of a hidden bent or drift in their evolution: it moves under systematic pressures which favour some kinds of development and disfavour others. This line of thought, however, does not seem easy to apply to decisions taken in full self-consciousness and freedom. Here talk of structures that constrain and forces that incline has less resonance than at lower dialectical stages. How can such decisions be regarded as even partially determined in the manner outlined? If they cannot be so regarded, how are they to be represented as what is rationally to be expected? It appears that the considerations drawn from the theory of history work best for agents with a limited consciousness of self and of society, operating in the twilight regions of the historical dialectic. Hence, these considerations offer least help where the need is greatest, in theorizing the culminating transition of Marx's system.

It is clear that other theoretical resources have to be drawn on if the task is to be accomplished. The example set by Hegel suggests that social ontology is the appropriate region in which to seek them, and this is a powerful precedent here. It seems entirely reasonable to suppose that what is required to complete the edifice of Marx's system is an ontology of class subjects. This now emerges as the crux on which the argument of the present inquiry turns. When attention is fixed on it, to anticipate the discussion a little, it soon appears that Marx's work does not contain an adequate body of theory of the kind required. His thinking in this involves too many rigidities and absences for that to be possible. Hence, as will also emerge more fully later, it is precisely to this area that one should look for the sources in his work of the current 'crisis of Marxism'. To link the crisis in this way with the foundations of the tradition is, from another point of view, just to highlight the failure of his followers and successors to repair the gaps and weaknesses in their intellectual inheritance. What is needed in the case of Marx and Marxists alike is a historical perspective within which their achievements and failures become intelligible, and this we must also attempt to supply. Of course, to specify the true nature of the crisis is also in principle to indicate where progress must be made if it is to be overcome. It tells one, at least in general terms, what is to be done if it is indeed to be a time of rebirth, of the liberation of 'something vital and alive'. Despair on this account in the present situation would, as we shall see, be both pusillanimous and irrational.

PART III

The Crisis of Marxism

The Ontology of Crisis

The discussion has reached a stage where it needs to examine the materials Marx provides for a social ontology whose basic elements are classes. A starting-point may be found in one of his best-known pronouncements on the subject:

> It is not a question of what this or that proletarian, or even the whole proletariat, at the moment *regards* as its aim. It is a question of *what the proletariat is*, and what in accordance with this *being (Sein)*, it will historically be compelled to do.[1]

These claims have an unmistakably 'ontological' ring: the question is one of what the proletariat '*is*', of the 'being' whereby its path of development is compelled. They put squarely on the agenda the problem of the ontological grounding of a familiar theme, Marx's overriding interest in the taking shape of the 'revolutionary, united mass'. What has now to be clarified is the extent to which such a grounding is actually achieved in his writings. It should be conceded in advance that the results never attain the status of a comprehensive, formal theory. There is, nevertheless, a formidable array of evidence, possessed of both breadth and depth, to be taken into account. Thus, for instance, the immediate context of the agenda-setting remarks is itself of considerable theoretical richness. It involves a number of ideas which, taken together, amount at least to a sketch for a portrait of the proletariat as revolutionary subject.

A striking feature of the context is the explicitly 'dialectical' manner of treatment, reflected in the Hegelian language:

> Proletariat and wealth are opposites (*Gegensätze*); as such they form a single whole. . . . The proletariat . . . is the *negative* side of the antithesis (*Gegensatz*),

its restlessness within its very self, dissolved and self-dissolving private property.... The class of the proletariat feels annihilated in estrangement (*Entfremdung*); it sees in it its own powerlessness and the reality of an inhuman existence. It is, to use an expression of Hegel, in its abasement the *indignation* at that abasement, an indignation to which it is necessarily driven by the contradiction (*Widerspruch*) between its human *nature* and its condition of life, which is the outright, resolute and comprehensive negation of that nature.[2]

With this contradiction between the proletariat's human nature and its condition of life one comes in touch with yet another aspect of Marx's historical dialectic. It is the aspect that is crucial for present purposes, and each term of the contradiction needs close scrutiny. In attempting this, one should be careful not to take them in abstract isolation from each other. It is a dialectical relation that is in question here, a relation of dialectical opposition. When different elements of one half are emphasized it is bound to bring corresponding elements of the other into prominence, so long as the tension between them is maintained. In particular, Marx's account of the conditions of life, much the more detailed and discursive side of things, will, as it develops, provide a changing perspective on the conception of human nature. It is always worth while to ask, at any particular point, what human nature must be if these conditions contradict it.

Some light is shed on both terms of the contradiction in the continuation of the passage:

> private property . . . produces the proletariat *as* proletariat, poverty which is conscious of its spiritual and physical poverty, dehumanization (*Entmenschung*) which is conscious of its dehumanization, and therefore self-abolishing (*sich selbst aufhebende*). . . . Since in the fully-formed proletariat the abstraction of all humanity, even of the *semblance* of humanity, is practically complete; since the conditions of life of the proletariat sum up all the conditions of life of society today in their most inhuman form; since man has lost himself in the proletariat, yet at the same time has not only gained theoretical consciousness of that loss, but through urgent, no longer removable, no longer disguisable, absolutely imperative *need* – the practical expression of necessity – is driven directly to revolt against this inhumanity, it follows that the proletariat can and must emancipate itself. But it cannot emancipate itself without abolishing the conditions of its own life. It cannot abolish the conditions of its own life without abolishing *all* the inhuman conditions of life of society today which are summed up in its own situation.[3]

The conditions of life of the proletariat are characterized in a general way by Marx as conditions of poverty, and this is both 'spiritual' and 'physical'. Once again, no rigid demarcation lines should be drawn, and yet the implied contrast is instructive and useful for present purposes. It will be convenient to follow a conventional, and surely correct, pattern of interpretation by taking the concepts of estrangement and self-estrangement as the chief means by which the category of spiritual poverty is given substance. These concepts are, of course, part of a considerable body of theory in the early Marx and have been the subject of extensive commentary and criticism. The issues involved will come in for some attention later. It is, however, the theoretically less striking notion of physical poverty that should be considered first.

The notion is filled out in the most dramatic and drastic terms in *The Holy Family*, as, indeed, elsewhere in the writings of the 1840s. This tendency is discernible in the passage quoted above in so far as physical poverty has a part in generating the 'absolutely imperative need'. A little later the situation of the proletariat is described as a 'having of hunger, of cold, of disease, of crime, of debasement, of hebetude, of all inhumanity and abnormity'.[4] The early text which is the chief source for the concept of spiritual poverty tells us that: 'So much does labour's realization appear as loss of realization that the worker loses realization to the point of starving to death.'[5] In *The German Ideology* we are assured that 'things have now come to such a pass that the individuals must appropriate the existing totality of productive forces, not only to achieve self-activity, but, also, merely to safeguard their very existence'.[6] Later in the work the tone is equally emphatic; 'the poverty of the proletarian assumes an acute, sharp form, drives him into a life-and-death struggle, makes him a revolutionary'.[7] The conception operative in these passages is of a class compelled to revolt by the realization that even its most basic physical needs, including the maintenance of life itself, cannot be satisfied within the existing system. Thus, historical necessity is given the starkest 'practical expression' through what are at root biological imperatives, mediated, as always with Marx, by forms of social consciousness.

After the period of the 'hungry forties' and as Marx's understanding of the political economy of capitalism matures, his treatment of these issues undergoes a perceptible change. Yet this by no means amounts to a radical break, and indeed the basic insights and inspiration of the earlier phase may be traced into the mature economic writings. It is illuminating here to counterpose to the discussion in *The Holy Family* a passage from the first volume of *Capital*:

> within the capitalist system all methods for raising the social productivity of labour are put into effect at the cost of the individual worker; ... all means for the development of production undergo a dialectical inversion so that they

become a means of domination and exploitation of the producers; they distort the worker into a fragment of a man, they degrade him to the level of an appendage of a machine, they destroy the actual content of his labour by turning it into a torment; they alienate (*entfremden*) from him the intellectual potentialities of the labour process in the same proportion as science is incorporated in it as an independent power; they deform the conditions under which he works, subject him during the labour process to a despotism the more hateful for its meanness; they transform his life-time into working-time, and drag his wife and child beneath the wheels of the juggernaut of capital. But all methods for the production of surplus-value are at the same time methods of accumulation, and every extension of accumulation becomes, conversely, a means for the development of those methods. It follows therefore that in proportion as capital accumulates, the situation of the worker, be his payment high or low, must grow worse. Finally, the law which always holds the relative surplus population or industrial reserve army in equilibrium with the extent and energy of accumulation rivets the worker to capital more firmly than the wedges of Hephaestus held Prometheus to the rock. It makes an accumulation of misery a necessary condition, corresponding to the accumulation of wealth. Accumulation of wealth at one pole is, therefore, at the same time accumulation of misery, the torment of labour, slavery, ignorance, brutalization and moral degradation at the opposite pole, i.e. on the side of the class that produces its own product as capital.[8]

It is plain both that this passage employs the language and mode of treatment of traditional dialectics and that it is filled with echoes of the philosophical anthropology of the early writings. That such features do persist into the later period is, perhaps, not all that surprising in the light of recent scholarship, nor is it the most significant aspect of the passage for present purposes.[9] For that one has to return to the question of the physical conditions of life, the empirical correlates of the theoretical claims. The qualification 'be his payment high or low' is itself enough to indicate that some shift has taken place in this respect. It signifies the abandonment by Marx of any version of the 'iron law of wages' doctrine which influenced his writings of the 1840s and helps to account for their distinctive tone. The change is easy to document from elsewhere in the major economic works.[10] In spite of it, he is quite unwilling to give up the idea of the 'accumulation of misery': what the phrase about payment qualifies is, after all, the claim that 'the situation of the worker ... must grow worse'. It is clearly, moreover, some kind of 'absolute' immiseration he has in mind, a conception whose substance is not difficult to detect from this passage and elsewhere. It is partly a matter of deteriorating work conditions with mechanization, of the worker becoming 'an appendage of a machine'. Another aspect of the accumulating misery was spelled out in the immediately preceding paragraph of *Capital*: 'the higher the productivity of labour, the greater is the pressure of the workers on the means of employment, the more precarious therefore becomes the condition for their existence, namely the sale of their own labour-power for the increase of alien wealth'.[11] Thus, technical progress also spells increased insecurity of employment for the labour force. More generally, it brings a worsening of the power relationship of labour and capital. As dead labour replaces living in the work process, the worker becomes ever more firmly 'riveted' in subordination and dependence. What underlies all this accumulation of misery is, of course, the basic logic of the profit-seeking, capital-accumulating economic system.

It will help to bring this picture into sharper focus if one considers the specific issue of wages. The implications for wages of the accumulation process were indicated a little earlier in *Capital*:

> the increasing productivity of labour is accompanied by a cheapening of the worker ... and it is therefore accompanied by a higher rate of surplus-value, even when real wages are rising. The latter never rise in proportion to the productivity of labour.[12]

'Real wages' should be understood here in the usual sense of the purchasing power of the wage payment, its command over use-values.[13] Clearly, Marx regarded any enlargement in this respect as compatible with the thesis of increasing misery. The standard gloss which the situation receives in the mature writings is fully anticipated in a text of the 1840s: 'Real wages may remain the same, they may even rise, and yet relative wages may fall.' He gives a simple illustration of what he has in mind, and continues:

> The share of capital relative to the share of labour has risen. The division of social wealth between capital and labour has become still more unequal.... If the income of the worker increases with the rapid growth of capital, the social gulf that separates the worker from the capitalist increases at the same time, and the power of capital over labour, the dependence of labour on capital, likewise increases at the same time.[14]

Thus, there is also a 'relative' element in the worsening situation of the workers: their share of total social wealth as represented by wages declines in proportion to the share of capital. There seems no doubt that Marx regarded this widening social gulf as crucial for the progress of the class struggle: 'on the present false base, every fresh development of the productive powers of labour must tend to deepen social contrasts and point social antagonisms'.[15] It is, one may assume, the deepening of the contrast that points the antagonisms. As the *Grundrisse* explains: 'in the struggle between the two classes – which necessarily arises with the development of the working class – the measurement of the distance between them, which, precisely, is expressed by wages itself as a proportion, becomes decisively important'.[16]

Thus, in dealing with Marx's position on these matters, one has to recognize a significant change of emphasis within an overall continuity from early to late. In both phases the centre of interest is a dialectical movement of consciousness under the pressure of unnatural conditions of life. The early writings tend to characterize these conditions in extreme terms, as posing a constant threat to physical existence itself. Later a more complex picture emerges. The notion of great and in-creasing misery is retained, but is to be understood as deteriorating work conditions, deepening insecurity and increasingly one-sided power relationships. All of this is compatible with improving living standards in the sense of enhanced purchasing power over commodities. Wages continue, nevertheless, to decline as a proportion of social wealth. Hence, the social gap continues to widen between the proletariat and the class that is the promoter of the capital accumulation process. The workers' awareness of the gap is taken to be decisive for the develop-ment by them of revolutionary consciousness.

As a sketch for a portrait of the revolutionary subject, these claims are open to a familiar kind of objection. In terms of our discussion it may be put by suggesting that, so far as the empirical conditions for the formation of the subject are concerned, Marx is in close touch with the basic requirements of his own argument only in the earlier writings. This is to imply that the later, more complex and qualified, account, whatever its other merits, contains no substitute for the absolutely imperative, biologically grounded need as originally conceived. Putting the point more concretely, it is that the mature doctrine is vulnerable to the charge of failing to give due weight to the significance of the rising living standards that it can in theory readily envisage. Though criticisms of this sort often take a simplistic and reductionist form, a serious concern lies behind them. A secular improvement in real wages, such as actually occurred in Marx's lifetime and thereafter, is not a trivial matter in the present context.[17] Its effect is to subvert his dialectical procedure by eroding the antitheses on which the procedure depends. What it signifies is not merely the abrogation of the necessity for life-and-death struggle in any literal sense. It signifies also that the subject class, or a substantial element of it, is beginning to acquire a stake in the existing order. Hence, it becomes all the more difficult to insist that the true material interests of the class are unequivocally opposed to that order. The pro-letariat is ceasing to be the 'class that is not a class' of civil society but rather its living negation, as in the early writings.[18] It is being incorporated into the society as one of its functioning parts. By the same token the workers have now to be considered as producing their own product not only as capital but also in some measure as a return for their labours. Thus, the antithesis presented in *Capital* of the accumulation of wealth and the accumulation of misery must also suffer a loss of sharpness and vitality.

In order to decide how much should be conceded to this line of thought, the argument has to be given a further dialectical twist. For Marx's writings contain elements which may be thought to anticipate the difficulties in all essentials. The chief piece of evidence derives from the way the emphasis shifts as he moves from general theory to assessing revolutionary prospects in particular situations. This distinction corresponds reasonably well to that between the major scientific writings and the correspondence, journalism and polemical works. In the latter context he shows himself to be highly sensitive to the level of prosperity of the workers as determined by the trade cycle. Thus, for instance, the upswing after 1848 leads him to conclude that 'With this general prosperity in which the productive forces of bourgeois society develop as luxuriantly as is at all possible within bourgeois relationships, there can be no talk of a real revolution.'[19] The same view is taken a couple of years later in a letter which attributes the 'flaccid condition of politics' to the 'period of prosperity', a prosperity which he fears will be 'of exceptionally long duration'.[20] The downswing of 1857–8, on the other hand, leads him to suppose that revolution may again be on the agenda. In *Herr Vogt* he reaffirms the judgement on the immediate post-1848 situation, but adds that things have now changed in a crucial respect: 'in fact European history has only re-entered an acute and, if one wishes, revolutionary phase since the crisis of 1857–8'.[21] It seems clear that when it comes to the concrete judgement of concrete cases Marx attaches great importance to the actual living standards of the workers. This is to recognize a causal link between those standards and the prospects for the revolutionary overthrow of capitalism. The official doctrine of the scientific writings is thereby liable to a kind of empirical undermining, should an improvement in standards be significant and sustained. This possibility does not, however, figure seriously in Marx's theoretical treatment of the socialist revolution. The awareness of it may be numbered among the ingredients of what István Mészáros has called an 'alternative perspective' which 'had to be confined to the margin of his conception, appearing there from time to time as somewhat isolated insights, but never fully integrated into his theory as a whole'.[22]

I

A wide variety of reasons could, no doubt, be adduced for the failure to achieve integration in the present case. It seems as likely a candidate to be overdetermined as one can conceive. The reasons would surely have to include recognition of the fact that, whatever may be licensed in principle, Marx is in practice markedly reluctant to allow that rising wages could ever be other than a limited and temporary phenomenon. This is the tendency in his work which sustains underconsumptionist readings of his view of capitalist crises.[23] In consequence of it the need to revise theoretically grounded expectations of revolution in the light of evidence about wages cannot appear in a pressing form. More speculatively, it may be suggested that unwillingness to adjust the theory so as to reflect the changing face of physical poverty owes something to the conviction that the significance of spiritual poverty under capitalism remains undiminished and inescapable. It is scarcely contentious by now to insist that the key notion of estrangement continues to operate in the mature writings.[24] It presupposes there, as elsewhere, a conception of human nature which specifies that from which the workers are estranged. This conception will be such as to maintain the dialectical tension between their human nature and their conditions of life. In the intellectual tradition in which Marx has his roots, a tradition encompassing Aristotle as well as Hegel, human nature is understood in the most general terms as the nature of a rational and social being. So far in the present discussion account has been taken of rationality as inconsistency-avoidance and as the adjustment of means to ends. What should now be recognized is the human capacity, in virtue of human nature, for the life of reason in a richer sense. This richness is best explicated by invoking once more a basic theme of dialectical thought, the inner connection of reason and freedom.[25] For Marx, as much as for Hegel, the 'culmination' of reason in history is self-conscious freedom, and the rationality of the socialist society is in large part constituted by the freedom of its members. In his most sustained discussion of these matters it is freedom in action that concretely defines human nature: 'free, conscious activity is man's species-character'.[26] The idea is echoed, with changes of idiom, throughout the later writings, most notably in the insistent concern in *Capital* for 'the free intellectual and social activity of the individual' and for 'the free play of the vital forces of his body and his mind'.[27] An immediate use to which this aspect of Marx's thought can be put is in tying up some loose ends in the preceding discussion.

To begin with, it suggests a formal solution to a problem which arose earlier, that of grasping how free, conscious decisions of the proletariat can be, as it were, sufficiently determined to be predictable. This is possible, it now appears, because such a decision, though not externally determinable, is subject to a kind of internal determination. It is so determined in so far as it is grounded in, and required by, the nature of the decider. The discussion in *The Holy Family*, among many other sources, makes plain that the proletariat, in emancipating itself, is to be thought of as abolishing all the 'inhuman conditions' of life of its society. It is, in a Hegelian phrase which Marx plays on elsewhere in the same connection, the 'universal class' whose emancipation signifies that of humanity in general.[28] Hence, its radical rejection of the existing system is a decision in favour of a rational, that is, freedom-embodying, social order for all human beings. The decision is predictable since the deciding subject is to be conceived of as having reached, in the course of the historical dialectic, a stage of development where it is fully expressive of its being, and any other outcome would be in contradiction with that being. There can be a well-founded confidence that the free choice of such a subject will be a choice of freedom for itself and others. It will not matter here how strongly one emphasizes the level of 'scientific insight' and 'theoretical consciousness' through which the choice is mediated. This emphasis is, as we have seen, entirely characteristic of Marx's treatment of the matter.[29] The higher the level of insight and consciousness the deeper is the subject's recognition of a necessity inherent in its own nature. Recognition of this inner, ontological necessity constitutes the freedom of the subject in such a case. Yet, of course, from another standpoint the subject's decision will appear as determined, and hence as what is rationally to be expected.

This is so far merely a formal solution of the problem or, rather, perhaps a demonstration of the possibility of solving it. Much detailed theoretical work needs to be carried out before a full solution could emerge, and something should be said here as to the lines it must take. Before doing so, however, there is another aspect of the preceding discussion to be completed. The attempt to vindicate the project of a materialist historical dialectic had drawn from Marx's work on the theme of instrumental reason and on the conception of human nature and its fulfilment. It is worth noting how strongly the inquiry has come by now to suggest the necessity of integrating these elements in order to construct an adequate theory. There is a tradition of disjoining instrumental reason not only from the context of authentic communication but also from the related one of human freedom and emancipation.[30] That this tendency is quite foreign to Marx's thought is shown by a representative passage in *Capital* which conveniently brings together many of the ideas we have been discussing:

the realm of freedom actually begins only where labour which is determined by necessity and mundane considerations ceases; thus in the very nature of things it lies beyond the sphere of actual material production. Just as the savage must wrestle with Nature to satisfy his wants, to maintain and reproduce life, so must civilized man, and he must do so in all social formations and under all possible modes of production. With his development this realm of physical necessity expands as a result of his wants; but, at the same time, the forces of production which satisfy these wants also increase. Freedom in this field can only consist in socialized man, the associated producers, rationally regulating their interchange with Nature, bringing it under their common control, instead of being ruled by it as by the blind forces of Nature; and achieving this with the least expenditure of energy and under conditions most favourable to, and worthy of, their human nature. But it nonetheless still remains a realm of necessity. Beyond it begins that development of human energy which is an end in itself, the true realm of freedom, which, however, can blossom forth only with this realm of necessity as its basis.[31]

Thus, the sphere of material production is, and must remain, a realm of necessity. In this sphere as elsewhere freedom has to be understood as a mode of rationality, as the rational regulation of the interchange with nature. The regulation will be rational, and hence an instantiation of freedom, in so far as the satisfaction of wants is achieved with the minimum of toil under conditions appropriate to the human nature of the producers. Clearly, it is instrumental reason that is primarily involved in such regulation: the moral is that it is, and must be, the basic form of rationality so far as the sphere of material production is concerned. Yet the partial freedom which thereby pertains to that sphere is, we are given to understand, the necessary basis of true freedom. A form of order incorporating the rationality of means and ends is to be conceived of as the indispensable precondition of the kingdom of ends. In the terms of our discussion it may be said that the instrumental rationality of the labour process is instrumental also for the life of non-instrumental reason. It would not be too much to suggest that this connection belongs to the essential structure of Marx's social theory. A large part of the unfinished business of the theory has to do with articulating and grounding the vision of human history which has the connection at its centre.

It should be possible to advance this business a step or two by means that are fruitful also for the question of the historical subject. What is required is a deeper exploration of the conceptual region in which both sets of issues are situated. For we have not yet reached rock-bottom there. The residual difficulties concern the vindication of the claim that the proletariat will by its own decision constitute itself as a revolutionary subject, and the vindication of the claim that the realm of true freedom is the uniquely authentic matrix of human life. In more concrete terms, they are the difficulties of demonstrating the feasibility of socialism and of justifying a particular view of the process by which it is achieved. In the context of Marx's thought their solution must lie in finding rational foundations for the belief in a nisus towards, and capacity for, emancipated existence, and for the way in which this belief comes to be focused on a specific historical actor. A possible model for a solution is suggested by the conception of historical subjects as instruments of the progress of *Geist*. Clearly, however, a conception of this sort is not as such available to a materialist dialectic. The ontological foundations of such a dialectic must surely by contrast have something of a naturalistic character. The conception of human nature and of the 'world-historical' role of the proletariat have alike to be grounded ultimately in a view of what belongs to human beings and proletarians as members of the natural order. It was noted above that Marx's early writings rely on a notion of an absolutely imperative need which is, though expressed through social forms, a biological need in a relatively straightforward sense. The question now is whether higher-order needs can be traced through more complex mediations to biological roots. In particular, it is whether the need for freedom and emancipation can be conceived in such terms.

The general area of theory to which these questions belong is that of philosophical anthropology and of the ontology of social being. Marx's writings can at the very least be relied on to furnish their pursuit with a context and a source of inspiration. A key text here is the *1844 Manuscripts* with its insistent refrain that 'man' is 'a part of nature', is 'directly a *natural being*', 'at bottom . . . is *nature*', and so on.[32] The spirit of Marx's thinking in this area is more concretely expressed in the conception of the emancipation of this 'real, corporeal *man*, man with his feet firmly on the solid ground, man exhaling and inhaling all the forces of nature'.[33] For such a being, emancipation is 'the complete *emancipation* of all human senses and qualities'.[34] Emancipated 'man' is, we are given to understand, 'affirmed in the objective world not only in the act of thinking, but with *all* his senses'.[35] A mode of description applied again and again to this state is that in it what is human comes also, for the first time, to be natural or, alternatively, nature becomes a truly human nature. Thus, the significance of the '*natural* species-relationship' of 'man to woman' is that it reveals the extent to which 'man's *natural* behaviour has become *human*, or the extent to which the *human* essence in him has become a *natural* essence – the extent to which his *human nature* has come to be *natural* to him'.[36] It is wholly in keeping with this theme of synthesis and reconciliation that the outcome of the emancipatory process should be a society which is 'the complete unity of man with nature – the true resurrection of nature – the consistent naturalism of man and the consistent humanism of nature'.[37]

Throughout the discussion the historicist character of Marx's vision never wavers. Human emancipation has always to be conceived as a project whose indispensable medium of existence is historical time. This awareness is a pervasive, shaping influence which crystallizes here and there in striking phrases, as when we learn that it is in 'human history – the genesis of human society' that 'man's *real* nature' develops.[38] A recourse to the notion of natural history seems inescapable in this connection: 'History itself is a *real* part of *natural history*'. It is 'the true natural history of man'.[39] There is no form of expression which could more effectively capture the union of naturalism and historicism in Marx's thought. This union has to be postulated as the framework within which the account of needs is set. Thus, it is only as the outcome of historical development, working on the '*natural* species-relationship', that 'man's *need* has become a *human* need' and, hence, that 'the *other* person as a person has become for him a need'.[40] The need for the other 'as a person' is undoubtedly a need with a natural basis, founded ultimately in aspects of our biological constitution. Yet it requires the passage of vast stretches of historical time to become a living reality in human life. The same requirement applies more generally to the emergence of the '*rich human being* and the rich *human* need': 'The *rich* human being is simultaneously the human being *in need of* a totality of human manifestations of life – the man in whom his own realization exists as an inner necessity, as *need.*'[41] Self-realization is, as Marx constantly asserts or implies, the realization of an essentially social being. The need for 'a totality of human manifestations of life' is only to be met in and through emancipated social existence. It seems plain that the conception of the individuals for whom such an existence is an 'inner necessity' has to be integrated with our earlier theme of the revolution of freedom and self-consciousness. The revolution will then, it may be suggested, begin to be intelligible as itself a stage in the natural, that is real, history of humanity.

It seems reasonable to conclude that Marx's writings contain the basic elements of a foundational theory for the materialist historical dialectic. Yet the theory itself has to be accounted among the projects he never completed and, indeed, which he can scarcely be said to have systematically addressed. Moreover, and again as part of a familiar pattern, the naturalism emphasized here is, one must concede, less prominent in the later work.[42] Marx's followers and successors have, with few exceptions, done little to restore and theorize its strategic place. Among the thinkers discussed in the present study it is undoubtedly Marcuse who deserves pride of place. His efforts in this field, plainly inspired by early Marx, are instructive in a number of ways. The most rewarding text is *An Essay on Liberation*, with its proposals for 'a biological foundation for socialism'.[43] What motivates the proposals is a conviction that 'the radical change which is to transform the existing society into a free society must reach into a dimension of the human existence hardly considered in Marxian theory – the "biological" dimension in which the vital, imperative needs and satisfactions of man assert themselves'.[44] In keeping with this impulse, Marcuse wishes to be able to speak of 'the instinctual basis for freedom' and of freedom and liberation as 'biological' needs.[45] It is at work also in the requirement that 'the economic, political and cultural features of a classless society must have become the basic needs of those who fight for it'.[46] In all of this Marcuse may be said to display an accurate sense of how 'Marxian theory' has to develop if it is to remain a revolutionary theory for the world of advanced capitalism. Yet there are also some serious reservations to be entered against his manner of proceeding.

The first stems from the familiar pessimism concerning the power of the existing system, a power which extends downwards into the 'biological' dimension. Thus, for instance: 'The need for possessing, consuming, handling and constantly renewing the gadgets, devices, instruments, engines, offered to and imposed upon the people, for using these wares even at the danger of one's own destruction, has become a "biological" need.' By such means the counter-revolution too is 'anchored in the instinctual structure'.[47] Indeed, the clear message of the text is that it is more firmly anchored there than is any need for revolution. That need is consistently presented under a qualification or question mark, or in the optative mode as a desideratum rather than an existing reality. The effect is to draw the issue within the problematic of the 'vicious circle', as Marcuse explicitly recognizes. The revolution with a biological foundation demands to be conceived as both a consequence of, and a precondition for, the 'rupture with the self-propelling conservative continuum of needs'.[48] Thus, the search for a naturalistic basis for the theory of revolution becomes itself subject to the disabling double-mindedness of Marcuse's later thought.

There is another feature of this thought with a more general cautionary significance for the search. Marcuse's attempt to enrich the biological dimension of 'Marxian theory' is accompanied by a substantial shift of perspective on the revolutionary subject as traditionally viewed in the theory. It is true that in *An Essay on Liberation* the working class retains 'its historical role as the basic force of transformation'. In consequence, however, of its integration within advanced capitalism it has in practice assumed 'a stabilizing, conservative function', constituting at best a revolutionary class '"in-itself" but not "for-itself", objectively, but not subjectively'. Hence, 'its radicalization will depend on catalysts outside its ranks', chiefly the young intelligentsia and the ghetto population.[49] It is on the catalysts that the force of the newly theorized biological needs is in the first instance assumed to be exerted. This line of thought is persuasive in its own terms. If freedom is a biological need, a need only to be satisfied in a free society, its frustration is liable to affect any or all members of unfree society, and perhaps most strongly, as Marcuse supposes, the least integrated elements of that society. The cautionary note derives from the fact that the recourse to the biological is now beginning to reveal an unsurprising tendency to erode categorial divisions within its species-wide field of reference. It may have been reasonable for Marx to have assumed that the criterion of imperative need was uniquely met by the proletariat as the prime locus of distress and deprivation in the world around him. With more complex and diffused biological needs such precision of reference is unlikely to be achieved. Moreover, as Marcuse's discussion suggests, there is no particular reason why those who do meet the requirements should constitute a class in the traditional sense. The difficulty, it appears, is one of combining the biological turn with the logic of a class-based theory.

It is a difficulty which deserves to be taken seriously, and would have to be comprehensively dealt with in a full-scale discussion of the issues. All that can be done at present is to remind ourselves of the chief resource provided by Marx for tackling it. This is the conception, already encountered, of the ontological significance of labour, a conception which is crucial to the intellectual structure of the *1844 Manuscripts*: 'for the socialist man the *entire so-called history of the world* is nothing but the creation of man through human labour, nothing but the emergence of nature for man'.[50] This formulation, in a context bearing the imprint of both historicist and naturalistic concerns, is of particular interest. For the conception forms the main theoretical link between those concerns. The ability to labour is grounded in our natural endowments, and, on the other hand, its continuous exercise is, in Marx's view, constitutive of our history; that is, of the self-creation of humanity. The strategic role of the conception is shown more specifically in the way it serves to hold in a single framework of thought the theme of Marx's naturalism and his sense of the historical importance of classes. The categorial status of classes is ultimately intelligible only in the light of an ontology in which the natural capacity for labour has a central place. Thus, the proletariat is a collective actor whose identity derives from a specific social form of the expenditure of human energy in the labour process. Yet in this actor the creative power of labour is crystallized in a way that is decisive for the development of humanity in the current phase of its history. The concept of labour may be seen as fulfilling here its role of mediating between the naturalistic foundations of the system and the reality of the structural divisions of human society. In doing so it offers a barrier to the universalizing drift which, as we noted, attends the opening up of the biological dimension. The way in which the barrier operates cannot be explored in detail at present. Our aim has simply been to insert the final building block in a schematic reconstruction of Marx's historical dialectic. It remains an important task for Marxist philosophy to give substance to such a scheme by systematically working out the ontological implications of the thesis that human beings are a part of nature. This is, as we have argued, the only form a truly materialist foundational theory can take. The discharge of the task is, it may be added, the best contribution which philosophy can make to showing the way forward in the current 'crisis of Marxism'. For the full significance of this claim to be appreciated, however, one needs to be clear as to the true nature of the crisis.

II

The crisis is, as one would expect, a complex phenomenon, not to be captured in a simple formula. Nevertheless, it is not difficult to see where the task of characterizing it should start. The starting-point is suggested directly by the discussion of Marcuse and by some preceding episodes of the present inquiry. The suggestion is that the crisis is to be understood as, in the first instance, a crisis of the identification of the revolutionary subject. The fundamental thesis of Marx's social theory is that capitalism contains within it the emergent structures of the rational form of society which is socialism. The emergence of socialism depends on the agency of a subject which must, within Marx's theoretical framework, be a social class. He identifies the revolutionary class as the proletariat of the most advanced capitalist countries of his time. Against this background the immediate source of the present crisis has to be seen as the failure of that class to play its historical role. Some rather obvious and familiar grounds for such a judgement will be adduced in the course of the discussion. It should be made clear, in getting our initial bearings, that it will not be substantially contested here. Indeed it is, one may suggest, difficult to see how anyone in the contemporary West, aware of the history of their own society and not deaf and blind to what is happening around them, could wish to maintain Marx's original identification unrevised. A willingness to revise it is now a condition of seriousness, at any rate of a serious intent to work within the live tradition he founded. For his failure has in the end to be reviewed as a failure of identification within a theoretical framework, not as a failure of the framework itself. This basic structure is logically prior to any particular solution to the problem of historical agency and is left unscathed by premature or inadequate solutions to it. Hence, the authentically Marxist response to the situation is to try again.

As a preliminary indication of the nature of the crisis and of the way forward from it, this will do well enough. It would, however, be unwise to place much reliance on it in its present form. For one thing it has something of the character of a bare result which is here, as elsewhere, lifeless and liable to mislead if taken in abstraction from the process that engenders it. More significantly, the verdict is too schematically convenient even by the standards of such cases. To bring this out, one should note the sense in which it may be said to let Marx off rather too lightly. His misidentification of the subject is not simply, as it were, a poor shot at the target. It signals also the omission of some of the preparations required for taking aim. That is to say, it reflects a theoretical weakness, though still of a kind which leaves the structure of the theory intact and, indeed, which presupposes that structure for its diagnosis.

Towards a Resolution

It would be a significant step forward from this point to put in place the elements of the historical perspective promised earlier. Misgivings concerning the proletariat as the revolutionary subject of Marx's conception go back a long way and have taken a variety of forms. They had a crucial role in, to take some egregious instances, the debate over revisionism around the turn of the century, the Frankfurt School's abandonment of the Marxism of Lukács in favour of the critical theory of society, and the rather numerous 'farewells to the working class' delivered in our own time.[1] These developments are the products of a complex set of historical determinants, a set which, fully specified, would include the main sources of Second International, and Western, Marxism as a whole. Among the more prominent landmarks one may cite the following. There is the growing conservatism of the German Social Democratic Party before the First World War, and the acceptance by it and other socialist parties of nationalist aims in that war. There is the failure of proletarian revolutionary movements in Western Europe after the war, followed by the rise of Fascism and Stalinism. From another direction there impinges the success of socialist revolutions after the Second World War on the peripheries of the capitalist world and as essentially the class achievements of peasants rather than proletarians. There is the consolidation of capitalism in its heartland in the same period, and the initiation of the most intense and sustained phase of growth in its history. There is the progressive integration of the working class during this phase, most strikingly in the United States, the most 'advanced' of all capitalist countries. The process culminates in what is widely agreed to be the general weakness and disorientation of working-class organizations in the West. This state of affairs is symbolized by the massive electoral support given by trade-union members to parties and governments of the radical right. It has continued beyond the end of the capitalist boom, leaving these organizations unable and unwilling to offer an effective challenge to the established order. More fundamentally, there is the continuing decline within advanced capitalist economies, both in quantitative terms and in terms of strategic importance, of the industrial working class in the traditional sense. Moreover, there are few serious observers, even among those most convinced of the indispensability of a class basis for radical politics, who would claim to detect any movement by this class towards the achievement of a revolutionary consciousness. Instead, one has at best to recognize stagnation at much lower levels or, more plausibly, a steady drift away from any such achievement.

The discussion has so far yielded an all too familiar list of defeats and lost opportunities. It speaks of a vast historical burden which seems unambiguously thrown in the scales against any projection it would be natural to make from Marx's original doctrine of revolution. The implications for Marxist theory have now to be considered in more detail. Within a materialist perspective it is inconceivable that the fortunes of theory should fail to reflect such unpropitious developments in social reality. The case of the Frankfurt School thinkers has once more an exemplary significance here. It arises in large part from the high level of self-consciousness which mediated their theoretical shifts. They display, it must be said, a sharp sense of where they had come from and of the direction in which they were heading, a historical awareness that was again to become rare in later Western Marxism. The key Marxist influences on the early Frankfurt School are Lukács and, in a lesser degree, Korsch, the chief rediscoverers of the dialectical dimension of Marxist theory in the twentieth century. The major writings of both contain, as one might expect, emphatic statements of an authentically Marxist conception of the role of theory. Thus, one may cite Korsch's assertion that 'the Marxist system is the theoretical expression of the revolutionary movement of the proletariat'.[2] Lukács declares, in the same vein: 'the theory is essentially the intellectual expression of the revolutionary process itself'.[3] It is not difficult to show that the transition through which such formulations lost their hold on the Frankfurt School thinkers was accomplished more or less consciously by them. In this context Horkheimer's 'Traditional and Critical Theory' is once again a seminal document.

The essay contains statements on the nature and status of social theory which seem of impeccably orthodox provenance. Thus, it advocates a conception in which 'the theoretician and his specific object are seen as forming a dynamic unity with the oppressed class', and so 'his profession is the struggle of which his own thinking is a part and not something self-sufficient and separate from the struggle'. What is opposed to traditional ideas of theory is the 'idea of a theory which becomes a genuine force, consisting in the self-awareness of the subjects of a great historical revolution'.[4] Clearly, these may be taken as reflecting formulations in Marx's writings which have already been noted here. It seems reasonable to take them as reflections mediated through the work of Lukács and Korsch, the immediate inspirers of earliest Frankfurt School Marxism. In spite of the obvious affinities, it has to be said that some crucial positions taken up in *History and Class Consciousness* have begun to be abandoned in Horkheimer's essay. This is most evident in the persistent concern to detach the fate of critical theory from that of the proletariat: 'even the situation of the proletariat is, in this society, no guarantee of correct knowledge'. There is no 'social class by whose acceptance of the theory one could be guided'. The conclusion is that, in words already quoted, 'the critical theory has no specific influence on its side, except concern for the abolition of social injustice'.[5] The key to the enigmatic quality of the essay surely lies here: it subscribes to a conception of theory as the self-awareness of revolutionary subjects, and yet on the identification of those subjects it has suffered a drastic failure of nerve. Hence, it also offers an alternative conception, juxtaposed to the first, of theory as social, and specifically moral, criticism, directed to all who care about injustice. The essay is a transitional and ambiguous work, marking the high point of Lukács's influence on the Frankfurt School and pointing to its inexorable decline as pessimism over the proletariat deepened. There is a certain symbolic significance in the fact that one and the same brief text attests the birth of critical theory and the death of the classical Marxist view of the proletariat. The truth it symbolizes is that social criticism was to become for socialist intellectuals a functional substitute for the loss of the subject. In the later development of the Frankfurt School the tension between the two conceptions, present in Horkheimer's essay, dissolves as the second of them comes to appropriate the entire field of discourse. This is in itself entirely understandable. It is hard to sustain a conception of theory which defines it by reference to revolutionary subjects when one no longer has any confidence in the existence of such subjects. Horkheimer's essay offers a final gloss on the situation in an image central to the later Frankfurt School's idea of itself: 'given the impotence of the workers', he remarks, 'truth sought refuge among small groups of admirable men'.[6] It makes these men no less admirable to point out that the vision of them as the sole guardians of truth exudes a stoically pessimistic spirit which is a world removed from classical Marxism.

A remarkable characteristic of the Frankfurt School thinkers, it was suggested earlier, is their level of understanding of the historical developments of which they were part. That Marcuse has a deep sense of what was being left behind is sufficiently indicated by the insight into the nature of dialectical thought shown in his exegetical work. It is further witnessed in such details as his enduring belief that Korsch and Lukács represented the 'most authentic' current of Marxism.[7] Adorno is able to view departures from this current with greater equanimity as he had always been less impressed by its conception of the significance of the proletariat for socialist theory. In some respects, however, he shows the sharpest awareness of the overall contours of the movement of ideas in which the critical theory of society was lodged. Here one may refer once more to his recognition that the theory involves a return to the standpoint of Left Hegelianism, a move enforced by the world's recalcitrance to the Marxist theoretical project.[8] It is in this context also that one should view his taking to task the attitude to criticism which Marx had developed by the time of the 'Theses on Feuerbach': 'In his youth he had demanded the "ruthless criticism of everything that exists". Now he mocked criticism. But his famous joke about the Young Hegelians, his coinage "critical criticism", was a dud and went up in smoke as nothing but a tautology.'[9]

If it is assumed that Adorno understands Marxist social theory as a critical theory of society, he is presumably to be regarded as rebuking Marx here for not being in his mature work properly Marxist. But this would be a fatuous opinion to attribute to Adorno. It is surely better to take the passage as another sign of his awareness that classical Marxism is not essentially social critique, and that the project of such critique is a reversion to a position which Marx had left behind with his youth, to a pre-Marxist conception of how thought is to be radical in relation to society.

In the most general terms the conception is, of course, that radical thought takes the form of social criticism. It is altogether natural, indeed inevitable, that such a conception should be widely accepted within Western Marxism. For it answers to the deepest needs of the historical situation of that movement. Marx's dialectical view of the role of theory had been crystallized in a particular solution to the problem of agency. Its ability to convince rested on the assurance of the existence of a collective actor engaged in realizing the potentiality of capitalist society by extracting its kernel of socialism. Marx's historical dialectic is ultimately, as is that of Hegel, a dialectic of the subject. Reason is actual in history in so far as it is embodied in a subject which is the vital force of the movement of objective reality. A loss of confidence in Marx's candidate for this role and the absence of any feasible alternative combine to create a strategic dilemma for socialist intellectuals. It is a dilemma which was to be negotiated unselfconsciously for the most part by those who lacked the vantage point of the first-generation Frankfurt

School. If theory can no longer be the expression of a transformative movement, the obvious way for it to maintain a relationship of opposition to the existing order is by being critical of that order. It will be socialist theory simply by virtue of speaking for socialism and against capitalism. The provision of such a theory is then the basic way in which socialist intellectuals can discharge their responsibilities, by going beyond a merely contemplative attitude to the social world to establish in principle a link with the impulse to change it. This view draws, as is to be expected, much of its appeal from the assumption that Marx was himself engaged in essentially the same enterprise. That is to say, it rests on a certain reading of the intellectual tradition within which it sought to locate itself. There is, it must be said, a genuine insight into the character of that tradition which points in the same direction or, at any rate, away from the most prominent alternative. There are complex reasons, by no means all to do with the internal history of ideas, why the standpoint of the Second International should have become decisively unavailable to serious thinkers in the formative period of Western Marxism. Some importance must, however, be given to the realization that it involves resolutely shutting one's eyes to all that is most distinctive in Marx's own claims for his work. His social theory refuses to be content with being descriptive and explanatory in relation to its object, and insists in having a practical significance for it. In this situation the critical turn may be said to be fully determined and over-determined. If positivism is conclusively ruled out, and dialectic is no longer possible, the only option for a Marxist thinker is to be a critic. For this role to be accepted in good faith by such a thinker, it has to be taken as embodying the authentic example and teaching of Marx himself. Hence, it requires a general, but unnoticed, reinterpretation of the meaning of his life-work.

In the shift to social criticism which overcame the Marxist tradition, the Frankfurt School writers display not only the deepest historical sense but also the strongest wish to retain something of a dialectical character. This is shown most clearly in their concern with immanence. If theory cannot be the voice of what is coming to be, it can at least take its vision of an ought from the highest ideals of what is. With scientific critique one finds no such level of historical awareness nor of engagement with dialectic. The project has its immediate source in the analytical movement in philosophy, a movement notoriously indifferent, or hostile, to Hegelian influences.[10] To engage with it is to enter instead the orbit of the thinker who represents the major influence on the movement from the direction of classical German philosophy. Scientific critique is essentially, as we have seen, a project of Kantian practical reason. It is, not surprisingly, innocent of any desire to secure immanence in the dialectical sense, an immanence geared to the specificity of the object being addressed. What its standards derive from, and may be said to be immanent with regard to, is the nature of rational inquiry as such, regardless of the object. Indeed, the pure abstraction of the procedure is, by virtue of its apparent certainty and economy, a commendation and point of pride for its adherents. Here the, theoretically crucial, locus of rational subjectivity completes the transition from the makers of history to the commentators on the process of its making. Their messages, in being addressed to the universe of rational beings in general, must, as was noted earlier, fail to connect uniquely with any particular category of them. All members of the audience will stand in essentially the same relationship to the deliverances of this abstract rationality. It is true that some advocates of scientific critique seem haunted by Marx's pronouncements on the expressive significance of theory for the revolutionary subject and the constitutive significance of the subject for the possibility of revolutionary theory. They are, however, quite unable to integrate their sense of the importance of such formulations with their critical rationalism. Being also unable to contemplate giving up this framework, they are cut off from any prospect of inquiring into what, in the contemporary world, could be the substance of a dialectical social theory.

I

The critical turn is, it has been argued, part of a large-scale historical development. As such it is rooted in the structural determinants of Western Marxism as a whole. In view of this, it is entirely to be expected that the assumption that Marxist, or indeed any radical, social theory must be social criticism should now be so pervasive in the West. Over a wide range of intellectual production it is simply taken for granted as not requiring explicit comment, still less defence. Where it is presented with any deliberation, this is usually just in order to exhibit it as a mark of enlightenment by contrast with the benighted empiricism and positivism of the past, or of the contemporary mainstream. What one has to deal with is a whole climate of opinion, and it may seem almost invidious in the circumstances to single out individual cases. Anyone acquainted with the literature could readily provide a score of references with much the same claim to attention. Nevertheless, our argument will have to be grounded in details if it is to make solid progress. Moreover, it should be possible to choose instances with a particular theoretical interest in the light of the preceding discussion. It will be best to consider writers of genuine competence and scholarly integrity. These qualities are what give their work its special value for illustrating the insidious power of the ruling paradigm.

Norman Geras has, with some others discussed in this study, a better claim to the title 'analytical Marxist' than most of those conventionally enlisted under that term of art. His book *Marx and Human Nature* sets out to 'refute the legend' that Marx in his mature work 'came to reject the idea of a human nature'.[11] In this it is entirely successful and, thereby, has significantly and, one hopes, permanently shifted the terms of the debate. The precise and detailed analysis leaves no room for doubt that the idea of human nature is present and operative in Marx's writings, early and late. Yet Geras misconceives the significance of his own achievement and does so in a way that has a general interest. He is well aware that, to use the idiom of the present discussion, 'human nature' is not simply a theoretical or explanatory category for Marx, but has inescapably a practical role. Where he reveals the grip of the ruling paradigm is in being unable to conceive of this role except as one of providing a normative dimension for theory, specifically of constituting it as moral critique. He recognizes that 'statements about human nature are not themselves necessarily value judgements'. Nevertheless, he wishes to argue, no doubt correctly or at any rate unobjectionably, that they can 'form part of the basis', or play a role 'in contributing to the reasons', for such judgements.[12] The distinctive legacy of the strange career of Western Marxism is contained in the assumption that it is only in virtue of doing so that they can have a practical bearing on reality. What the 'normative usage of human nature' amounts to is 'adverse judgement upon social conditions which fail the very needs common and intrinsic to humankind, adverse because they fail them'.[13] This 'normative function' is 'as prominent as ever' in the mature work: 'Whatever else it is, theory and socio-historical explanation, and scientific as it may be, that work is a moral indictment resting on a conception of essential needs, an ethical standpoint, in other words, in which a view of human nature is involved.'[14] Thus, we arrive once more at the anthropological mode of critique, at the idea that Marx's work is a moral indictment of capitalist social conditions in the name of human nature and its needs.

It should scarcely be contentious by now to assert that such an interpretation flies directly in the face of Marx's most explicit utterances on the subject of morality and of much other textual evidence. Grounds for this assertion have been adduced at various points above and need not be rehearsed here.[15] There is in any case a sense in which Geras is as alive to them as anybody. In a paper published shortly after the book on human nature he writes:

> Marx, as is well known, was quite impatient and dismissive of overt theoretical reflection about normative questions, condescending only rarely to engage in it himself. He was hostile, not neutral, towards the explicit elaboration of

socialist ethical theory, disdained in this area the kind of rigorous examination
of problems and concepts he so insisted upon elsewhere.[16]

The subject of the paper is 'the controversy about Marx and justice', a
controversy whose nub is the question of whether Marx condemned
capitalism as unjust. It should be noted that, as Geras reports, all parties
to the dispute agree that Marx did condemn capitalism. They agree, in
what Geras says are 'other words' for the same point, though the words
surely involve an appreciable upward shift in generality, that 'there is
some such normative dimension to his thought'. The question at issue is
the more specific one of whether he condemned capitalism 'in the light
of any principle of *justice*', and not simply in the light of such values as
freedom, self-realization, well-being and community.[17] Although Geras
does not think the denial of the normative dimension 'worth taking
seriously any longer', he has to confront the awkward fact that whenever
Marx addresses the issue he does quite explicitly deny any such dimension: 'Early and late, Marx's denials in this matter (efforts of repression,
so to speak, of the normative dimension of his own ideas) are quite
general in scope'. He proceeds to cite some familiar textual evidence for
this claim and concludes: 'Marx's impatience with the language of norms
and values is global in range.' Geras's response to the problem he
perceives here is to maintain that there is a 'pervasive contradiction', a
'real and deep-seated inconsistency on Marx's part', an 'aboriginal self-
contradiction and confusion in this area' which Marxists should not any
longer continue to propagate.[18] This is a verdict which we should now be
in a position to resist by undermining the reasoning from which it
derives. Marx's emphatic repudiation of any normative dimension to his
thought can, and should, be respected without charging him with self-
contradiction. To show this, it will be necessary to observe some distinctions which are frequently neglected in the debate over Marx and
morality, a tendency which vitiates the discussion wherever it appears.

The first is not so much an analytical distinction as a contrast, already
hinted at, between different kinds of evidence, a contrast in levels of
generality. It is implicit in Geras's presentation, though unremarked
there. The evidence he takes to be decisive for establishing the normative dimension consists of a number of adverse judgements by Marx on
particular aspects, often in themselves substantial and important, of
capitalist society. Geras has an accurate sense of the character of this
material: 'like just about everyone else he was given to the use of moral
judgement. Normative viewpoints lie upon, or just beneath the surface
of, his writings, and they lie there abundantly, albeit in an unsystematic
form.'[19] This unsystematic abundance of detailed judgements is what, in
Geras's view, sets up the contradiction with the official, global rejection

of the normative. It may be doubted, however, whether genuine contradictions are quite so easily established, and it is far from obvious, in view of the difference in levels of generality, that there is one here. The doubt may be linked with the distinction noted earlier between the context in which Marx reveals his personal moral opinions and that of his view of what constitutes revolutionary social theory. If one bears this in mind, what the textual evidence taken as a whole suggests is that while he does indeed regard capitalism as immoral in various ways, he does not suppose that making or elaborating such judgements is a necessary part of his role as revolutionary theorist. Neither, to make a separate but related point, does he appear to believe that their enunciation, however elaborated, can contribute significantly to the process of overthrowing capitalism. This scepticism is an aspect of his rooted hostility to all idealist and utopian tendencies in the socialist movement.

The distinctions suggested here are simple enough, and yet, it seems, easy to overlook. Thus, Geras, in speaking of Marx's work as a 'moral indictment', is offering a general characterization of it, a comment on its logical status. What he immediately cites in support of this is, however, a list of specific responses by Marx to the manifold evils wrought by capitalism.[20] The assumption that the accumulation of such instances suffices to establish the general thesis surely involves a too easy traversing of conceptual boundaries. Geras has himself noted that Marx uses moral judgement 'like just about everyone else'. If one were to comb the writings of the more humane and honest bourgeois economists from Adam Smith to Keynes, one could compile a comparable anthology of negative reactions to aspects of capitalism.[21] By parity of reasoning one would presumably then have to allow a normative dimension to their work, which puts it in the same category as that of Marx. But this would be to obliterate the specificity of bourgeois and revolutionary social science alike. It is surely better to block such absurdities by acknowledging that the virtually unavoidable occurrence of adverse moral judgements in a work of social science does not in itself establish that the work is essentially a moral indictment or, indeed, that there is anything significant about its identity to be captured in such a form of description. It would then be possible to hold together in a unitary framework Marx's occasional outbursts of savage indignation and his resolutely non-normative conception of the status of his work. The possibility suffices to acquit him of any deep-seated inconsistency in this area.

The discussion should now return to Geras's assumption that the true significance of the idea of human nature in Marx must be normative and, specifically, moral. What has to be noted is how precisely his stance mirrors the structural situation of Western Marxism. In Marx's thought the idea belongs, as we have seen, to ontology and the philosophy of history. It is the ultimate guarantor of the dialectical thesis that human history is a species of natural history, the natural history of social beings whose rationality develops in and through history from potential to fulfilment. In classical Marxism this vision is balanced, as it were, on the assurance of a collective subject with responsibility for realizing the immanent rationality of the existing order of things. With the fading of that assurance the vision must prove increasingly difficult to sustain. For socialist intellectuals in this situation the doctrine of social critique is an obvious and tempting recourse. Deprived of the possibility of being the mouthpiece of a world-transforming movement, they may seek to retain a link with practice by becoming providers of practical reasons; that is, reasons for acting to bring about change. These reasons have to be grounded in a negative evaluation of the object to be changed. Thus, socialist theory becomes in essence normative theory. Given the common assumption that morality is the most general, fundamental and authoritative sphere of normative judgement, the inner logic of this process drives theory to take on an explicitly moral character. Ethics has in the end to replace ontology in the manner illustrated so vividly by Geras. The exemplary value of his work derives precisely from the fastidiousness and transparency of its procedure. These are the qualities that make it an effective window on the operation of the historical mechanism as a whole. When such writers are found to be calmly subject to systematic misconceptions, it is a sign that a major intellectual displacement has occurred unnoticed.

Another kind of sign is provided by a second illustration of the workings of the ruling paradigm. Although not possessing the theoretical interest of Geras's case, it has an undeniable resonance against the background of our preceding discussion. In Douglas Kellner's study of Marcuse, once again a work of genuine scholarship, there is cited a definition from Marcuse's first published essay: 'Marxism is the theory of proletarian revolution and the revolutionary critique of bourgeois society.'[22] This should itself be viewed as the kind of transitional, ambivalent formulation characteristic of the first stirrings of Frankfurt School critical theory. It looks backward to the classical sources and forward to Western Marxist developments in a way reminiscent of Horkheimer's 'Traditional and Critical Theory'. Kellner's gloss is equally typical and revealing so far as the intellectual climate of our own time is concerned. 'This definition of Marxism', he comments, 'is taken almost verbatim from Lukács's book on Lenin.'[23] Nowhere in that book, however, is Marxism characterized as 'the revolutionary critique of bourgeois society', and such a characterization would be wholly at odds with the conception of Marxism which animates it. Neither does Marcuse make any attempt to foster the phrase on to Lukács, and doing so represents a further step in the progress of Western Marxism's historical amnesia. Kellner's taking of this step is not to be ascribed to carelessness in any ordinary sense. It signifies rather a kind of liberality which genially assumes that the great figures of the past share one's own certainties. Thus, it illustrates the continuous, largely unconscious, process of reshaping such figures in the light of current preconceptions. Moreover, Kellner's gloss is by no means wholly gratuitous: it embodies quite literally a half-truth. The first sentence of Lukács's book on Lenin reads as follows: 'Historical materialism is the theory of the proletarian revolution.' The significance of this claim for Lukács is best revealed by quoting the continuation:

> It is so because its essence is an intellectual synthesis of the social existence which produces and fundamentally determines the proletariat; and because the proletariat struggling for liberation finds its clear self-consciousness in it. The stature of a proletarian thinker, of a representative of historical materialism, can therefore be measured by the depth and breadth of his grasp of this and the problems arising from it; by the extent to which he is able accurately to detect beneath the appearances of bourgeois society those tendencies towards proletarian revolution which work themselves in and through it to their effective being and distinct consciousness.[24]

What we have here is an extended statement of the foundational thesis of classical Marxism as interpreted in this study. Marxist theory expresses the self-consciousness of the proletarian movement, and its task is to bring to that consciousness the hidden tendencies within bourgeois reality which are working towards its revolutionary transformation. The statement is an echo of numerous passages in Marx, some of which have already been cited. The story may be rounded off by noting in particular that it echoes the well-known passage we used to introduce the question of the nature and status of his social theory.[25] This is the section of the Postface to the second German edition of *Capital* in which he offers some reflections on dialectical method. The method is 'a scandal and an abomination to the bourgeoisie' because, among other things, 'it includes in its positive understanding of what exists a simultaneous recognition of its negation, its inevitable destruction; because it regards every historically developed form as being in a fluid state, in motion, and therefore grasps its transient aspect as well'.[26] This is, of course, the now familiar thesis that the dialectical character of the theory is essentially bound up with its cognitive insight into the unfolding potentialities of present existence. As an isolated thesis stated in such terms, it would itself, however, have the undialectical status of an abstract summary. By this stage our discussion should have overcome this danger by providing the elaboration which enables it to be grasped concretely in its proper setting.

Lukács's purpose in starting his book with a definition is to incorporate his subject within the understanding of Marxism it embodies. The sentence immediately following the passage quoted above assures us that 'By these criteria Lenin is the greatest thinker to have been produced by the revolutionary working-class movement since Marx.' His greatness consists precisely in the grasp of essentials:

> *The actuality (Aktualität) of the revolution: this is the core of Lenin's thought* and his decisive link with Marx. For historical materialism as the conceptual expression of the proletariat's struggle for liberation could only be achieved and formulated theoretically when revolution was already on the agenda as a practical reality; when, in the misery of the proletariat, in Marx's words, was to be seen not only the misery itself but also the revolutionary element 'which will bring down the old order'.[27]

In these words Lukács rehearses once again the central themes of the present discussion. What is of particular interest now is the sense of the historical linkages which they reveal, and to which they seek affiliation. The basic pattern may be traced in detail elsewhere. In the case of ideology too there exists a unitary tradition whose major figures are Marx, Lenin and Lukács.[28] The tradition is defined by the fact that for it the concept serves to theorize the role of ideas in class struggle. It may reasonably, in view of its membership, be accorded a classic status within Marxist approaches to the subject. In the formative period of Western Marxism, however, after the publication of *History and Class Consciousness* and the death of Lenin, the concept of ideology underwent a transformation. It came to acquire the incongruous epistemological and sociological burdens which distinguish its later career in the West. This development reflects in a specific area the forces which shaped the larger terrain of conceptions of social theory in general. On this terrain, too, one has to acknowledge a distinctive position shared by Marx, Lenin and Lukács, an immanently dialectical view centred on the actuality of the revolution of which the theory is the conceptual expression.[29] On the other side there is the emergence of a view of theory as a mode of adverse judgement on existing society which is by no means dependent for its formulation on that actuality. It is available to 'admirable men' regardless of whether revolution is on the agenda as a practical reality and, indeed, has all the greater appeal for them as its presence there begins to fade. With ideology conceived as false consciousness and social theory as social critique, the main pillars of the intellectual structure of Western Marxism may be said to be firmly in place.

These pillars mutually support each other, creating an appearance of great strength and cohesion. Thus, to identify ideology with what is, in one way or another, cognitively defective is to make the concept a potential instrument of a critical social science. The assumption that socialist science must be such a critique serves in its turn to motivate and ratify the process of reading the cognitive defect view into Marx.[30] In this way ideology comes to conform to, and reinforce, the general pattern of Western Marxism's normative reappropriation of Marx's thought. The outcome is a critical apparatus which has considerable scope and versatility and is, in particular, well adapted to tackling the superstructure of bourgeois society. The social critique doctrine is an ideal vehicle of the superstructural obsession which, together with the epistemological, serves to define Western Marxism through the contrast with Marx's lack of serious theoretical interest in either area. Within this perspective ideology readily figures as a formation of the superstructure, albeit one charged with a negative significance as, most typically, the disreputable 'other' of science. The project of a normative theory of bourgeois institutions, which includes the concept of ideology in its critical armoury, is without precedents or foundations in classical Marxism. It answers very well, however, to the needs of the succeeding era in which revolution has ceased to be an actuality in the West.

II

As a preliminary to taking more positive steps, it may be helpful to review, in the light of the discussion, the options for a social theory that now aspires to be socialist. To avoid begging the question, the notion of socialist theory will be taken in a wide sense. It will encompass any body of theory which can reasonably claim to belong as of right on the side of the movement or goal of socialism and to be opposed to its enemies. An obvious possibility is that it takes the form of social critique; that is, of a system of normative, and characteristically moral, indictment of non-socialist reality. This is, of course, a viable and honourable enterprise and, indeed, the standard model for contemporary socialist thought in the West. Moreover, it is a form of theoretical intervention that should be welcome to the socialist movement. Even if one doubts the effectivity of moral reasoning in shaping the forces that lie at the heart of historical change, it must be accorded an influence at the margins. In terms of Marxist tradition this is most obvious in the case of bourgeois intellectuals. As bourgeois they lack organic roots in socialist practice, and as intellectuals they are imbued with the conviction that for action to be rational it must be mediated by general reflection. In this situation moral critique may have a useful role to play. The contribution of ethical socialism should neither be despised nor allowed to fill the whole perspective. It is also worth remembering that some versions of critique have striven to maintain a link with dialectical thought by requiring that critical standards be drawn from the ideals of the object of criticism itself. This betrays a sound impulse, even though, as we have seen, it will not yield the true immanence of being the self-consciousness of a rational order emerging through existing forms. There remains the disparity between theory as the appeal to an ought and theory as the revelation of what the subject is and what, in accordance with its nature, it will be compelled to do.

A survey of options has to acknowledge that theory may be socialist and dialectical, in a legitimate sense of those terms, without being Marxist. The obvious suggestion is that it may rely on subjects other than classes as the agents who release the rational kernel of socialism from the capitalist shell. The politics of revolution will not then be conceived as class politics. Theory will be the conceptual expression of a process whose dynamic derives from non-class forces. They may perhaps be identified as intellectuals, students, women, blacks, or lesbian and gay people, or the emphasis may be on the socialist potential of groups concerned with nuclear disarmament or environmental sanity. These, it will be recognized, are the components of what have in recent years come to be known as the 'new social movements'. Another possibility, taking one further from Marx's form of dialectic, is that the socialist influences may be conceived, in the style of late Marcuse, as too amorphous to qualify as a subject or collection of subjects in a traditional sense. They consist in a certain subjectivity, a liberating mode of sensibility widely diffused within society without ever, as it were, gathering to a point of agency. Taking a step still further from Marx, the socialist dialectic may be viewed as not essentially phenomenological in character. It expresses rather a logic embedded in capitalism which, of course, is not as such independent of human consciousness but nevertheless does not require, in the manner of a phenomenology, to be experienced by a subject at successively higher levels of awareness in order to be constituted as dialectic. Some versions of 'technological determinism' could, perhaps, be read dialectically along these lines. A liberating potential inherent in technology might be made to yield a 'dialectic of enlightenment' in a non-ironic, non-catastrophic sense different from that of Horkheimer and Adorno.

As in the case of social critique, it must be acknowledged that these are all, on the face of it, viable and even persuasive lines of thought. As before also, one should be careful not to draw rigid lines of demarcation around, and within, the socialist project. Thus, a 'new social movements' approach may not only take the strongly dialectical form envisaged here but may instead, and more predictably in current circumstances, be linked to ideas of social critique. It may look to those ideas for intellectual foundations and, in turn, the new movements may be thought to provide the most fertile ground for the critical message. Moreover, these movements constitute a source of potential support which only the crassest conception of class-based politics could wish to ignore. The reservations about non-Marxist forms of dialectic that concern us at present arise chiefly from their relative lack of theoretical specification. Nearly all the serious work in this field remains to be done. A sense of what is missing and a hint of how it might be supplied are conveyed in Marcuse's late proposal to identify the liberating forces with those who, in the societies of corporate capitalism, experience most keenly with least distortion the biological need for freedom and happiness. This remains, however, a directional pointer rather than an achieved solution. The issue may be highlighted by comparing the position with that of the dialectic of classes. This is underpinned by a detailed and sophisticated political economy which demonstrates the crucial role of classes in the material production of life. Beyond that there is an admittedly incomplete but still imposing edifice of theory comprising the ontology of labour and the philosophy of history which rests upon it. At this point too Marx's thought engages with, and draws strength from, that of Hegel; more especially from the fundamental theme of humanity's self-creation through labour. It is a connection with the deepest roots of the dialectic of history which is lost to a theory that categorizes human beings not in terms of the social forms of the exercise of their vital, natural powers but as citizens, consumers, enlightened ones or potential victims, or by gender, ethnic origin or sexual identity. It is true that dialectic, as the least sentimental of philosophies, is the least imbued with piety and the least susceptible to a cult of the founders. Anyone seriously committed to it must in principle find it thinkable that its future should in substance lie quite outside the sphere of Hegel and Marx, that, to put it crudely, as friends of dialectic we must cease to be Marxists. For this to be more than an abstract possibility, however, it requires an alternative theoretical setting of comparable depth and richness to the one we have inherited. Such an achievement is at present nowhere in sight.

This brief survey has ranged over non-dialectical and, *a fortiori*, non-Marxist conceptions of social theory and over others which are dialectical without being Marxist. It returns us in the end to the idea of a theory which is authentically Marxist and, hence, dialectical. This idea belongs to, and crystallizes, a tradition of thought with many achievements of unsurpassed brilliance and power to its credit from *The German Ideology* to *History and Class Consciousness*. It would be foolish, not just faint-hearted, to abandon it without the most sustained resistance. In general the cause of intellectual progress is served not by tamely surrendering traditions of demonstrated range and fertility in the face of the inevitable difficulties but by holding fast through the difficulties, using them as means of renewed development. The resolve to do so should be all the stronger when, as here, the resources of the position have never been fully mobilized in the context in which the difficulties arise. That this should be so in the case of Marxism is partly explained by aspects of its history which have already been considered. In particular, there is the simple fact that in Western Marxism the dilution or relinquishing of the problematic of the revolutionary class subject has not by any means been accompanied by the most sustained resistance. Yet, as we have seen, the specific identity of classical Marxism is bound up with this problematic and, hence, a tradition which claims organic descent therefrom must stand or fall with it. If the problematic has now to be rejected as exhausted or barren, it would be well to recognize that an era in intellectual history has decisively closed. Whatever stray influences may continue to emanate, the core of its significance is dissolved. In such circumstances socialist theorists would still be able to pursue their post-Marxist projects with a clear conscience and a clear head. To conclude, however, that this is our actual world would itself be wilful and premature. It is not, as we shall see, a verdict enforced by objective features of the situation.

To be reminded of the identity of classical Marxism is also to be brought in touch again with the most pressing difficulty that faces anyone who today would be a Marxist in social theory. It is that the original nomination of the revolutionary subject cannot now be sustained. The crisis of Marxism is at root a crisis occasioned by the absence of this subject as Marx conceived it. At the most general level the response characteristic of Western Marxism is to assume that its presence is not, after all, constitutive of the possibility of Marxist theory. The missing element is written out of the definition, so that the theory ceases to be conceived as its self-consciousness. No longer the cognitive expression of a movement of reality, it becomes instead a testament to what reality ought and sometimes aspires to be and is not. Since the classical dialectic is essentially a dialectic of the subject, theory loses its dialectical character in the process. It is for this reason that one may speak of a specific historical event, the loss of the subject, as inaugurating an intellectual crisis affecting the system as a whole. It is in this context too that one must understand the claim that Western Marxism fails to carry forward the substance of the classical programme in social theory. Given the centrality of that programme for Marx's thought in general, there is plainly a straightforward sense in which Western

Marxism is not Marxist. This is in itself an unpleasantly melodramatic thesis. Nevertheless, when, on being given a reasonably precise reading, it is forced upon one by sober consideration of the evidence, it has to be accepted.

The chief implication for the future is that any hopes of renewal must depend on setting aside the immediate past and reaching across the historical gulf to the classic springs of Marxist thought. Such an enterprise will be immediately confronted by the fact that the crucial task of identifying the revolutionary subject has to be performed again. That task cannot be carried through here. It must itself be an achievement of substantive theory, not of the meta-theoretical reflection with which the present inquiry is concerned. All that can reasonably be expected of such inquiry is a perspective within which progress with the substantial issues is once more conceivable. It should, however, be possible to go a little beyond what this suggests by pointing out the first steps on the forward path. The obvious place to start, in the spirit of the overall enterprise, is with the circumstances of the original identification. To do so is instructive in a number of ways. For one thing, it soon becomes clear that Marx did not himself bring to bear all the resources of his own thought on the task. This opens up the possibility, if only in the mode normally available to pygmies resting on a giant, that contemporary Marxists may be able to perform it more adequately. At least they may reasonably hope to achieve a denser mediation of theory and a deeper awareness of the complexities and contingencies of the situation. These qualities are themselves in large part, of course, the bitter fruit of a history hidden from Marx.

The issues of present concern in Marx's thinking are best presented in terms of a contrast. In its immediate aspect it is one between the first period of his socialist and materialist writings and all the rest of his intellectual career. Contrasts of this sort are a familiar, sometimes overused, device. The one in question here does not, however, fit well with the usual periodizations, nor is it intended to suggest any deep theoretical rupture. In the earlier period, which includes *The German Ideology*, there was a commitment, formed in the light of the reflective experience of the time, to the proletariat as the revolutionary class. It was, as was indicated earlier, a rational step in the circumstances. The class of the proletariat seemed capable of meeting the strictest requirements of dialectical theory. It could convincingly be said to be driven by imperative needs which the existing order was unable to satisfy. It could also be thought, in view of its strategic importance for that order, to have the power, as well as the incentive, to bring about its overthrow. Moreover, the signs of a developing socialist consciousness among the workers were incontrovertible, even if Marx inclined to be over-sanguine as to

what had already been attained. In the later period his commitment
remains the same in all outward respects. Yet a part of its original
meaning drains away as it comes to designate a somewhat lifeless area in
his thought. There was a kind of hardening of intellectual and imagina-
tive arteries, a closure shutting off the core of the theory of revolution
from fresh influences which were at best forced to cluster on the
margins. The contrast being displayed here may now be said to have an
aspect which is not simply chronological but which has an analogy in
Marx's registering of the political implications of the trade cycle. That is
to say, it corresponds in some measure to the distinction between
occasional writings and formal scientific work. The outcome is both
curious in itself and characteristic of Marx. Its peculiarity lies in the
remarkable way he anticipates problems that were to be central for his
successors without attempting to work the anticipations into the
substance of his official theory. This is both a testimony to his intellectual powers and a reminder of the limits of what can be achieved in a
single human life under the constraints of time and circumstances.

These remarks may be illustrated by a topic which has received much
attention from commentators. It is, for instance, the main focus of attention in the discussion by Mészáros referred to earlier. The topic is what
he identifies as 'the *fragmentation* of the working class' arising from its
'position in the existing *division of labour*'. He argues that in Marx's
work in general the fragmentation is 'greatly underestimated' and that its
'necessary political consequences' remain largely unexplored. This is, he
points out, all the more remarkable since in *The German Ideology* Marx
had insisted: 'The more the division of labour develops and accumulation grows, the further fragmentation develops. *Labour itself can only
exist on the premise of this fragmentation.*' This is an insight with far-
reaching implications, which are, however, as Mészáros notes, never
spelled out by Marx. Instead, there is the stipulation of a 'natural
progression' from 'occasional and partial' to 'permanent and comprehensive' trade unionism, and thence to 'the politically conscious assertion of the interests of universal emancipation accomplished by the
united proletarian "class for itself"'.[31] Once again, *The German
Ideology* had taken a more sober view: 'Both for the production on a
mass scale of this communist consciousness, and for the success of the
cause itself, *the alteration of men on a mass scale is necessary.*'[32] What
characterizes the later writings, however, is, Mészáros argues, a postulating, 'even if in an ambiguous form', of the 'accomplished *actualization*
of that communist mass consciousness whose *production* was presented
in *The German Ideology* as a challenging historical task for the future'.[33]
Indeed, he insists on speaking of a 'contradiction' in this body of work
'between the fact that the task of "transforming circumstances and men"

is far from accomplished, and the assumption that the communist consciousness of the working class is *already given*'.[34]

It is clear that Mészáros is focusing here on a highly vulnerable area and one that poses a considerable challenge for Marxist theory. It does so precisely because the phenomenon of fragmentation is not merely incidentally or intermittently part of the capitalist mode of production. It is, on Marx's own showing, grounded in the development of the division of labour and in the process of accumulation. Hence, it belongs to the basic logic of the system. Moreover, it has important implications for the scenario of revolution which is dominant in Marx's thinking. For it works to produce a myriad of forms of sectional consciousness, rather than the unitary class consciousness on which the scenario depends. Marx is, as the writings of the earlier period show, well aware of this aspect of the logic of capitalism. Yet he makes no serious attempt to integrate the awareness with his mature theory of its overthrow. It would be hard to find a more telling illustration of the fact that the theme of the revolutionary subject identifies a once vital, but later petrified, region in his thought.

If it is to be reclaimed for life and movement, one should be able to explain the onset of petrification. There is a remark by Mészáros which places the issue in a helpful context. He refers to the gap that separates the present conditions of life from 'the "new historic form" aimed at', and adds: 'under the historically *premature* conditions of the advocated "social revolution" – when capitalism is acknowledged by Marx to be in its *ascendancy* on by far the greater part of the planet – only the stipulated communist mass consciousness can bridge this great historical gap and provide the desired guarantee for maintaining the impetus of the necessary struggle'.[35] What is particularly helpful here is the suggestion of the importance of the planetary perspective. Once again, Marx is well aware of the point without managing to embody it discursively within the framework of his mature theory. In displaying such awareness he could, of course, be said to be building on an insight of Hegel's which has already been noted. It is the idea that the 'inner dialectic' of bourgeois society drives it 'to push beyond its own limits and seek markets' specifically through 'colonizing activity'.[36] Strikingly similar formulations occur in Marx: 'The need of a constantly expanding market for its products chases the bourgeoisie over the whole surface of the globe. It must nestle everywhere, settle everywhere, establish connections everywhere.'[37]

It should be said that Marx is wholly convinced that the consequences of all this activity require full-scale theoretical treatment. For the evidence one has, however, to turn to his various statements of a programme of work rather than to any achieved results. Thus, in the plan presented in *Grundrisse* the final section is to be devoted to 'the world market and crises'.[38] The juxtaposition here is exact and signifi- cant. Later in the same text the content envisaged for the section is elaborated as follows: 'the world market the conclusion, in which production is posited as a totality together with all its moments, but within which, at the same time, all contradictions (*Widersprüche*) come into play'. The fundamental importance of the topic is recognized at once: 'The world market then, again, forms the presupposition of the whole as well as its substratum. Crises are then the general intimation which points beyond the presupposition, and the urge which drives towards the adoption of a new historic form.'[39]

The specific terms of this recognition are worth noting. It is partly a question of the dialectical character of the theory. The world market must be invoked to yield the standpoint of the totality from which alone all the contradictions can be seen to 'come into play'. It has also to do with the status of the theory as a theory of revolution. For it is only in the context of the world market that the crises of capitalism assume their full significance. Thus, it appears that this context is uniquely appropriate as the crown of a body of social theory that aspires to be dialectical and revolutionary. Marx was never to write the final section of the *Grundrisse* programme, nor the book which corresponds to it in some versions of his plans.[40] 'The world market and crises' is perhaps the most important of the various studies he projected but never carried out, an even greater loss to us than those on the state and on the nature of the materialist dialectic. It represents an absence with the largest significance for his life-work as a whole, and for the subsequent history of Marxism.

An explanation of Marx's failure to complete all that he proposed would have to draw on biographical data of various kinds. It would, for instance, have to take account of the unfavourable circumstances of his life and of his exceedingly painstaking method of composition. It would also in the case in question here have to recognize the peculiar sensitivity of the task. This is partly a reflection of Marx's sense of its sheer theoretical difficulty. Thus, in *Theories of Surplus Value* he refers to 'the world market crisis' as 'the most complicated phenomenon of capitalist production'.[41] The difficulty derives not just from complexity but also from the fact that what is involved is a dynamic process still in its labile, expansionary, phase. This aspect is captured in a letter of 1858 to Engels:

> The specific task of bourgeois society is the establishment of a world market, at least in outline, and of production based upon this world market. As the world is round, this seems to have been completed by the colonization of California and Australia and the opening up of China and Japan. The difficult

question for us is this: on the Continent the revolution is imminent, and will immediately assume a socialist character. Is it not bound to be crushed in this little corner, considering that in a far greater territory the movement of bourgeois society is still in the ascendant?[42]

The passage suggests that the sensitivity of the world market project is not simply a matter of being theoretically daunting but has also to do with its practical and political implications. It leaves no doubt of Marx's awareness that in a global perspective bourgeois society still appears as ascendant, and by no means at the point of systematic crisis. It is a sobering, indeed chilling, perspective for a serious revolutionary, bent on the overthrow of the existing order and ever anxious, as in the letter to Engels, to detect signs of imminent transformation in any corner of it. What the global perspective enjoins is the vision of a long haul which may turn out to be very long indeed. To speak once more at a biographical level, it seems altogether understandable in human terms if Marx were to shrink from the full implications of this. So far as the development of theory is concerned, the natural outcome is at least a partial turning away from the dialectical labour of finding a voice for what is latent in present reality towards premature solutions which can appear to work only by stipulating what should be fruits of discovery or proof. This is to suggest that Marx's sense of reality was overborne here by what must be considered a kind of wishful thinking. Such a verdict could seriously be held to affect his status as a thinker only by those who have ceased to view him in secular terms, or who in general insist on seeing the intellectual leaders of humankind as wholly transcending their own personal and historical situations. Nevertheless, the defeat of his realism in this area has to be acknowledged and its implications need to be faced.

To grasp the true proportions of the problem, it should be noted that the defeat also signals a rupture with the logic of his own system. This serves to open up the possibility that its logic, properly understood, may not after all be at odds with the movement of twentieth-century history. The suggestion then arises that the difficulties presented by that history, the source of the contemporary crisis of Marxism, do not strike at essentials and can in the end be negotiated within the framework of Marx's thought. The basic point to be made is implicit in the account already given of the status and role of dialectical theory. It may be drawn out with the help of one of Marx's best-known applications of a dialectical perspective to the development of human society. The passage in question dates from more or less the same time as the letter to Engels. Its theme is, with appropriate variations, strongly marked in Hegel also, thus testifying to its significance for the tradition of thought as a whole:

No social order is ever destroyed before all the productive forces for which it is sufficient have been developed, and new superior relations of production never replace older ones before the material conditions for their existence have matured within the framework of the old society. Mankind thus inevitably sets itself only such tasks as it is able to solve, since closer examination will always show that the problem itself arises only when the material conditions for its solution are already present or at least in the course of formation.[43]

Nothing could indicate more clearly the futility of unripe solutions; that is, those proffered by individuals before 'mankind' has 'set itself' the problem. Marx was well aware at the time of writing of the grounds there were for supposing that not all the productive forces for which the capitalist order sufficed had been developed. It is at this point, however, that the lack of an elaborated theory of the world market, of the international trading system in its global ascendancy, makes itself felt. It deprives him of the standpoint of totality which alone can integrate all components of the scene. As a consequence, the conception of revolution cannot be properly articulated with the rest of the theory and in particular with the insight into the still dynamic character of bourgeois society. Thus, the process of identifying the revolutionary subject takes place in a partial theoretical vacuum, insulated from, and unconstrained by, the fundamentals of the system. This is what opens the way for Marx to fall victim to the wishful thinking referred to earlier. It leaves him vulnerable to misjudging the identity and location of his own time in the historical sequence. The temptation is one to which proponents of historical dialectic are peculiarly liable. Hegel too was to succumb to it, more completely and with less excuse, in beginning to think of the Germanic period as the culmination of world history. What this illustrates is the fact that while the Absolute may, as he assures us, never be in a hurry, its mortal interpreters all too often are. Marx for his part saw with great clarity the folly of the political economists in assuming that 'there has been history, but there is no longer any'.[44] Yet later in life he himself came to snatch too eagerly at the moment when history ceases, or rather, to use a description only verbally at odds with this, when the prehistory of human society gives way to truly human history.

III

Against this background, it is plain enough what in general terms Marxist theorists now need to do. It involves, in as literal a sense as may be envisaged, a return to the classic sources, with the intention of carrying through their unfinished programme. The task is in part one for Marxist philosophy, a matter of completing the foundations of the materialist historical dialectic. For this dialectic, human history is the natural history of a rational species, or rather the record of a species whose rationality develops in historical time on the basis of natural endowments. What is required to complete the foundations is a philosophical account of the relationship between reason and nature; more specifically, a demonstration that the life of reason in emancipated society is to be conceived as the satisfaction of a natural need. Such an achievement would have considerable importance for dialectical thought as a whole. The meeting ground of the categories of nature and reason has been for it an obscure and undertheorized region, forming, for instance, a notorious crux in the philosophy of Hegel. A successful materialist treatment of it would repair a historic weakness in the tradition.[45] It would also be a major event on the philosophical scene in general. In this context it could scarcely avoid having a familiar kind of practical, that is, ideological, significance. This is so just in virtue of the role, intelligible in terms of the semantic, evaluative model of ideology, of philosophy as a source of legitimation in the intellectual world. The subject is still widely assumed to be a repository of ultimate or, at any rate, otherwise unanswerable, questions. Hence, it has an authority which, however reduced and battered, is felt throughout the whole domain. Claims and assumptions are made elsewhere with a good conscience in the belief that they could, if necessary, be subjected to a justificatory process resting in the end in philosophical considerations. Thus, analytical philosophy has played a part in underpinning the empiricist practice of science, if only, at the limit, by reassuring its practitioners that any 'metaphysical' worries can be resolved somewhere out of sight in a sense favourable to their activities. Given this situation, the suggestion must arise that a revitalized materialist philosophy could serve as a cornerstone of an alternative intellectual culture, a counter-hegemony. It should not aspire to anything lower, though the aspiration may itself strike some as impracticable, or even absurd. Here one has to reckon with the loss of nerve and corresponding poverty of ambition, which has, regrettably but understandably, overcome sections of the left in recent years. As always, however, it should be remembered that everything appears overwhelming if one is on one's knees and a simple change of attitude greatly improves the perspective. Moreover, there are in the present case auspicious omens that may be pointed to in a spirit of the most sober realism.

An obvious, but important, truth to bear in mind is that analytical philosophy, for long the dominant force in the academic world of Britain and the United States, is itself a historical product. Indeed, the main contours of its rise and fall are already plainly visible. It is perhaps worth remembering in particular that its immediate predecessor in the early years of this century was a form of dialectical philosophy, albeit a form of idealism. This serves at least to show that no immutable 'Chinese wall' can be relied on to protect the Anglo-Saxon academy from all influences of dialectic. What we are witnessing at present, however, is the other extremity of the historical lifespan of the analytical movement. Signs of its dissolution are now widespread, and the intellectual scene begins to darken with obituary notices.[46] The collapse of its dominance is what provides a revitalized Marxist philosophy with the opportunity to become a substantial presence on that scene. In doing so, it should, of course, seek to preserve in dialectical fashion the best features of what it supersedes, in this case the virtues of clarity and rigour. These are at any rate what the analytical school has most prided itself on, though, as Sean Sayers points out, they are 'the virtues of *good* philosophy, of *good* thought in all fields', and 'no monopoly of analytical philosophy'.[47] In doing so, moreover, the new philosophy will obviously have to move Hegel and Marx, and such other key figures in its past as Feuerbach and Engels, closer to the centre of intellectual attention and debate. It is also important for it to establish a pantheon of twentieth-century thinkers different from that of the dissolving orthodoxy and from the various alternatives waiting in the wings. It will have to consist of those major socialist thinkers who have striven to give substance to a dialectical perspective in philosophy. Such thinkers comprise the only significant tradition of radical philosophy we possess, the only one with the authority and resources to offer a serious challenge to the hegemony of bourgeois thought. Their work is crucial for the present proposal, not in the sense that it is to be the subject of uncritical celebration but just by virtue of the centrality of the problems it grapples with and the enduring interest of its solutions; by virtue, that is, of its worthiness to be the focus of sustained critical attention. The obvious names to mention here are Lukács, Adorno and Sartre.[48] It may perhaps be thought, in view of this list, that what is being proposed is an updated version of Left Hegelianism. This is by no means the intention. Hegelianism is emphatically not what we need and its claims are not improved by the assumption that all will be well if it is rotated leftwards. The result must in its own way be just as much an undialectical harnessing together of elements from bourgeois and socialist thought as is analytical Marxism. In both cases it is the bourgeois component that retains its identity and dominates the whole, while what is socialist survives largely as rhetorical colouring. What we need is a materialist and dialectical philosophy which has its own integrity while incorporating what is of value in Hegelianism, as in the analytical school and, indeed, in all the thought of the past.

It will not devalue such a philosophical achievement to point out that it could not of itself resolve the crisis of the Marxist intellectual tradition. For it does not go to the core of the matter. The crisis is ultimately not one of Marxist philosophy but of Marxism as revolutionary social theory. What philosophy can contribute is, as usual, a framework which provides guidelines for other sorts of inquiry, enabling them to be pursued with vigour and a good conscience in the assurance of a rooted legitimacy. It is, however, the success of the main inquiry which is thereby legitimated that is in this instance vital. In describing the object of that inquiry one can hardly do better in a shorthand phrase than to say it is the missing theory of 'the world market and crises'. It is, that is to say, a political economy of the international capitalist system as the setting for a grasp of its potential for revolutionary change. In still other terms, it is the location of the problematic of the class subject, the hall-mark of Marx's conception of revolution, within the perspective of the totality, the vantage point which alone yields the entire manifold of contradictions. It is essential here that general theory and the search for the solution to the problem of agency should go together in what may legitimately be considered a dialectical interaction. The search has, as it were, to be permeated by theoretical insight at the appropriate level, and it serves in turn as an urgent stimulus to the further development of theory. It is the weakness of such interaction in Marx's thinking in this area that largely accounts for the impression of lifelessness it conveys. In a sense he found the solution to the problem of agency too easily and too soon, and his absolute commitment to it once found was to be a brake, rather than a spur, to theoretical progress. This diagnosis offers a way of stating the condition under which the current crisis may be truly a time of birth and of liberation. It will be so only in so far as contemporary Marxists overcome the weakness in their inheritance by creating and maintaining the dialectical tension that properly belongs at the heart of it. The substance of such an achievement has so far eluded Marx's successors. It is true that there are important and valuable Marxist contributions to the political economy of global capitalism.[49] These must be preserved and built on for the future. Nevertheless, the divorce of philosophy and the study of the material base which is so striking a feature of Western Marxism in general has been particularly unfortunate in its effect here. It has served to weaken the hold of the dialectical perspective on the political economy, thereby permitting the problematic of the class subject to drift from its anchorage at the fixed centre of things. A great merit of that perspective is that it forces one to attend constantly to the question of agency, to insist on asking what the specific vehicle is by which the rationality of the actual is realized. It is in this sense the least abstract of standpoints and the enemy of all abstraction.

Hence, it is the appropriate standpoint from which to pursue Marxist political economy as the core of a revolutionary social theory. In particular, it alone can sustain the reciprocal development of general theory and of the concrete grasp of possibilities for change that constitutes the way forward from the present situation.

It is, of course, impossible to say in advance whether Marxist philosophy and political economy will actually develop along the lines proposed here. The discussion has attempted to show that the proposals are coherent and feasible and that they embody what is indispensably required if Marxism is to be again a vital intellectual force. The first of these aims may be pursued a little further so far as political economy is concerned. The grounds for confidence which general theory yields in this case are not yet exhausted. It is worth pointing out to begin with that capitalism remains in its global form as contradictory as ever. No engagement with its political economy is needed to state the contradiction which is of chief interest now. This is, rather, a matrix into which all the more technical sorts of contradictions of the system may be fitted. The contradiction is the primary one identified by the young Marx between the conditions of life of the masses under capitalism and their human nature. In a global perspective it is plain that this has lost none of its sharpness since his time. Indeed, the inability of the system to meet elementary human needs is more apparent than ever. The relevant facts are well known and copiously documented and will not be rehearsed here.[50] The crucial point is the existence on a vast scale in countries locked into the capitalist world system of poverty, illiteracy, disease, hunger, starvation and backbreaking toil. These unnatural conditions are integrally bound up with the system and their removal cannot be seriously envisaged except in terms of its coming to an end. In the meantime it sustains itself in the face of them through organized violence; by means of hit men, death squads, 'freedom fighters', beatings, imprisonment, exile, torture, executions and other devices of state terrorism. From the standpoint of Marxist theory such a situation is inherently unstable and contains the seeds of its own destruction. This is most fundamentally so not because the recital of its many evils arouses moral condemnation but because it involves a contradiction of the nature of the beings who suffer and inflict suffering under it. Such a deep ontological divide must ultimately, the theory holds, impose its logic on history, as the course of events comes to reflect, with whatever digressions and regressions, a unifying movement. Thus, there are resources in Marxist thought for placing scientific inquiry into the contradictions of the capitalist mode of production within a context of rational optimism.

There is another, more concrete, kind of guidance to be had from general theory. It makes use of two prominent themes there. The first is that of the primacy of labour; more specifically of what is the main lesson of the master–slave dialectic on a materialist reading, that the human future belongs to the labourer who through the work of fashioning the thing 'becomes conscious of what he truly is'.[51] The second, also to be found in Hegel, is the idea that social forms do not perish before all their potentialities are developed; the dialectical insistence that, as one might say, 'ripeness is all'. Taken together, what these imply for the problem of agency is that prospects of social transformation have to be located in the most alienated and exploited of direct producers at the point of maximum expansion of the system. Marx's solution to the problem meets this requirement only in part. It identifies the alienated and exploited, but at a point when bourgeois society is still 'in the ascendant'; that is, prior to the critical moment of the dialectic of forces and relations of production. It is impossible, at least in abstraction from substantive analysis, to form a judgement of the stage which that society has now reached in its historical life-process. Nothing useful can be said on the question in advance of the work of political economy referred to above, and a significant part of the value of such work should consist in providing a purchase on it. For the present, one has to return to the other element in the guidance, the reference to the extremity of exploitation. This suggests a direction in which one should look, and the advice may be reinforced and sharpened by other considerations.

It was shown earlier that Marx's writings contain penetrating, even if not systematically maintained and integrated, insights into the resources available to bourgeois society. In particular, he takes over and enlarges Hegel's sense of the significance of the drive for markets through colonization and the annexation of outlying regions. This process has a consequence which he may be excused for not focusing precisely since the main development took place after his death, in the classic age of imperialism. It is noted by Mészáros in the course of amplifying the claim that 'some important characteristics of working-class existence cannot be given their full weight in the Marxian perspective'. The characteristics are said to include 'the exploitative relationship of the Western working classes in general to the "Third World"'.[52] This is a somewhat bald formulation of an idea which merits more nuanced language. At least it should be said that the relationship of the Western working classes in general to the 'Third World' cannot be regarded as exploitative in the same sense as is that of the Western capitalist classes in general. It has to be seen as, by contrast, subordinate, unconscious and adventitious, less comprehensive in scope and less ramified in its implications. It is not unlikely, of course, that Mészáros would wish to take account of such complications in a fuller treatment of the matter. Nevertheless, the substance of his point is surely incontrovertible and, so far as it goes, decisive. Even the qualified role of the Western working classes in the exploitative relationship suffices to constitute a characteristic which indeed cannot be given its full weight within Marx's original perspective. For it is in its own right destructive of that perspective. It signifies the inability of these classes to meet the criteria for the revolutionary subject which the perspective enjoins. As classes benefiting, however indirectly, from exploitation, they cannot be thought to represent exclusively the universal interest of human emancipation. They are caught up in local and sectional interests whose realization is bound to the well-being of bourgeois society. They have become not merely incorporated into that society but partners in some measure of its ruling classes in the exploitation of others. The claim to be the absolute negation of it thereby loses all credibility. Yet, fortunately, the line of thought which leads to this conclusion also points beyond it. For it suggests where the search for negation should be redirected. It should quite plainly look towards the victims of the exploitative relationship; that is, towards the masses of the 'Third World'.

The only branch of theory with a significant contribution to make from this point onwards is the political economy of the world system and its crises, an enterprise lying outside the scope of the present work. It is scarcely presumptuous, however, to suggest that its first tasks should include a critical examination of an idea which has arisen in the course of the discussion, that of the 'Third World'. Referring as it does to a vast and heterogeneous collection of societies, it is virtually useless as an analytical category. It may serve well enough for the immediate purpose of shifting attention away from the 'First World', from, roughly speaking, the countries which formed the basis of Marx's model of capitalism, as the focal point of world history. But scientific inquiry with a view to specifying potentialities for change will need more refined instruments. For the rest the obvious point to note is that the account given here of the identity of the Marxist intellectual tradition implies constraints on what could count as a Marxist solution to the problems. Historical agency in this tradition is the agency of class subjects, and socialist politics is class politics. It was shown earlier that it is not necessary, or indeed possible, to maintain unrevised Marx's identification of the agent with the 'First World' proletariat. Neither, one may add, is it necessary, within the confines of Marxist thought, to insist that the agent be a proletariat in a narrow sense. It is perhaps particularly important in a 'Third World' context to bear in mind that the distinction between industrial workers and the wage labourers of capitalist agriculture has little theoretical significance.[53] The argument of this study has concluded by pointing to the workers of 'Third World' capitalism as crucial for the future development of Marxism, and it is not as yet possible to be any more specific. The requirement that class remains the basis for conception of agency does, however, have some cutting edge within socialist theory. It serves to warn against bourgeois nationalist positions with which some forms of the theory within a 'Third World' perspective have become entangled. It is important here to insist on the class analysis of 'Third World' societies and to resist tendencies to represent national entities rather than classes as the chief actors on the global scene. It is important also that the 'Third World' class analysis be integrated with that for the 'First World' and that the political prospects in the two 'worlds' be articulated as arising within a unitary field of force. Putting the point more generally, and in the traditional language of dialectics, the inquiry has to be conducted from the standpoint of the totality. Such a standpoint allows the light to fall on particular aspects and regions of the whole, on specific points of tension and sources of energy, on – to use one useful kind of formal terminology – principal rather than secondary contradictions and on the principal aspects of those contradictions. The proposals made here fall easily within the freedom thus allowed. In taking advantage of it, the primacy of the category of totality in science, as 'the bearer of the principle of revolution', is not disturbed.

The standpoint of the totality is, not surprisingly, difficult to adopt and to maintain. The difficulty is in one aspect a reflection of capitalism's logic of fragmentation which puts constant pressure on conceptions of socialism as a global project.[54] A dialectical perspective is, however, by nature, as its major exponents have always acknowledged, peculiarly liable to seem inaccessible and bleak. For socialists it is partly a matter of the large vistas it reveals, more particularly their temporal extension. This is the problem of the long haul referred to earlier. It is true that without adequate scientific knowledge no informed judgement can be made of capitalism's current stage of development and capacity for future development. Nevertheless, it may be supposed that it is far from decrepit and, if so, the future still has many adventures of its dialectic in store. It is necessary to be prepared for this prospect in all its ramifications. There is also the fact that the central substantive insight of dialectics is a demanding kind of truth. It is, as we have seen, the idea that behind the phenomenal forms of existing society there is a more rational order struggling to be born. This is demanding in virtue of the duality of vision it imposes, the requirement always to look through the forms to their hidden actuality. It is bound to be easier to go with the drift of things, the current that moves on their surface. This is so at least for all those who are not impelled beyond the appearances by the material circumstances of existence, a group which includes intellectuals in general. It is perhaps a measure of their situation in our society that the fundamental tenets of the founders of dialectical thought should now be so little appreciated. It is, quite simply, not easy to accept that Hegel and Marx literally and consistently believed what they believed. There is a standing temptation, some of whose traces have been examined here, to dilute their beliefs so as to be more congenial to our mundane and shrunken selves. The remedy, of course, is to insist on the integrity of those ideas. It is also vital to bear in mind that, as the present study has tried to show, Marx's rationalism at any rate has not been refuted or bypassed by the course of events, but rather has yet to face the true test of history. Even when this is recognized, however, we should not expect that we shall find it easy to assimilate the ideas of such thinkers, or to live by them.

Notes

Preface

1. L. Althusser, 'The Crisis of Marxism', *Power and Opposition in Post-revolutionary Societies*, trs. P. Camiller and J. Rothschild, London, Ink Links, 1979, pp. 229, 237.
2. G.W.F. Hegel, *Hegel: Texts and Commentary*, trs. W. Kaufmann, New York, Anchor Books, 1966, p. 20.
3. Althusser, 'Crisis', pp. 225, 229.

Chapter 1

1. K. Marx and F. Engels, *Selected Works*, Volume 2, Moscow, Foreign Languages Publishing House, 1958, p. 155.
2. See below, e.g. p. 81.
3. A. Gramsci, *Selections from the Prison Notebooks*, ed. and trs. Q. Hoare and G. Nowell-Smith, London, Lawrence and Wishart, 1971, pp. 364–5.
4. K. Marx, *Capital*, Volume 1, trs. B. Fowkes, Harmondsworth, Penguin Books/NLR, 1976, p. 103.
5. It has been attempted in J. McCarney, *The Real World of Ideology*, Brighton, Harvester Press, 1980.
6. For discussion of these examples see ibid., pp. 22–31.
7. A longer look is taken ibid., especially ch. 3.
8. J. Elster, *Logic and Society: Contradictions and Possible Worlds*, Chichester, John Wiley and Sons, 1978, p. 65.
9. Ibid., p. 65.
10. Ibid., p. 70.
11. Ibid., p. 4: J. Elster, *Making Sense of Marx*, Cambridge, Cambridge University Press, 1985, p. 48.
12. Elster, *Logic*, p. 158.
13. Elster, *Making Sense*, p. 44.
14. Elster, *Logic*, p. 110; for the source see J.-P. Sartre, *Critique of Dialectical Reason*, trs. A. Sheridan-Smith, London, Verso, 1982, pp. 161–96.
15. Elster, *Making Sense*, p. 48.
16. Elster, *Logic*, p. 122.
17. Ibid., p. 159.
18. Elster, *Making Sense*, p. 10.

19. J. Elster, *Ulysses and the Sirens*, Cambridge, Cambridge University Press, 1979, p. 20.

20. Elster, *Logic*, p. 134.

21. Ibid., p. 150.

22. Ibid., pp. 134–5.

23. G.W.F. Hegel, *The Science of Logic*, trs. A.V. Miller, London, Allen and Unwin, 1969, p. 439; *Hegel's Logic*, trs. W. Wallace, Oxford, Clarendon Press, 1975, p. 174.

24. Elster, *Making Sense*, p. 43.

25. Ibid., p. 50.

26. K. Marx, *Economic and Philosophical Manuscripts of 1844*, Moscow, Progress Publishers, 1974, p. 87. The conclusion of *The Poverty of Philosophy* is worth noting in this connection. There Marx refers to the 'antagonism' (*antagonisme*) between the proletariat and the bourgeoisie as 'a struggle of class against class' (*une lutte de classe à classe*), and asks, 'Is it at all surprising that a society founded on the opposition (*sur l'opposition*) of classes should culminate in a brutal *contradiction* (*contradiction brutale*), the shock of body against body, as its final denouement?' K. Marx, Moscow, Progress Publishers, 1955, p. 153; *Misère de la Philosophie*, Paris–Brussels, Frank-Volger, 1847, p. 117. The standard German translation, which was supervised by Engels, uses *Gegensatz* for both *antagonisme* and *opposition* and *Widerspruch* for *contradiction*, K. Marx and F. Engels, *Werke*, Band 4, Berlin, Dietz Verlag, 1959, p. 182. Compare also: 'In a crisis, the antithesis (*Gegensatz*) between commodities and their value-form, money, is raised to the level of an absolute contradiction (*Widerspruch*)', *Capital*, Volume 1 (1976), p. 236; *Das Kapital*, Band 1, Frankfurt, Ullstein, 1969, p. 111.

27. Elster, *Logic*, p. 134.

28. Ibid., p. 97.

29. Ibid., p. 67.

30. 'Es ist der reine Wechsel oder *die Entgegensetzung in sich selbst, der Widerspruch zu denken*', G.W.F. Hegel, *Phänomenologie des Geistes*, Frankfurt, Suhrkamp, 1970, p. 130.

31. Elster, *Logic*, p. 65; *Making Sense*, p. 37.

32. Ibid., pp. 71–2.

Chapter 2

1. M. Horkheimer, *Critical Theory: Selected Essays*, trs. M.J. O'Connell *et al.*, New York, Herder and Herder, 1972, pp. 188–252.

2. Ibid., p. 206.

3. The immediate source of the borrowing is P. Connerton, *The Tragedy of Enlightenment: An Essay on the Frankfurt School*, Cambridge, Cambridge University Press, 1980, p. 25.

4. T.W. Adorno, *Against Epistemology: A Metacritique*, trs. W. Domingo, Oxford, Basil Blackwell, 1982, p. 5.

5. G.W.F. Hegel, *The Science of Logic*, trs. A.V. Miller, London, Allen and Unwin, 1969, p. 581.

6. Adorno, *Against Epistemology*, p. 5.

7. M. Horkheimer, 'Notes on Institute Activities', *Studies in Philosophy and Social Science*, Volume 9, no. 1 (1941), p. 122.

8. T.W. Adorno *et al.*, *The Positivist Dispute in German Sociology*, trs. G. Adey and D. Frisby, London, Heinemann, 1976, p. 115.

9. H. Marcuse, 'Some Social Implications of Modern Technology', *The Essential Frankfurt School Reader*, ed. A. Arato and E. Gebhardt, Oxford, Basil Blackwell, 1978, p. 147.

10. 'This study attempts to evaluate some main trends of Soviet Marxism in terms of an "immanent critique", that is to say it starts from the theoretical premises of Soviet

Marxism, develops their ideological and sociological consequences and re-examines the premises in the light of these consequences.' H. Marcuse, *Soviet Marxism: A Critical Analysis*, Harmondsworth, Penguin Books, 1971, p. 1.

11. T.W. Adorno, *Prisms*, trs. S. and S. Weber, Cambridge, Mass. MIT Press, 1981, p. 65.

12. T.W. Adorno, *Minima Moralia: Reflections from Damaged Life*, trs. E. Jephcott, London, Verso, 1974, p. 93.

13. Ibid., p. 93.

14. Ibid., pp. 210–11.

15. Ibid., p. 95.

16. K. Marx, *Early Writings*, Harmondsworth, Penguin Books/NLR, 1975, pp. 212–41.

17. K. Marx, *Capital*, Volume 1, trs. B. Fowkes, Harmondsworth, Penguin Books/NLR, 1976, p. 280.

18. Adorno, *Minima*, p. 211.

19. For a sample of Adorno's dealings with 'morality', see discussion below. For Marcuse, see e.g. *An Essay on Liberation*, Harmondsworth, Penguin Books, 1969, pp. 18–19; *Five Lectures: Psychoanalysis, Politics and Utopia*, trs. J. Shapiro and S. Weber, Boston, Mass., Beacon Press, 1970, p. 96. Horkheimer's status as the Institute's 'moralist' was well recognized: see letter from Adorno quoted in S. Buck-Morss, *The Origin of Negative Dialectics: Theodor W. Adorno, Walter Benjamin and the Frankfurt Institute*, Brighton, Harvester Press, 1977, p. 236; see also the associated discussion by Buck-Morss.

20. Horkheimer, *Critical Theory*, p. 248.

21. Adorno, *Minima*, pp. 155–6.

22. Ibid., p. 157.

23. T.W. Adorno, *Negative Dialectics*, trs. E. Ashton, London, Routledge and Kegan Paul, 1973, pp. 203–4.

24. Ibid., p. 285.

25. Ibid., p. 365.

26. Adorno, *Minima*, p. 18; see also M. Horkheimer, *Eclipse of Reason*, New York, Oxford University Press, 1947, p. vii.

27. Horkheimer, *Critical Theory*, pp. 199, 245, 242.

28. H. Marcuse, 'Philosophy and Critical Theory', *Negations: Essays in Critical Theory*, Harmondsworth, Penguin Books, 1968, pp. 136–7.

29. Marcuse, 'On Hedonism', *Negations*, p. 180.

30. Ibid., p. 154.

31. Adorno, *Prisms*, pp. 92–3.

32. G.W.F. Hegel, *Lectures on the Philosophy of World History: Introduction*, trs. H. Nisbet, Cambridge, Cambridge University Press, 1975, pp. 27, 29.

33. A central difficulty may, however, be posed in terms, relevant to the present discussion, of the traditional distinction between immanence and transcendence. It seems essential to Hegel's conception that the dialectical subject be, in some sense, immanent, that it should not confront the historical movement in blank externality and that its purposes be realized only in and through that movement. Yet, its purposes are not simply exhausted in, or identical with, the historical details, and it must have enough transcendence to be intelligible as the source of the teleological energy on which the movement as a whole depends. It is not easy to see how, or whether, these requirements can be reconciled.

34. Adorno, *Positivist Dispute*, p. 23; *Negative Dialectics*, p. 144.

35. Adorno, *Positivist Dispute*, pp. 33, 34.

36. The first sentence in this passage is rendered in accordance with *Negative Dialectics*, p. 177. The translation of the second is taken from M. Rosen, 'Critical Theory: Between Ideology and Philosophy', *The Need for Interpretation*, ed. S. Mitchell and M. Rosen, London, Athlone Press, 1983. German text is *Negative Dialektik*, Frankfurt am Main, Suhrkamp, 1966, pp. 176–7. My discussion of the theme in connection with *Negative Dialectics* is influenced by Rosen's treatment.

37. Adorno, *Negative Dialectics*, p. 316.

38. Ibid., p. 38; translation amended, see *Negative Dialektik*, p. 46.

39. T.W. Adorno and M. Horkheimer, *Dialectic of Enlightenment*, trs. J. Cumming, London, Verso, 1979, p. 4.

40. Ibid., p. 3.

41. Ibid., pp. 3-4, 104. In general, the hallmark of formalized reason is the adjustment of details within a framework taken for granted. Thus, as well as instrumentality it is also subsumption under principles; ibid, p. 82. Clearly, this strand in Frankfurt School theory owes more to Weber than to Marx.

42. Adorno, *Negative Dialectics*, p. 118.

43. Ibid., p. 355.

44. Ibid., p. 320.

45. Ibid., p. 320.

46. Adorno and Horkheimer, *Dialectic*, p. 217.

47. K. Marx and F. Engels, *Collected Works*, Volume 5, London, Lawrence and Wishart, 1976, pp. 52, 206. It may be added that Proudhon's partiality to the 'fiction of the person, Society' forms an important part of the case against him; K. Marx, *The Poverty of Philosophy*, Moscow, Progress Publishers, 1955, p. 83; see also ibid., p. 79.

48. K. Marx, *Grundrisse: Foundations of the Critique of Political Economy*, trs. M. Nicholaus, Harmondsworth, Penguin Books/NLR, 1973, p. 94.

49. Adorno, *Positivist Dispute*, p. 128.

Chapter 3

1. H. Marcuse, *Studies in Critical Philosophy*, trs. J. De Bres, London, New Left Books, 1972, p. 26.

2. H. Marcuse, *Eros and Civilization: A Philosophical Inquiry into Freud*, New York, Vintage Books, 1962, p. 4.

3. H. Marcuse, *Negations: Essays in Critical Theory*, Harmondsworth, Penguin Books, 1968, p. 143.

4. H. Marcuse, 'A Note on Dialectic', *The Essential Frankfurt School Reader*, ed. A. Arato and E. Gebhardt, Oxford, Basil Blackwell, 1978, p. 449. This essay was written in 1960 as a new Preface to *Reason and Revolution*. The claim quoted here may be seen as implied by the interpretation of Hegelian 'real possibility' in that work; see H. Marcuse, *Reason and Revolution: Hegel and the Rise of Social Theory*, London, Routledge and Kegan Paul, 1969, pp. 150-2.

5. H. Marcuse, *One-Dimensional Man: Studies in the Ideology of Advanced Industrial Society*, London, Routledge and Kegan Paul, 1964, p. xv.

6. Ibid., pp. xiv-xv.

7. Ibid., p. x.

8. Ibid., pp. xi-xii.

9. Ibid., p. xii.

10. Ibid., p. xiv.

11. Ibid., p. xiii.

12. Ibid., p. 253.

13. Ibid., pp. 254-5.

14. Marcuse, *Studies*, p. 40.

15. Marcuse, *Reason and Revolution*, e.g. pp. 52, 259. For the suggestion that 'Marcuse has a quite Fichtean-Kantian reading of Hegel which stresses the absolute sovereignty of the subject', see D. Kellner, *Herbert Marcuse and the Crisis of Marxism*, Basingstoke, Macmillan, 1984, p. 443, n. 10.

16. Marcuse, *Reason and Revolution*, p. 291; *One-Dimensional Man*, p. 31.

17. Marcuse, *One-Dimensional Man*, p. 252.

18. H. Marcuse, *Counterrevolution and Revolt*, London, Allen Lane; 1972, see successively pp. 16, 71, 21, 41, 82, 31, 93, 25.

19. See, e.g. B. Katz, *Herbert Marcuse and the Art of Liberation: An Intellectual Biography*, London, New Left Books, 1982, p. 165, n. 8.

20. H. Marcuse, *An Essay on Liberation*, Harmondsworth, Penguin Books, 1969, p. 27.

21. H. Marcuse, *Five Lectures: Psychoanalysis, Politics and Utopia*, trs. J. Shapiro and S. Weber, Boston, Mass., Beacon Press, 1970, p. 80.

22. Marcuse, *Negations*, p. xvi.

23. Ibid., p. xx.

24. Marcuse, *Essay*, p. 13.

25. What appear to be exceptions are so only in a verbal sense; see e.g. *Five Lectures*, p. 64. The position that Marcuse there denies is 'utopian' is elsewhere taken by him to be the essence of the utopian strain, i.e. complete reliance on purely 'technical possibility'.

26. 'Protosocialism and Late Capitalism: Towards a Theoretical Synthesis Based on Bahro's Analysis', *Rudolf Bahro: Critical Responses*, ed. U. Wolter, New York, M.E. Sharpe, 1980, p. 26.

27. Marcuse, *Essay*, pp. 58–9, 82.

28. See Kellner, *Herbert Marcuse*, pp. 317–18 and p. 467, n. 95. There is some tension between Kellner's position in the note, where he accepts that in Marcuse's late writings the revolutionary subject becomes revolutionary subjectivity, and his position in the main text, where this is represented as a shift that Marcuse should have made but did not.

29. Marcuse, *Essay*, p. 59.

30. Ibid., p. 31.

31. Ibid., p. 33.

32. Marcuse, 'Protosocialism', p. 27.

33. Ibid., p. 39.

34. Ibid., pp. 28–9.

35. Ibid., p. 32.

36. A useful index to the process is provided by the increasing influence on Marcuse of Adorno's aesthetic theory; for instance, of his obsessive anti-identitarian stance and of his view of autonomous form as the sole carrier of the radical significance of art. See e.g. H. Marcuse, *Counterrevolution*, p. 198; *The Aesthetic Dimension: Towards a Critique of Marxist Aesthetics*, London, Macmillan, 1978, pp. xi, 8, 13.

37. For an introduction to this strategy, see J. Habermas, 'A Postscript to *Knowledge and Human Interests*', *Knowledge and Human Interests*, 2nd edn, trs. J. Shapiro, London, Heinemann, 1978, pp. 351–86. For the transcendental method in general, see B. Stroud, 'Transcendental Arguments', *The Journal of Philosophy*, LXV, no. 9 (1968), pp. 241–56; C. Taylor, 'The Validity of Transcendental Arguments', *Aristotelian Society Proceedings* (1979), pp. 151–65.

Chapter 4

1. T.W. Adorno, *Aesthetic Theory*, London, Routledge and Kegan Paul, 1984, p. 378.

2. T.W. Adorno, *The Positivist Dispute in German Sociology*, trs. G. Adey and D. Frisby, London, Heinemann, 1976, p. 83.

3. Ibid., pp. 96–7.

4. For the commentators see e.g. ibid., p. 124 and for Adorno see ibid., p. 22.

5. Ibid., p. 23.

6. Ibid., p. 27.

7. Ibid., p. 114.

8. Ibid., p. 27.

9. Ibid., pp. 24–5.

10. Ibid., p. 90.

11. Ibid., p. 16.

12. R. Bhaskar, 'Scientific Explanation and Human Emancipation', *Radical Philosophy*, 26 (Autumn 1980), p. 22.

13. Ibid., p. 21. Here, as elsewhere in Bhaskar citations, 'CP' signifies *ceteris paribus*.

14. Ibid., p. 16.

15. It provides at least part of the basis for the persistent theme in Adorno's work of criticism of a society through criticism of its cultural products: 'Musical sociology is social critique accomplished through that of art.' Adorno recognizes, however, that 'the genetic contexts' in this case are extraordinarily complex. *Introduction to the Sociology of Music*, trs. E.B. Ashton, New York, Seabury Press, 1976, pp. 63, 218.

16. Bhaskar, 'Scientific Explanation', p. 23.

17. Ibid., p. 23.

18. Ibid., p. 16.

19. Ibid., p. 25.

20. Ibid., p. 26.

21. Ibid., p. 27.

22. Ibid., pp. 21, 23.

23. Ibid., p. 24.

24. Ibid., p. 25.

25. Ibid., p. 28, n. 1, n. 29.

26. R. Edgley, 'Philosophy', *Marx: The First Hundred Years*, ed. D. McLellan, Oxford, Fontana, 1983, p. 296.

27. R. Edgley, 'Marx's Revolutionary Science', *Issues in Marxist Philosophy*, ed. J. Mepham and D.H. Ruben, vol. 3, Brighton, Harvester Press, 1979, p. 19.

28. Edgley, 'Philosophy', p. 299.

29. R. Edgley, 'Science, Social Science and Socialist Science: Reason as Dialectic', *Radical Philosophy*, 15 (Autumn 1976), p. 6.

30. See e.g. 'What Is Dialectic?', *Conjectures and Refutations*, London, Routledge and Kegan Paul, 1963, pp. 316–17, 322.

31. R. Norman and S. Sayers, *Hegel, Marx and Dialectic: A Debate*, Brighton, Harvester Press, 1980, pp. 50, 51.

32. W. Empson, *Seven Types of Ambiguity*, London, New Directions, 1947, p. 197.

33. Samples of the views of Engels and Lenin may be found in D. Craig, ed. *Marxists on Literature*, Harmondsworth, Penguin Books, 1975, sections 12, 13, 16. For Lukács see *The Historical Novel*, trs. H. and S. Mitchell, Harmondsworth, Penguin Books, 1969, ch. 1.

34. Adorno, *Prisms*, p. 32.

35. Thus, for instance: 'even traditional art perceives all the more, the more deeply it expresses the contradictions present in its own material', *Philosophy of Modern Music*, trs. A.G. Mitchell and W.V. Blomster, London, Sheed and Ward, 1973, p. 135. Indeed, Adorno tends to regard consistency in works of art as a symptom of ideology, which for him always carries the suggestion of 'false consciousness'. See e.g. *Aesthetic Theory*, p. 84.

36. S. Freud, *Jokes and Their Relation to the Unconscious*, trs. J. Strachey, Harmondsworth, Penguin Books, 1976.

37. S. Freud, *The Interpretation of Dreams*, trs. A.A. Brill, London, Allen and Unwin, 1915.

38. Edgley, 'Science', p. 6.

39. R. Edgley, *Reason in Theory and Practice*, London, Hutchinson, 1969.

40. Edgley, 'Philosophy', p. 296n.

41. Edgley, *Reason*, p. 134.

42. Ibid., p. 50.

43. R. Edgley, 'Dialectic: The Contradictions of Colletti, *Critique*, 7 (Winter 1976–7), p. 51.

44. Edgley, *Reason*, p. 110.

45. Ibid., p. 86.

46. Ibid., p. 166.
47. Ibid., p. 121.
48. Ibid., p. 85.
49. Ibid., pp. 85–6.
50. It would also serve to ground Bhaskar's version of the idea: see n. 16 above and corresponding discussion in text.
51. Edgley, 'Science', p. 7.
52. Ibid., p. 7.
53. A more mediated route is taken in J. McCarney, 'Social Science as Dialectic', *Explorations in Knowledge*, 1 (1984), pp. 129–32.
54. Edgley, 'Dialectic', p. 52.
55. R. Edgley, 'Structures Don't Take to the Streets' (unpublished paper), p. 17; I am grateful to Roy Edgley for providing me with a copy of this.
56. Edgley, 'Science', p. 7.
57. Edgley, *Reason*, p. 108.
58. Edgley, 'Structures', p. 13.
59. Edgley, 'Philosophy', p. 269.
60. It would surely strike Bhaskar, for instance, in this way; see his distinction between 'social sciences' which 'abstract from human agency' and have 'social structure' as their object, and the 'social psychological sciences' whose object is 'social interaction', 'Scientific Explanation', p. 18.
61. Edgley, *Reason*, pp. 86–7.
62. Edgley, 'Philosophy', p. 298.
63. Edgley, 'Marx's Revolutionary Science', p. 24; see also R. Edgley, 'Dialectic: A Reply to Keat and Dews', *Radical Philosophy*, 21 (Spring 1979), p. 31.
64. Edgley, 'Philosophy', p. 297.
65. R. Edgley, 'Revolution, Reform and Dialectic', *Marx and Marxism*, ed. G.H.R. Parkinson, Cambridge, Cambridge University Press, 1982, p. 29.

Chapter 5

1. R. Norman and S. Sayers, *Hegel, Marx and Dialectic: A Debate*, Brighton, Harvester Press, 1980, p. 48; the passage is also cited by Sayers, ibid., p. 111.
2. Ibid., p. 48.
3. Ibid., p. 47.
4. Ibid., p. 51.
5. Ibid., p. 51.
6. Ibid., p. 49.
7. Ibid., pp. 60–2.
8. Ibid., pp. 60–4.
9. Ibid., p. 61.
10. See e.g. K. Popper, 'What Is Dialectic?', *Conjectures and Refutations*, London, Routledge and Kegan Paul, 1963, pp. 317–22. Various attempts have, of course, been made to show that contradictions may be admitted into logical systems if their ramifications are restricted; see e.g. N. Rescher and R. Brandom, *The Logic of Inconsistency*, Oxford, Basil Blackwell, 1980, section 6. Such attempts can draw inspiration from quite un-Hegelian sources, e.g. the treatment of contradiction in L. Wittgenstein, *Remarks on the Foundations of Mathematics*, trs. G.E.M. Anscombe, Oxford, Basil Blackwell, 1978, especially part VII.
11. S. Haack, *Deviant Logic*, Cambridge, Cambridge University Press, 1974, p. 36.
12. P.F. Strawson, *Introduction to Logical Theory*, London, Methuen, 1952, p. 3.
13. P. Feyerabend, *Against Method: Outline of an Anarchistic Theory of Knowledge*, London, Verso, 1975, p. 260.
14. P. Feyerabend, *Science in a Free Society*, London, Verso, 1982, p. 36.

15. Feyerabend, *Against Method*, p. 155n.

16. Norman and Sayers, *Hegel, Marx*, p. 63.

17. For confirmation of this in Edgley's case, see above, p. 62.

18. Norman and Sayers, *Hegel, Marx*, p. 66, n. 3.

19. See above, pp. 31–2, and the additional references in n. 47 corresponding.

20. Norman and Sayers, *Hegel, Marx*, p. 140.

21. R. Keat, 'Comment', *Radical Philosophy*, 16 (Spring 1977), p. 48.

22. R. Keat, 'Scientific Socialism: A Positive Delusion?', *Radical Philosophy*, 23 (Winter 1979), p. 22.

23. Ibid., p. 23.

24. R. Edgley, 'Dialectic: A Reply to Keat and Dews', *Radical Philosophy*, 21 (Spring 1979), p. 29.

25. R. Edgley, 'Marx's Revolutionary Science', *Issues in Marxist Philosophy*, ed. J. Mepham and D.H. Ruben, vol. 3, Brighton, Harvester Press, 1979, p. 25.

26. R. Edgley, 'Philosophy', *Marx: The First Hundred Years*, ed. D. McLennan, Oxford, Fontana, 1983, pp. 299–300.

27. Ibid., p. 292.

28. Norman and Sayers, *Hegel, Marx*, p. 63.

29. R. Edgley, *Reason in Theory and Practice*, London, Hutchinson, 1969, p. 91; here Edgley is quoting D.G. Brown, *Action*, London, Allen and Unwin, 1968, 1.9.

30. Edgley, *Reason*, p. 89.

31. Ibid., p. 121.

32. Norman and Sayers, *Hegel, Marx*, p. 60.

33. Compare 'It is not just a conflict between opposing forces, it is also a conflict within a single potentially rational agent. And it is just for that reason that we can describe the behaviour as *self-contradictory, self-defeating, irrational.*' Ibid., p. 61.

34. Keat, 'Scientific Socialism', pp. 22–3.

35. Edgley, 'Philosophy', pp. 290–1.

36. Edgley, 'Revolution', p. 27.

37. Edgley, 'Dialectic: A Reply', p. 31.

38. Edgley, 'Marx's Revolutionary Science', p. 26.

39. Ibid., p. 17.

40. Norman and Sayers, *Hegel, Marx*, p. 135.

41. Ibid., pp. 135, 137–8.

42. Ibid., p. 170.

43. Ibid., p. 173, n. 12.

44. Ibid., p. 139.

45. Ibid., p. 139. This is Sayers's way of making the point; for Norman's acknowledgement of it, see ibid., p. 173, n. 12.

46. Ibid., p. 170.

Chapter 6

1. K. Marx and F. Engels, *Collected Works*, Volume 5, London, Lawrence and Wishart, 1976, p. 323.

2. K. Marx and F. Engels, *Selected Correspondence*, London, Lawrence and Wishart, n.d., p. 182.

3. K. Marx, *Critique of the Gotha Programme*, Moscow, Progress Publishers, 1971, p. 18.

4. Marx and Engels, *Selected Correspondence*, pp. 375–6.

5. Marx and Engels, *Collected Works*, Volume 5, p. 49.

6. K. Marx, *Early Writings*, Harmondsworth, Penguin Books/NLR, 1975, p. 415.

7. K. Marx, *The Civil War in France*, Moscow, Progress Publishers, 1972, p. 58.

8. K. Marx and F. Engels, *The Communist Manifesto*, Harmondsworth, Penguin Books, 1967, p. 95.

9. Marx and Engels, *Selected Correspondence*, pp. 410–11.

10. Marx, *Early Writings*, pp. 207, 244, 248, 246.

11. It is employed in *The German Ideology*, though with reference to, and in the course of a polemic against, the work of Max Stirner; *Collected Works*, Volume 5, p. 377.

12. The main German terms standardly translated as 'political economy' are *National-ökonomie* and *politische Ökonomie*. Nineteenth-century political economy differed significantly in subject-matter and methodology from neo-classical and other forms of modern economics. It was defined by the *Encyclopaedia Britannica* (1885), following J.B. Say, as the 'science of the production, distribution and consumption of wealth', and succinctly by Marx as the 'science of wealth', *Economic and Philosophic Manuscripts of 1844*, Moscow, Progress Publishers, 1974, p. 104. Incorporating more of his own distinctive standpoint, he defines 'English political economy' as 'the scientific reflection of the state of the economy of England', *Early Writings*, p. 406. Say's work was, of course, well known to Marx and usually dealt with scathingly; e.g. 'In no science other than political economy does there prevail such a combination of great self-importance with the mouthing of elementary commonplaces. For instance, J.B. Say sets himself up as a judge of crises because he knows that a commodity is a product.' K. Marx, *Capital*, Volume 1, trs. B. Fowkes, Harmondsworth, Penguin Books/ NLR, 1976, pp. 209–10, n. 24. The *Encyclopaedia Britannica*'s definition is quoted in the editor's Preface to ed. T. Carver, *Karl Marx: Texts on Method*, Oxford, Blackwell, 1975, p. 6; see this source of further discussion.

13. The impression is probably strongest in K. Marx and F. Engels, *The Holy Family, or Critique of Critical Criticism*, Moscow, Progress Publishers, 1975. This work is foreshadowed in a letter from Marx to Feuerbach of 11 August, 1844: 'I am going to publish a short booklet attacking this aberration of criticism'; K. Marx and F. Engels, *Collected Works*, Volume 3, London, Lawrence and Wishart, 1975, p. 356.

14. Marx, *Early Writings*, p. 251.

15. Ibid., p. 158.

16. See *The Fiery Brook: Selected Writings of Ludwig Feuerbach*, trs. Z. Hanfi, New York, Anchor Books, 1972, p. 86; for discussion, see H. Marcuse, *Reason and Revolution: Hegel and the Rise of Social Theory*, London, Routledge and Kegan Paul, 1969, pp. 267–73, and M. Wartofsky, *Feuerbach*, Cambridge, Cambridge University Press, 1977, especially pp. 92–4, 192–93, 342.

17. *Capital*, Volume 1, p. 638 n.

18. G.W.F. Hegel, *Hegel: Texts and Commentary*, trs. and ed. W. Kaufmann, New York, Anchor Books, 1966, p. 10; *Phänomenologie des Geistes*, Frankfurt, Suhrkamp, 1970, p. 13.

19. Hegel, *Hegel: Texts*, p. 90; *Phänomenologie*, p. 56.

20. Another version of the tendency is found in F.H. Bradley's 'My Station and Its Duties', *Ethical Studies*, Oxford, Clarendon Press, 1927, pp. 160–206.

21. Within the ranks of 'Marxism' the distaste is perhaps most strongly marked in the work of Lukács and Adorno, in most other respects very different thinkers.

22. G.W.F. Hegel, *Phenomenology of Spirit*, trs. A.V. Miller, Oxford, Clarendon Press, 1979, pp. 50–1.

23. See e.g. K.R. Dove, 'Hegel's Phenomenological Method', ed. W.E. Steinkraus, *New Studies in Hegel's Philosophy*, New York, Holt, Rinehart and Winston, 1971, pp. 34–56; C. Taylor, *Hegel*, Cambridge, Cambridge University Press, 1975, part 2; G. Rose *Hegel Contra Sociology*, London, Athlone, 1981, ch. 2.

24. Hegel, *Phenomenology*, p. 50.

25. Ibid., pp. 52–3.

26. K. Marx, *The Poverty of Philosophy*, Moscow, Progress Publishers, 1955, p. 96.

27. Ibid., p. 97.

28. Ibid., pp. 98–9.

29. An introduction to the possibilities on each side is provided by the Norman–Sayers debate. R. Norman and S. Sayers, *Hegel, Marx and Dialectic: A Debate*, Brighton, Harvester Press, 1980.

30. T.W. Adorno, *Against Epistemology: A Metacritique*, trs. W. Domingo, Oxford,

Basil Blackwell, 1982, pp. 78–80; *Negative Dialectics*, trs. E. Ashton, London, Routledge and Kegan Paul, 1973, pp. 151–3.

31. Hegel, *Hegel's Logic*, trs. W. Wallace, Oxford, Clarendon Press, 1975, pp. 116–17.

32. This is so constant a refrain that citation seems superfluous. Indeed, it is a source of embarrassment to commentators who tend to feel with Kaufmann that 'Hegel often uses "necessary" quite illicitly as the negation of "utterly arbitrary"', Hegel, *Hegel: Texts*, p. 11.

33. 'The dialectical movement, this way that generates itself', Hegel, *Hegel: Texts*, p. 98; '[the] self-moving soul, the principle of all natural and spiritual life', G.W.F. Hegel, *Science of Logic*, trs. A.V. Miller, London, Allen and Unwin, 1969, p. 56; compare 'Movement and "self-movement" (this NB! arbitrary (independent), spontaneous, *internally necessary* movement), "change", "movement and vitality", "the principle of all self-movement", "impulse" (Trieb) to "movement" and to "activity" – the opposite to "dead Being" – who would believe that this is the core of "Hegelianism", of abstract and abstrusen (ponderous, absurd?) Hegelianism??', V.I. Lenin, *Collected Works*, Volume 38, London, Lawrence and Wishart, 1972, p. 141.

34. G.W.F. Hegel, *Philosophy of Right*, trs. T.M. Knox, Oxford, Oxford University Press, 1967, pp. 34–5.

35. This applies not merely to the writings of Bhaskar, Norman and Edgley, discussed above, but to other recent contributions to the literature; for discussion of some of them see J. McCarney, 'Recent Interpretations of Ideology', *Economy and Society*, Volume 14, no. 1 (February 1985), especially section 3.

36. This charge is developed from a somewhat different standpoint in Sayers's contributions to Norman and Sayers, *Hegel: Marx*, see especially pp. 126, 131, 135–8.

37. I. Kant, *Fundamental Principles of the Metaphysics of Ethics*, trs. T.K. Abbot, London, Longmans, 1955, p. 11; Marx, *Early Writings*, p. 252.

Chapter 7

1. K. Marx, *Early Writings*, Harmondsworth, Penguin Books/NLR, 1975, p. 247.

2. Ibid., p. 209.

3. Ibid., p. 206.

4. K. Marx, *Capital*, Volume 1, trs. B. Fowkes, Harmondsworth, Penguin Books/NLR, 1976, p. 92; another much-cited instance occurs in K. Marx, *Critique of the Gotha Programme*, Moscow, Progress Publishers, 1971, p. 16.

5. K. Marx, *The Civil War in France*, Moscow, Progress Publishers, 1972, p. 58.

6. G.W.F. Hegel, *Hegel's Logic*, trs. W. Wallace, Oxford, Clarendon Press, 1975, p. 117.

7. G.W.F. Hegel, *Philosophy of Right*, trs. T.M. Knox, Oxford, Oxford University Press, 1967, p. 10.

8. See M.J. Inwood, *Hegel*, London, Routledge and Kegan Paul, 1983, ch. XI, sections 7–10.

9. K. Marx and F. Engels, *The Communist Manifesto*, Harmondsworth, Penguin, 1967, pp. 114–15.

10. K. Marx, *The Poverty of Philosophy*, Moscow, Progress Publishers, 1955, pp. 109–10.

11. K. Marx, *Karl Marx: Early Texts*, trs. D. McLellan, Oxford, Basil Blackwell, 1972, p. 7.

12. Hegel, *Philosophy of Right*, p. 10.

13. Hegel, *Hegel's Logic*, p. 9.

14. W. Kaufmann, 'The Hegel Myth and Its Method', *Hegel: A Collection of Critical Essays*, ed. A. MacIntyre, Notre Dame, University of Notre Dame Press, 1976, p. 37.

15. For the enduring significance for Marx of the Hegelian distinction between the 'real' or 'existent' and the 'actual', see S. Avineri, *The Social and Political Thought of Karl Marx*, Cambridge, Cambridge University Press, 1968, p. 106, and T. Ball, 'Marxian

Science and Positivist Politics', *After Marx*, ed. T. Ball and J. Farr, Cambridge, Cambridge University Press, 1984, p. 242.

16. Hegel, *Philosophy of Right*, p. 12.

17. Marx, *Early Writings*, pp. 160, 163, 185, 193, 196, 197.

18. Ibid., pp. 146–7.

19. Hegel, *Philosophy of Right*, pp. 151–2. On the significance of the working class for Hegel's social theory see B. Cullen, *Hegel's Social and Political Thought: An Introduction*, Dublin, Gill and Macmillan, 1979.

20. To take an obvious, but crucial, point, much emphasized in Marx's critique, Hegel cannot, after the very earliest period of his thought, envisage the abolition of private property. Once arrived at, he never departs from the conviction that 'The fate of property has become too powerful for us to tolerate reflections on it, to find its abolition thinkable', *Early Theological Writings*, trs. T.M. Knox, Chicago, University of Chicago Press, 1948, p. 221. Hegel had, of course, theoretical grounds, connected with the idea of property as the necessary embodiment of freedom and personality, for his stance, *Philosophy of Right*, paras. 41–71.

21. G.W.F. Hegel, *Phenomenology of Spirit*, trs. A.V. Miller, Oxford, Clarendon Press, 1979, p. 49.

22. K. Marx, *Economic and Philosophic Manuscripts of 1844*, Moscow, Progress Publishers, 1974, p. 127.

23. See e.g. S. Haack, *Philosophy of Logics*, Cambridge, Cambridge University Press, 1978, ch. 6; R. Edgley, *Reason in Theory and Practice*, London, Hutchinson, 1969, pp. 169–76.

24. L. Wittgenstein, *Philosophical Investigations*, trs. G.E.M. Anscombe, New York, Macmillan, 1968, p. 161. For a discussion of the issues in a Wittgensteinian framework, see P. Winch, *The Idea of a Social Science*, London, Routledge and Kegan Paul, 1958, ch. 5, and for a discussion in a Hegelian framework, see C. Taylor, 'Hegel and the Philosophy of Action', *Hegel's Philosophy of Action*, ed. L.S. Stepelevich and D. Lamb, Atlantic Highlands, Humanities Press, 1983, pp. 1–18.

25. In particular, perhaps, by those drawing some inspiration from Durkheim.

26. J. Elster, *Making Sense of Marx*, Cambridge, Cambridge University Press, 1985, pp. 6, 359, 363.

27. Ibid., p. 426, n. 1.

28. Ibid., pp. 35, 116.

29. Ibid., p. 434.

30. K. Marx and F. Engels, *Selected Works*, Volume 1, Moscow, Foreign Languages Publishing House, 1958, p. 370.

31. For further discussion, see J. McCarney, *The Real World of Ideology*, Brighton, Harvester Press, 1980, pp. 36–7, 99–100, 118; 'Recent Interpretations of Ideology', *Economy and Society*, vol. 14, no. 1 (February 1985), section 2.

32. McCarney, *Real World*, pp. 115–21.

33. Marx, *Capital*, Volume 1, p. 97.

34. Marx and Engels, *Selected Works*, Volume 1, p. 386.

35. K. Marx, *Das Kapital*, Band 1, Frankfurt, Ullstein, 1969, p. 23.

36. Marx, *Poverty*, p. 150.

37. K. Marx and F. Engels, *Selected Correspondence*, London, Lawrence and Wishart, n.d., p. 328.

38. K. Marx and F. Engels, *Collected Works*, Volume 5, London, Lawrence and Wishart, 1976, p. 469.

39. Marx, *Poverty*, p. 150.

40. F. Engels, *Anti-Dühring: Herr Eugen Dühring's Revolution in Science*, London, Lawrence and Wishart, 1975, p. 151.

41. G. Lukács, *History and Class Consciousness*, trs. R. Livingstone, London, Merlin Press, 1971, p. 29.

42. Ibid., p. 27.

43. For a discussion of the role of theoretical concepts as depicted in modern philosophy of science, and of Marx's compatibility with these findings, see J. McCarney, 'Social

Science as Dialectic', *Explorations in Knowledge*, 1 (1984), pp. 127–53.
    44. Lukács, *History*, p. 171.

Chapter 8

    1. K. Marx, *Capital*, Volume 1, trs. B. Bowkes, Harmondsworth, Penguin Books/
NLR, 1976, p. 102.
    2. Compare K. Marx, *Early Writings*, Harmondsworth, Penguin Books/NLR, 1975,
p. 65; K. Marx and F. Engels, *The Holy Family or Critique of Critical Criticism*, Moscow,
Progress Publishers, 1975, pp. 71, 93–4, 100, 161.
    3. G.W.F. Hegel, *Lectures on the Philosophy of World History: Introduction*, trs. H.
Nisbet, Cambridge, Cambridge University Press, 1975, p. 27.
    4. There are, of course, various 'anthropological' and 'non-metaphysical' readings of
Hegel which interpret him on quite different lines from Marx and the mainstream; see e.g.
K. Hartmann, 'Hegel: A Non-Metaphysical View', *Hegel: A Collection of Critical Essays*,
ed. MacIntyre, University of Notre Dame Press, 1976 pp. 101–24; and R.C. Solomon, *In
the Spirit of Hegel*, New York, Oxford University Press, 1983.
    5. K. Marx and F. Engels, *Selected Correspondence*, London, Lawrence and Wishart,
n.d., p. 379.
    6. Here again one may have doubts as to whether in following Marx one is doing full
justice to Hegel. Thus, for instance, it is worth noting that the dramatic pronouncement
quoted above in the text is immediately followed by some less dramatic qualifications. For
Hegel appears to recognize another kind of proof, not derived from philosophy and
brought to history as a presupposition but, lying 'in the study of world history itself'. Hegel,
Lectures, p. 28. Moreover, he warns that the statements quoted are not 'to be regarded
simply as prior assumptions, but ... as the *result* of the ensuing inquiry', and he insists that
in this inquiry 'we must be sure to take history as it is; in other words, we must proceed
historically and empirically'. Ibid., p. 29. For the conception of two kinds of proof here,
see 'Taylor, Hegel and the Philosophy of Action', *Hegel's Philosophy of Action*, ed. L.S.
Stepelevich and D. Lamb, Atlantic Highlands, Humanities Press, 1983, pp. 219–20.
    7. K. Marx, *A Contribution to the Critique of Political Economy*, Moscow, Progress
Publishers, 1970, pp. 20–2.
    8. Ibid., p. 21.
    9. It has been argued that Marx had tactical reasons, having to do with fear of the
Prussian censor, for not using the terms 'class' or 'class struggle' in the 1859 Preface; see
A.M. Prinz, 'Background and Ulterior Motive of Marx's "Preface" of 1859', *Journal of the
History of Ideas*, 30 (1969), pp. 437–50.
    10. G.W.F. Hegel, *Hegel: Texts and Commentary*, trs. and ed. W. Kaufmann, New
York, Anchor Books, 1966, p. 34.
    11. Marx, *Capital*, Volume 1, p. 284.
    12. K. Marx, *Economic and Philosophic Manuscripts of 1844*, Moscow, Progress
Publishers, 1974, p. 131.
    13. See e.g. special issue of *Theory and Society*, 11 (1982).
    14. Marx, *Capital*, Volume 1, pp. 878–9.
    15. Ibid., pp. 883–4.
    16. Ibid., pp. 884–5.
    17. Ibid., p. 876.
    18. Ibid., p. 303, n. 18.
    19. K. Marx, *Theories of Surplus Value*, Part 2, London, Lawrence and Wishart, 1969,
p. 528.
    20. See reference in previous note, and the discussion in J. Elster, *Making Sense of
Marx*, Cambridge, Cambridge University Press, 1985, especially p. 276.
    21. Marx, *Capital*, Volume 1, pp. 432–5.
    22. Ibid., p. 617; K. Marx and F. Engels, *The Communist Manifesto*, Harmondsworth,
Penguin, 1967, p. 83.

23. 'Marx did not believe that any technical change occurred in pre-capitalist societies.' Elster, *Making Sense*, p. 250. Elster's merits as a commentator are, unfortunately, flawed by a tendency to attribute to Marx more extreme and implausible views than his own documentation shows are warranted. For further examples and discussion, see J. McCarney 'A New Marxist Paradigm?', *Radical Philosophy*, 43 (Summer 1986), pp. 29–31.

24. In considering these issues, one should perhaps bear in mind the way in which the dynamic, and, hence, ultimately progressive, character of capitalism tends to provoke Marx's most exalted rhetoric. *The Communist Manifesto* illustrates this tendency, as do his writings on British rule in India; K. Marx and F. Engels, *Selected Works*, Volume 1, Moscow, Foreign Languages Publishing House, 1958, pp. 345–58.

25. E.O. Wright, 'Giddens's Critique of Marxism', *New Left Review*, 138 (March–April 1983), p. 28.

26. 'Even the ordinary, run-of-the-mill historian who believes and professes that his attitude is entirely receptive, that he is dedicated to the facts, is by no means passive in his thinking; he brings his categories with him, and they influence his vision of the data he has before him.' Hegel, *Lectures*, p. 29.

27. K. Marx, *Capital*, Volume 3, London, Lawrence and Wishart, 1974, p. 232.

28. Marx, *Early Writings*, p. 208.

29. Most notably, perhaps, by G. Lukács: it forms a central theme of *History and Class Consciousness*, trs. R. Livingstone, London, Merlin Press, 1971.

Chapter 9

1. K. Marx and F. Engels, *The Holy Family, or Critique of Critical Criticism*, Moscow, Progress Publishers, 1975, p. 44.

2. Ibid., p. 43.

3. Ibid., p. 44.

4. Ibid., p. 51.

5. K. Marx, *Economic and Philosophic Manuscripts of 1844*, Moscow, Progress Publishers, 1974, p. 63.

6. K. Marx and F. Engels, *Collected Works*, Volume 5, London, Lawrence and Wishart, 1976, p. 87.

7. Ibid., p. 219. For a powerful statement of the inability of the proletarian to satisfy 'even the needs that he has in common with all human beings', 'the needs arising directly from his human nature', see ibid., p. 289.

8. K. Marx, *Capital*, Volume 1, trs. B. Fowkes, Harmondsworth, Penguin Books/ NLR, 1976, p. 799.

9. It must be admitted that the translation used in the text overdoes things in referring to a 'dialectical inversion' of the means for the development of production where the original has 'alle Mittel zur Entwicklung der Produktion … umschlagen'; *Das Kapital*, Band 1, Frankfurt, Ullstein, 1969, p. 595. Nevertheless, as Martin Nicolaus makes clear in his 'Foreword' to *Grundrisse*, *Umschlag* is itself a technical term of dialectics for Hegel and Marx; *Grundrisse: Foundations of the Critique of Political Economy*, trs. M. Nicolaus, Harmondsworth, Penguin Books/NLR, 1973, p. 32. Moreover, the strongly dialectical tone of the particular passage is incontestable, and any general doubts about the persistence of this tone beyond the early writings should have been settled by the publication of *Grundrisse*. On the importance of the idea of human nature in the mature Marx, see N. Geras, *Marx and Human Nature: Refutation of a Legend*, London, Verso, 1983; this work is discussed below, Chapter 10.

10. In *Critique of the Gotha Programme*, Marx associates the 'iron law' with Lassalle, and attacks it as a 'truly outrageous retrogression' in the light of a more recent 'scientific understanding' of wages. He adds: 'It is as if, among slaves who have at last got behind the secret of slavery and broken out in rebellion, a slave still in thrall to obsolete notions were to inscribe on the programme of the rebellion: Slavery must be abolished because the feeding of slaves in the system of slavery cannot exceed a certain low maximum.' *Critique*

of the Gotha Programme, Moscow, Progress Publishers, 1971, pp. 22–3. In *The Poverty of Philosophy* he had declared 'The natural price of labour is no other than the wage minimum.' *The Poverty of Philosophy*, Moscow, Progress Publishers, 1955, p. 44. In a footnote in the 1885 German edition, Engels comments that this thesis 'was first put forward by me', and adds: 'As seen here, Marx at that time accepted the thesis. Lassalle took it over from both of us.' *Poverty*, pp. 44–5n.

11. Marx, *Capital*, Volume 1, p. 798.

12. Ibid., p. 753.

13. That is, not in the strict Ricardian sense of the amount of labour contained in the use-values which the payment commands.

14. K. Marx, 'Wage Labour and Capital', *Selected Works*, Volume 1, Moscow, Foreign Languages Publishing House, 1958, pp. 96–8.

15. K. Marx, 'Inaugural Address of the Working Men's International Association', Ibid., p. 381.

16. Marx, *Grundrisse*, p. 597.

17. For data on trends in wages, see H.P. Brown and S.V. Hopkins, *A Perspective of Wages and Prices*, London, Methuen, 1981.

18. K. Marx, *Early Writings*, Harmondsworth, Penguin Books/NLR, 1975, p. 256.

19. 'Review: May to October', K. Marx and F. Engels, *Collected Works*, Volume 10, London, Lawrence and Wishart, 1978, p. 510.

20. Letter to A. Cluss of 22 April 1852, K. Marx and F. Engels, *Collected Works*, Volume 39, London, Lawrence and Wishart, 1983, pp. 83–4.

21. K. Marx and F. Engels, *Collected Works*, Volume 17, London, Lawrence and Wishart, 1983, pp. 92–3.

22. I. Mészáros, 'Marx's "Social Revolution" and the Division of Labour', *Radical Philosophy*, 44 (Autumn 1986), p. 15.

23. The tendency finds expression in numerous passages. Thus, for instance: 'the sale of commodities, the realization of commodity-capital and thus of surplus-value, is limited, not by the consumer requirements of society in general, but by the consumer requirements of a society in which the vast majority are always poor and must always remain poor'. K. Marx, *Capital*, Volume 2, London, Lawrence and Wishart, 1956, p. 320. See, to similar effect, *Capital*, Volume 3, London, Lawrence and Wishart, 1974, pp. 244–5.

24. Once again, *Grundrisse*, is a decisive text here, and Nicolaus's 'Foreword' provides a convenient, brief introduction to the issues; Marx, *Grundrisse*, pp. 50–1.

25. See above, p. 26.

26. Marx, *1844 Manuscripts*, p. 68.

27. Marx, *Capital*, Volume 1, p. 375.

28. Marx, *Early Writing*, p. 256; *1844 Manuscripts*, p. 73.

29. See above, pp. 94, 150.

30. The obvious reference is, once again, the Frankfurt School: see discussion in D. Held, *Introduction to Critical Theory: Horkheimer to Habermas*, London, Hutchinson, 1980, part 1.

31. Marx, *Capital*, Volume 3, p. 820.

32. Marx, *1844 Manuscripts*, pp. 68, 135, 134.

33. Ibid., p. 134.

34. Ibid., p. 94.

35. Ibid., p. 95.

36. Ibid., p. 89.

37. Ibid., p. 92.

38. Ibid., p. 98.

39. Ibid., pp. 98, 136.

40. Ibid., p. 89.

41. Ibid., p. 98.

42. It also fits the pattern that the theme should surface strongly now and again, as in the remark in a letter of 1861 to Lassalle that Darwin's book *On the Origin of Species* serves 'as a natural-scientific basis for the class struggle in history'. K. Marx and F. Engels,

Selected Correspondence, London, Lawrence and Wishart, n.d., p. 151. Perhaps the best evidence for Marx's sustained interest in these matters is provided by the ethnological notebooks; see *The Ethnological Notebooks of Karl Marx*, ed. L. Krader, Assen, Van Gorcum, 1972.

43. This is the title of the first chapter; H. Marcuse, *An Essay on Liberation*, Harmondsworth, Penguin Books, 1969, p. 17. Some other figures in the Marxist tradition should be mentioned in connection with the concern for 'biological foundations'. Chief among them is Engels: this concern is integral to his project of a 'dialectics of nature'. Some issues of great interest from the standpoint of the present discussion are dealt with in his essay on 'The Part Played by Labour in the Transition from Ape to Man'; K. Marx and F. Engels, *Selected Works*, Volume 2, Moscow, Foreign Languages Publishing House, 1958, pp. 80–92. Among our contemporaries it is Sebastiano Timpanaro who should have pride of place; see S. Timpanaro, *On Materialism*, trs. L. Garner, London, Verso, 1980. An acute sense of the importance of these issues is shown in P. Anderson, *In the Tracks of Historical Materialism*, London, Verso, 1983; see especially the discussion of the idea that the major challenge to Marxism will in future come from 'naturalism', pp. 81–4.

44. Marcuse, *Essay*, p. 25.

45. Ibid., pp. 14, 20, 57.

46. Ibid., p. 91.

47. Ibid., pp. 20–1.

48. Ibid., p. 27.

49. Ibid., pp. 59–60.

50. Marx, *1844 Manuscripts*, p. 100.

Chapter 10

1. The basic understanding of the substantive, defining traits of Western Marxism employed in this chapter is derived from P. Anderson, *Considerations on Western Marxism*, London, Verso, 1976. The obvious divergence from Anderson is that *History and Class Consciousness* is interpreted here as a major text of the classical tradition while he locates it within Western Marxism. The work does not, however, meet the conditions he has convincingly laid down. In particular, it cannot reasonably be regarded as the product of a 'structural divorce' from political practice, nor of 'political isolation and despair', nor does it come anywhere near exemplifying a 'consistent pessimism'. Anderson, *Considerations*, pp. 29, 42–3. For further discussion, see J. McCarney, *The Real World of Ideology*, Brighton, Harvester Press, 1980, pp. 129–32. The problem with Anderson's placing of this text is that it suggests a non-existent measure of continuity between classical and Western Marxism. Hence, it may lend encouragement to the widely accepted view of the latter as essentially a Lukács-inspired engagement with the central philosophical tasks of the Marxist tradition. For a statement of this, see A. Arato and P. Breines, *The Young Lukács and the Origins of Western Marxism*, London, Pluto, 1979. It is strongly implied by the present study that such a view is an agreeable fantasy, and that Western Marxism is better understood as a historic evasion of those tasks, owing nothing of substance to Lukács. The archetype of the current spate of 'farewells' is A. Gorz, *Farewell to the Working Class*, London, Pluto, 1982.

2. K. Korsch, *Marxism and Philosophy*, trs. F. Halliday, London, NLB, 1970, p. 42.

3. G. Lukács, *History and Class Consciousness*, trs. R. Livingstone, London, Merlin Press, 1971, p. 3.

4. M. Horkheimer, *Critical Theory: Selected Essays*, trs. M.J. O' Connell *et al.*, New York, Herder and Herder, 1972, pp. 215, 216, 231.

5. Ibid., pp. 213, 242, 212.

6. Ibid., pp. 237–8.

7. Reported in D. Kellner, *Herbert Marcuse and the Crisis of Marxism*, Basingstoke, Macmillan, 1984, p. 69.

8. The chief reason he gives for being 'forced back' to this standpoint is that 'the theory developed by Marx and Engels' can no longer retain the significance it had for them: 'This results from the disposition of men who, as is well known, can no longer be aroused by theory in any way, and results from the form of reality which excludes the possibility of such actions which for Marx seemed to be just around the corner.' T.W. Adorno, *The Positivist Dispute*, in *German Sociology*, trs. G. Adey and D. Frisby, London, Heinemann, 1976, pp. 128–9.

9. T.W. Adorno, 'Resignation', *Telos*, 35 (Spring 1978), p. 166.

10. The analytical movement is, of course, standardly assumed to have its origins in Moore and Russell's break with the British Idealism of their time.

11. N. Geras, *Marx and Human Nature: Refutation of a Legend*, London, Verso, 1983, p. 19.

12. Ibid., pp. 98, 100.

13. Ibid., p. 71.

14. Ibid., pp. 83–4.

15. It may be useful to cite some further evidence concerning his views on the specific subject of 'morality'. To the proletarian, according to *The Communist Manifesto*, 'Law, morality, religion are ... so many bourgeois prejudices, behind which lurk in ambush just as many bourgeois interests.' K. Marx and F. Engels, *Communist Manifesto*, Harmondsworth, Penguin Books, 1967, p. 92. *The German Ideology* declares: 'The communists do not preach *morality* at all', and later speaks of the contradiction between the bourgeoisie and the proletariat as having, in giving rise to communist and socialist views, 'shattered the basis of all morality'. K. Marx and F. Engels, *Collected Works*, Volume 5, London, Lawrence and Wishart, 1976, pp. 247, 419. Finally, there is Vorländer's testimony that Marx 'burst out laughing every time anyone spoke to him of morality'. Quoted in L. Goldmann, 'Is There a Marxist Sociology?', *Radical Philosophy*, 1 (January 1972), p. 17.

16. N. Geras, 'The Controversy About Marx and Justice', *New Left Review*, 150 (March/April 1985), p. 62.

17. Ibid., pp. 47, 54, 55.

18. Ibid., pp. 84–5.

19. Ibid., p. 62.

20. Geras, *Marx and Human Nature*, p. 84.

21. This claim should be elaborated a little, at least for the two writers mentioned. Smith's account of the condition of the 'labouring poor' in the capitalism of his time is frequently condemnatory, rising at times to a moral indictment; A. Smith, *An Inquiry into the Nature and Causes of the Wealth of Nations*, Oxford, Clarendon Press, 1976, see especially V. i. f and V. i. g. His view of the class of employers is strongly normative: 'an order of men, whose interest is never exactly the same with that of the publick, who have generally an interest to deceive and even to oppress the publick, and who accordingly have, upon many occasions, both deceived and oppressed it'. Ibid., p. 267. For Keynes's opinion of 'the outstanding faults of the economic society in which we live', see J.M. Keynes, *The General Theory of Employment, Interest and Money*, London, Macmillan, 1973, ch. 24. More generally, he has expressed the view that although capitalism is efficient, 'in itself it is in many ways extremely objectionable', and adds: 'Our problem is to work out a social organization which shall be as efficient as possible without offending our notion of a satisfactory way of life.' *Laissez-Faire and Communism*, New York, New Republic, 1926, p. 77.

It may be useful to add here a list of some of the questions normally run together, or not adequately differentiated, in the contemporary debate over Marx and morality. Without any attempt to be exhaustive, the more important ones may be grouped as follows:

(1) Does Marx hold, and express in his writings, personal normative views? If so, are these specifically 'moral' views, or are they normative in some other way? Do they amount to something like a systematic and consciously held set of beliefs?

(2) Does he hold, and express, the view that capitalism is 'immoral', or that it is normatively defective in some other way? If he does, is it so in virtue of being unjust, or unfree, or failing to develop human potential, or to promote human well-being or self-realization, or in virtue of all of these, or in virtue of failing to meet some other standards?

(3) Does he think that normative, and specifically moral, ideas and judgements play a significant role in history, especially in bringing about social change? Does he think that they have such a role to play in the overthrow of capitalism?

(4) Does he think that socialist theory should have a normative dimension, drawing on the force for change of those ideas and judgements? Does he think that the theory should be essentially a normative, or moral, indictment of capitalism? Did he attempt to build such a dimension into his own theory, or does he think of it as such an indictment? If not, does he conceive of it as being practical and revolutionary in some other way?

The substance of the contemporary debate is mainly provided by the questions in groups (1) and (2), and the answers tend to be taken, usually implicitly, as decisive for those in groups (3) and (4). It is easy to see that this is in general terms an illicit procedure. Thus, one may readily combine a basically affirmative set of answers to the first two groups with either affirmative or negative answers to the others. It is certain that Marx, 'like just about everyone else', holds normative, and indeed moral, views, and that they are to be found in his writings. It is also true that he tends to be scathing about the historical effectivity of such views, and, specifically, about their value for the socialist cause. Whenever he addresses the questions in group (4) he emphatically denies that socialist theory should have a moral or normative dimension or character. Yet he holds with equal emphasis that his own theory has a practical and revolutionary significance. From one point of view the present study is an attempt to demonstrate that his position on these matters is entirely coherent and defensible.

22. Kellner, *Herbert Marcuse*, p. 39. It may be useful to add a third illustration, providing another perspective on the topic. This time it is from a work of pure scholarship with ostensibly no theoretical axes to grind. Allen Oakley's *The Making of Marx's Critical Theory* is subtitled *A Bibliographical Analysis*, London, Routledge and Kegan Paul, 1983. The object for analysis is presented right at the start as consisting of the phases of 'Marx's evolving critical theory of capitalist society' (p. ix). More fully specified, the focus is to be his 'critico-theoretical writings', those 'in which the analyses are the result of Marx's preoccupying intellectual activity, namely the pursuit and propagation of a *critical* comprehension of the nature and operations of capitalism as a social system that functions through human inequity and oppression' (p. 1). These formulations are offered as initial definitions of the task, and may be assumed to reflect the preconceptions Oakley brings to it. The argument of the present study suggests that, on a literal reading of the definitions, the task is not one that could detain a bibliographer for long. Fortunately, Oakley also reveals early in the book the true substance of his concerns. Shortly after the first formulation cited above he refers to the importance of an appreciation of the bibliographical framework of 'Marx's critique of capitalism and political economy' (p. x). Once introduced the project of the critique of political economy quickly takes over the field, and supplies all the material Oakley needs for his bibliographical labours. Thus, the task he actually discharges may be described simply as one of documenting the evolution of Marx's critique of political economy. The value of the results is not seriously affected by the misconceived rubric under which he seeks to subsume them. In practice it is not difficult to discount such attempts in order to obtain the benefits of the scholarship. The case is, nevertheless, significant for showing that the most scrupulous textual inquiry may be imposed on by the prevailing theoretical climate and for confirming the general character of the climate that currently obtains in Marx studies.

23. Ibid., p. 387, n. 6.

24. G. Lukács, *Lenin: A Study on the Unity of His Thought*, trs. N. Jacobs, London, Verso, 1970, p. 9.

25. See above, p. 5.

26. K. Marx, *Capital*, Volume 1, trs. B. Fowkes, Harmondsworth, Penguin Books/ NLR, 1976, p. 103.

27. Lukács, *Lenin*, p. 11; *Werke*, Band 2, Neuwied, Luchterhand, 1968, pp. 523–4.

28. For discussion, see McCarney, *Real World*, especially pp. 41–60.

29. Trotsky offers this version of the basic idea; 'Marxism considers itself the conscious expression of the unconscious historical process. But the "unconscious" process, in the historico-philosophical sense of the term – not in the psychological – coincides with its

conscious expression only at its highest point, when the masses, by sheer elemental pressure, break through the social routine and give victorious expression to the deepest needs of historical development. And at such moments the highest theoretical consciousness of the epoch merges with the immediate action of those oppressed masses who are farthest away from theory.' L. Trotsky, *My Life: An Attempt at an Autobiography*, New York, Pathfinder Press, 1970, p. 334.

30. For illustrations and further discussion of this tendency, see J. McCarney, 'Recent Interpretations of Ideology', *Economy and Society*, vol. 14, no. 1 (February 1985), especially Section 3.

31. I. Mészáros, 'Marx's "Social Revolution" and the Division of Labour', *Radical Philosophy*, 44 (Autumn 1986), pp. 17–18.

32. Quoted ibid., p. 16.

33. Ibid., p. 17.

34. Ibid., p. 16. Mészáros goes so far as to charge Marx with resorting to 'equivocation' to reconcile this contradiction, and refers a little later to a 'similar equivocation'. Ibid., pp. 16–17.

35. Ibid., p. 17.

36. G.W.F. Hegel, *Philosophy of Right*, trs. T.M. Knox, Oxford, Oxford University Press, 1967, pp. 151–2.

37. Marx and Engels, *Communist Manifesto*, p. 83.

38. K. Marx, *Grundrisse: Foundations of the Critique of Political Economy*, trs. M. Nicolaus, Harmondsworth, Penguin Books/NLR, 1973, p. 108.

39. Ibid., pp. 227–8.

40. See letters of early 1858 to Lassalle and Engels, Marx and Engels, *Selected Correspondence*, London, Lawrence and Wishart, n.d., pp. 124–30, and discussion in Oakley, *Makings*, especially ch. 4.

41. K. Marx, *Theories of Surplus Value*, Part 2, London, Lawrence and Wishart, 1969, p. 501.

42. K. Marx and F. Engels, *Selected Correspondence*, p. 134; quoted in Mészáros, 'Marx's "Social Revolution"', p. 14.

43. K. Marx, *A Contribution to the Critique of Political Economy*, Moscow, Progress Publishers, 1970, p. 21. Compare 'It is of the nature of truth to prevail when its time has come, and . . . truth appears only when its time has come – and therefore never appears too early, nor ever finds that the public is not ready for it.' *G.W.F. Hegel: Texts and Commentary*, trs. W. Kaufmann, New York, Anchor Books, 1966, p. 108.

44. K. Marx, *The Poverty of Philosophy*, Moscow, Progress Publishers, 1955, p. 105.

45. Compare Perry Anderson's discussion of the 'difficult questions' posed by the relation between nature and history; P. Anderson, *In the Tracks of Historical Materialism*, London, Verso, 1983, pp. 81–4. There is an obvious affinity between his argument that the articulation of these two terms poses a 'great crux' for Marxism and the programme outlined in the text above. For him, however, the problem is located explicitly in the context of Marxism as a critical theory and of socialist morality.

46. Perhaps the most remarkable of these notices is R. Rorty,*Philosophy and the Mirror of Nature*, Oxford, Basil Blackwell, 1980.

47. S. Sayers, 'Marxism and the Dialectical Method: A Critique of G.A. Cohen', *Radical Philosophy*, 36 (Spring 1984), p. 4. In Sayers's view these virtues are 'not even particularly characteristic' of analytical philosophy which has 'all too often' been 'needlessly obscure in style, cloudy in thought and not noticeably more rigorous in argument than the work of any other major school of philosophy'. Ibid., p. 4. That the birth of the analytical school marked a sharp decline in these respects will be obvious to anyone who compares, say, the breadth of outlook and passion for unrestricted argument of J.M.E. McTaggart with the cosy provincialism and reliance on the mental habits of one's own sort of people of G.E. Moore.

48. Continuing the triadic scheme, the previous pantheon may be said to have consisted of Russell, Wittgenstein and Quine, while the main alternative is Heidegger, Foucault and Derrida. Naturally enough, the suggestion is also occasionally heard that some or all elements of these lists be combined to form a new academic consensus

embracing both Anglo-Saxon and continental traditions.

49. In particular one may cite the work over many years of Paul Sweezy, Harry Magdoff and others associated with the journal *Monthly Review*. An introduction to their work is provided by S. Resnick and R. Wolff, eds, *Rethinking Marxism: Struggles in Marxist Theory*, New York, Autonomedia, 1985.

50. They are trenchantly summarized in Geras, *Marx and Human Nature*, pp. 104–5.

51. G.W.F. Hegel, *Phenomenology of Spirit*, trs. A.V. Miller, Oxford, Clarendon Press, 1979, p. 118.

52. Mészáros, 'Marx's "Social Revolution"', p. 19.

53. Once again the underlying point is anticipated by Marx: in bourgeois society 'Agriculture to an increasing extent becomes just a branch of industry and is completely dominated by capital.' *Contribution*, p. 213. In a similar vein it is worth noting the various occasions on which he recognizes the dynamic potential of outlying regions; e.g. 'Revolution in China and in Europe', K. Marx and F. Engels, *Collected Works*, Volume 12, London, Lawrence and Wishart, 1979, pp. 93–100; Marx and Engels, 'Preface to the Russian Edition of 1882', *Communist Manifesto*, pp. 55–6. A basic theme on these occasions is the recognition that 'Violent outbreaks must naturally occur rather in the extremities of the bourgeois body than in its heart, since the possibility of adjustment is greater here than there.' *The Class Struggles in France, 1848–50*, Moscow, Progress Publishers, 1972, p. 126.

54. The effects of this pressure have been particularly evident in Britain where the debate in recent years over the future of the left has been astonishingly narrow-minded and insular. It would at any rate have astonished earlier generations of socialists. The failure to come up with any satisfying answers suggests in itself that the questions are being unfruitfully posed. The best illustration is the phase of the debate that accompanied the Malvinas-Falklands war. This also shows clearly the way in which general perspectives influence concrete judgements. There was a case for holding that the left should support the war. It has various strands but two may be singled out here. Both are based on considerations available at the time to any newspaper reader. The first is that the war must cause significant problems for the United States, the chief pillar of the capitalist order in Latin America as elsewhere. Its strategy in this crucial region was bound to be disrupted by being forced to choose between its allies Britain and Argentina backed by the rest of Latin America. More specifically, it was certain to have an unfavourable impact on proposals, then much in the air, to use Argentinian and other Latin American forces against the revolution in Nicaragua and El Salvador. The second strand concerns the predictable effects of defeat in war on the military regime in Argentina, a regime which was, as the British press assured us, steeped in the blood of its own people. It was reasonable to assume that its downfall would involve progressive political and social change in that country, putting an end at least to the 'disappearances' and other horrors. These considerations should count for something for those who are not pacifists and would give intellectual assent to the proposition that capitalism, particularly in its Latin American form, is systematic violence and terror. Such people would surely have to agree that the choice was not between violence and the absence of violence, or indeed between war and peace, but between different modes of violence and war, charged with different kinds of significance. The present writer knows from personal experience, however, how difficult it was in conversations or public discussions with people on the left even to get them to take such arguments seriously. They are, of course, not decisive in themselves, though it is worth noting that they have been borne out reasonably well by events. Thus, changes of the kind postulated here occurred in Argentina, and, on the bearing of the war on the Nicaraguan and Salvadorean situations, there is the convincing testimony of John Lehman, then US Navy Secretary; see the *Observer*, 29 May 1988. The important point is that the arguments represent a dimension of the question which was almost entirely missing from the debate in Britain at the time, and which, had it been present, would have caused the true socialist case against the war, if there is one, to be formulated. Not least of the victories of Thatcherism is its success in convincing British socialists that the only real problem they face is defeating Margaret Thatcher. Even those most obsessed with that goal should, to focus the issues, consider the following thought experiment based on simplified but plausible assumptions. It consists in

asking which is preferable, so far as the cause of socialism is concerned, the actual world of Margaret Thatcher, civilian rule in Argentina, the Sandinistas in power in Nicaragua and continuing resistance elsewhere in Central America, or the possible world of a Foot or Kinnock government in Britain, military rule in Argentina, the crushing of all Central American opposition and a restored dictatorship in Nicaragua wreaking revenge for being interrupted.

Index

DATE DUE

FEB 1 2 1994			

GAYLORD   PRINTED IN U.S A.